SCOTLAND

FOR FISHING

2002

CONTENTS

This edition published by
Pastime Publications Ltd,
5/9 Rennie's Isle,
Edinburgh EH6 6QA
Tel/Fax: 0131 553 4444

2002 © Pastime Publications Ltd.

Printed and bound in Scotland.
UK and worldwide distribution.

It has been a torrid time. Since Scotland for Fishing last appeared, tourism has been slammed first by the foot and mouth crisis and then by the cataclysmic events of September 11. The first event caused us to think long and hard about the advisability of going ahead with our plan to publish in March 2001. At the risk of losing that all-important 'visibility' in the market place, we decided, nonetheless, to postpone publishing until now. A decision that has been vindicated by events and that has allowed us to re-vitalise the Guide.

First we must introduce you to our new Editor, Mike Shepley. To many of you, he needs no introduction but for those of you who are unfamiliar with his sea angling achievements he is twice a former winner of the SFSA Scottish Open Boat Championships, British National Boat Champion and EFSA European Champion. Nowadays, when not fly fishing for salmon and trout, Mike spends most of his time running a multi-media production business based in Dubai! With the aid of new technology and a few 'old tech' telephone calls, we bring to you the fruits of our endeavours.

The Editorial has been re-focused through Mike's eyes to bring to our readers fresher, less anecdotal and more objective content. We have introduced a similar 'Gems' theme to our Golf Guide. 'Scotland's Fishing Gems' cover rivers and lochs, game and coarse fish and sea angling. There are tips and hints galore, maps and an enormous wealth of information on where to stay.

And, last but not least, the directory has been completely updated to give you information on how much you will be charged for permits and where you can buy them. This exercise proved to be a mammoth task and our thanks go to Mike's son, Paul, for putting it all together.

We hope you enjoy the new 'Scotland for Fishing' and that it helps you to plan a successful return to our waters. One thing is for sure; there will be more than a welcome on the Hillsides and in the Glens after such an annus mirabilis: the welcome will be with wide-open arms everywhere. Scotland is open again – in fact it was never really closed.

Graham Wilson
Publisher

Scotland for Fishing

by *Mike Shepley*

Since the Scottish Tourist Board first launched Scotland for Fishing over 30 years ago, a great deal has changed – not least our fisheries and our sport.

Scotland for Fishing continues to be the definitive guide to fishing in Scotland, whether your interest lies in wonderful scenic river and loch fishing, or in the sea: there are gentle hills and pastureland, craggy mountains and glens carved by time itself. Great salmon rivers such as Spey, Dee, Tay, Forth and Tweed still support runs of wild fish throughout the season. And once again, Salmo Salar runs the River Clyde.

Central Scotland offers great stillwater trouting for browns and rainbows, from smaller put and take fisheries to natural waters such as the beautiful Lake of Menteith. There is the remote, unspoilt beauty of the Western Isles – the old Norse Earldom of Orkney – or Viking Shetland.

The islands offer anglers not only wonderful trout, sea trout and salmon fishing, but great sea angling opportunities too.

Not everything has been good news – it would be wrong to suggest otherwise, or ignore the problems: there are rainbow trout escapees which displace wild trout and eat the spawn laid by salmon and sea trout. And the proliferation and expansion of commercial fish farming has threatened to outstrip the essential care for the inshore environment and our wild stocks, particularly so on the west coast where some rivers have seen a major decline in sea trout and salmon.

And now the good news: The River Clyde is experiencing a growing number of salmon and sea trout where none has run for decades. Rivers such as the East Lothian River Tyne have salmon now as well as big sea trout – challenging fishing that is far cheaper than many day ticket trout waters further south.

Both west and east coast rivers experienced earlier runs of bigger-than-average sea trout in the 2000 season. And in 2001, some Scottish salmon rivers had their best runs in years.

As with rainbow trout, there is no statutory close season for coarse fishing in Scotland and sport can include specimen roach, pike, perch – even carp, bream and golden-olive tench.

There are excellent stocks of wild brown trout in both rivers and lochs: and excellent stillwater fisheries which offer year-round sport with rainbows.

The Solway rivers Nith and Annan offer excellent, value-for-money sport, with trout, salmon and sea trout.

Winter fishing for grayling can also be great fun with days of crisp frosts and blue skies. Grayling are often classed with coarse fish, but they are true *salmonids* as their adipose fin confirms. Recent seasons have produced a number of record-size grayling, including two remarkable specimens reputedly over 4 lbs from the River Nith.

Sea Anglers can get afloat from many centres, or take part in fishing festivals and competitions around the coast and islands.

And don't forget to pack some heavy gear: they may not turn up often, but Scottish porbeagle shark and Atlantic halibut do run to over 400 lbs!

Salmon fishing has traditionally been the near-exclusive pastime of the wealthier angler – it can be an expensive game costing several hundred pounds a day for a rod on the more exclusive beats. And having the necessary funds does not automatically guarantee you either access or a salmon at the end of the day.

I'm reminded of the ghillie who, when he finally netted his guest's first fish of the week with a feeling of triumph, was told it had cost its captor £750.

"Ah sir, it's jist as weel you didnae catch anothir yin at yon price!"

But in Scotland, there's another *price* to pay

offering seriously good value!

We have included amongst our *'gems'* a variety of rivers and lochs, some of them in fact quite famous, where anglers can catch salmon and sea trout on a very modest budget indeed.

Sometimes 'hidden' is not the right word. If you fish the wonderful Grantown on Spey club fishings, it can be very busy when the salmon and sea trout are running. Get up at 3.30am and fish through the dawn: the river will be quieter, you may even have a stream or tempting pool to yourself. And you will have an excellent chance of a salmon or brace of sea trout in the bag before a hearty highland breakfast. Then while the banks are busy with those perhaps less committed to their sport, you can take the family to the beach, or hit a little white ball on one of those wonderful undulating green swathes, that are never very far away.

If like me, golf clubs often go in the car alongside the rods – and you have enough time in the day – Scotland cannot be bettered for choice or value for money.

Many anglers enjoy a variety of aspects of the sport – sea fishing from shore and boat, loch and river fishing for game and coarse fish, or stocked rainbow fisheries.

Again look no further than Scotland: there are many centres where you can fish off the rocks or beaches for codling, flatfish, mackerel, coalfish and tackle-testing pollack.

There are harbours where you can get afloat at reasonable cost for a few hours. And then if the mood takes you, find a nearby loch where you can catch specimen perch and pike:

Or cast a fly in front of a drifting boat for wild brownies during the often prolific evening rise.

At dusk, there will be fresh-run sea trout to catch, or even that elusive grilse or summer salmon. And even when the rain doesn't come and the rivers run to summer lows – early morning will always hold a golden chance for the intrepid angler on the water before the sun. It's also a magic time of the day to watch wildlife, whether it's an otter in the river, perhaps a wily fox come to drink at his favourite pool: or an osprey circling a loch before swooping on its prey finning below. In Scotland, the choice is yours!

The editor with a fine 5lbs rainbow trout from Markle Fisheries near East Linton in East Lothian.

Readers are invited to visit us online at **www.rod-and-line.net** where they will find in-depth information on all aspects of Scottish sport featured in 'Scotland for Fishing'. All e-mail enquiries relating to freshwater and sea angling, tickets and accomodation, will be answered promptly. We would also welcome comments, recommendations and additions, so that we can continue to improve our guide and service to all anglers, whether welcome visitors or residents.

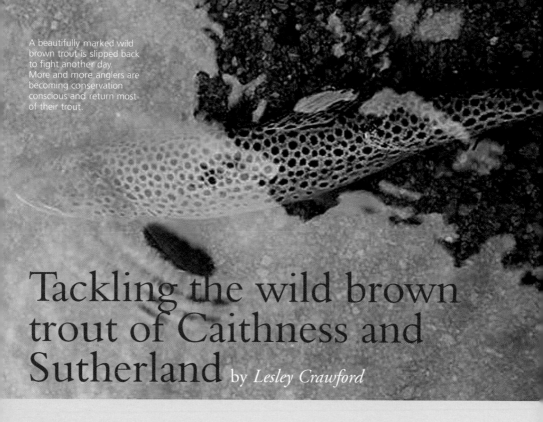

A beautifully marked wild brown trout is slipped back to fight another day. More and more anglers are becoming conservation conscious and return most of their trout.

Tackling the wild brown trout of Caithness and Sutherland *by Lesley Crawford*

The rugged yet beautiful lands of Caithness and Sutherland provide some of the finest wild trout angling in the UK. There are lochs galore, rivers and burns in abundance and panoramas to take your breath away. The county of Sutherland has over two thousand trout lochs pitted deep between mountain and glen, while smaller Caithness provides the ideal contrast with its 50 or so shallow, translucent waters surrounded predominantly by lush green agriculture. Forget any notion of dark peaty northern tarns producing nothing but small fish, numerous lochs in these more remote highland regions lie over a fertile limestone base. Virtually all the trout waters in Caithness are alkaline enriched by a limestone (marl) underlay and similarly lush lochs occur in Sutherland near Durness, Forsinard, Elphin, Achfary, Inchnadamph and Lochinver. Its a mistake to assume all the trout you catch out on the bleak heather/peat moor will be poor half starved specimens. Far from it for the fish of the Far North will average anything from half a pound to superb wild golden browns in the 1lb to 4lb plus range.

Most of the trout angling takes place in lochs rather than the rivers where migratory species like salmon also lurk. This is no hardship however, for the choice of waters is almost limitless. You can walk for miles into the wilderness and fish chains of sparkling lochans in total solitude or in the case of roadside waters, you can simply jump straight from the car into the boat.

As the loch environment is usually a less harsh one when compared to hill burns prone to heavy spate, the better/bigger trout are nearly always found in the 'stillwaters' rather than the dark peaty streams of the north.

In all cases the cost of a loch trout permit is minimal, normally £5 to £8 for a full day. Note there are also reasonable trout in various rivers, especially those with slower currents, however you may find you have to buy a (much more expensive) salmon permit in order to fish for the streams.

TACKLE

The trout of Caithness and Sutherland require traditional 'loch style' equipment. Normally a carbon fibre rod of around 10ft is used (wind resistance is considerable when using a longer rod for trout) and anything between 9-10ft will suffice. Use a reel that balances the rod (not too heavy) and allow a wide drum to take plenty of backing. Lines are usually floaters but there is scope for intermediates and occasionally a sinking line is employed. I prefer a WF floating line which copes much better with the high winds and use a WF intermediate if the trout appear to be lying a little deeper than normal. Nylon of 4 to 6lb is the most commonly used, 4lb being the most popular.

Fly selection covers a broad spectrum with nymph, dry fly and wet in sizes 10 to 16. Wet flies fished in teams are the accepted norm on the majority of lochs of the far North. A selection of the more successful sub surface patterns would include the Black Pennel, Zulu, Soldier Palmer and Invicta along with standards like the Kate McLaren, Wickhams, Claret and Golden Olive Bumbles, Butcher and Dunkeld.

Dry flies which do the business include the Grey Wulff, Green Drake and French Partridge for the mayfly season (which runs for almost 3 months from late May to the latter half of August) and the more multi purpose varieties of Wickhams, March Brown and Red Sedge also do well.

Nymphs are very effective both early and late in the season and in hard bright weather; most useful are variations of the Pheasant Tail, Damsel Nymph and Hares Ear.

TACTICS

The trout of Caithness and Sutherland have a wide ranging menu. Everything from shrimp, sedge, mayfly, damsel and olive is consumed along with caddis, snail, midge, bibio, crane fly and so on ad infinitum! Consequently there is scope for all types of fly fishing when hunting highland browns. Patterns and style can vary with the changing weather conditions also.

You can tactically employ anything from `fine and

Frying tonight – Lesley keeps a wild loch brownie for supper.

... and one to return – a River Tummel brown trout: note the wet mits to prevent scale damage.

far off' imitative work to straightforward searching of the depths with wets. When the trout are up and feeding well, strategic ploys need not be too ingenious but if the loch looks silent and still with little signs of activity then more subtle techniques may have to be employed.

In general terms, when you fish for wild trout in the northern highlands you will be fishing traditional `Loch Style'. While this tactic is often used from the boat, it's just as effective off the bank so do not be deterred if you cannot go afloat.

Normally you will work teams of 2 or 3 wet flies on a short line retrieved back just below the surface at a medium to fast pace.

Just before lifting off you should `dibble' the top dropper across the top of the water as this acts as a

Few anglers realise that the north of Scotland has excellent hatches of Mayfly.

You could be excused at times for thinking there was more water than land in Caithness and Sutherland and often lochs appear isolated and unpatrolled. Don't forget however that in Scotland it is a civil offence to fish for wild brown trout without permission – and where a Protection Order is place, it is also a criminal offence. All fishing is legally owned by the riparian owner .

Check before you go on the water – there could also be salmon in the river or loch you wish to fish and you must not go on the water without written permission. Also, please remember to observe local custom: in the Highlands and Islands, Sunday is a *day of rest* and not for trout fishing.

There is no angling for salmon and sea trout anywhere in Scotland on Sundays.

fish attractor. This method is highly successful providing you keep in contact with your flies and is ideal for the breezy, dull conditions frequently experienced in the north.

However, hot bright still weather is often experienced in May and June and this can call for a change of technique. Buzzers Nymphs, or traditional Spiders fished with a slow retrieve on floating or intermediate line often achieve results when standard wet fly fails. A single well ginked dry fly twitched slowly back can also produce a sudden savage response. Remember, dry fly can be of considerable use from as early as April so do not be afraid to use one on the top dropper whenever trout are showing on the surface. Just because you are fishing in the home of traditional wet fly you should not ignore the floating fly. Fish dries on a slightly slower retrieve and watch how they bring up trout you never knew were there! This is spectacular, visual fishing with trout often slashing at the flies.

BEST TIMES

Normally you can expect good trout angling from the middle of May to the latter half of September with a 'lull' during late August particularly if it's humid and thundery. Early and late in the season you should fish during the warmest part of the day from around 11am to 3pm when trout are more likely to be feeding. In high summer you can spread your efforts out a bit more as dawn and dusk are also good feeding periods for wild browns.

In truth the best time for wild trout in Caithness and Sutherland is anytime between March 15th and October 6th.

All you have to do is be there . . .

Lesley is in great demand as an angling guide for visitors in Caithness and Sutherland.

Scotland's stillwater fisheries by *Jim Boyd*

Scotland has a remarkably wide range of still water trout fishing facilities, from the wonderful lochs of Shetlands and Orkney, the magnificent machair lochs of the Hebrides, the numerous secret lochs of the western highlands and the rich and bounteous limestone lochs.

Then there are hill lochs, moorland lochs and the richer low-lying waters in the central and more southern parts of the country.

But what a lot of people are completely unaware of is the fact that around 85% of the people who fish for trout in Scotland do so at commercially operated stillwaters mainly stocked with rainbow trout.

Some fifty years ago, when I started out fishing, just about all we knew about a mysterious fish called the rainbow trout was that it was a highly colourful

species to be found in North America or New Zealand and that it was a bonny fighter. Frankly, few people had even heard of such a species. It goes without question that perhaps the biggest change in trout angling in Scotland has been the introduction and subsequent enormous geographic spread of the rainbow trout. But why did it all come about?

In these days we were still exporting considerable numbers of brown trout of the Loch Leven strain from the world renowned hatcheries at Howietoun and Solway, to places all over the world to satisfy a demand for this truly wonderful species. But at that time our own natural brown trout resource was in decline because of fishing pressure and lack of proper controls.

In the sixties, huge tracts of land in the north were

One of the lime-rich machair lochs of Lewis which abound with hard-fightingwild brown trout.

They don't come much nicer than this 8 pounder taken on a small size 16 black buzzer. Don't always believe in the old addage – Fish a big fly, catch a big fish!

being given over to afforestation and further south farm land was being fertilised with perticides, which in time, leeched into the low lying lochs, with adverse long term effects for wild brown trout stocks.

Loch Leven, at that time, was a classic example and one of the most wonderful brown trout fisheries in the world and angling sport suffered badly.

To reverse the trend in part, rainbow trout were imported from North America and New Zealand, with the end result being the creation of a brand new game fishing industry. At my last count there were well over 100 rainbow trout fisheries in Scotland being operated on a commercial basis.

Escapee rainbows mainly from commercial fish farms have caused problems, so not everyone is happy with the introduction. But I will happily defend their introduction as they came along just in time to offer the Scottish angler what then was an essential alternative to the brown trout: in time and essence rainbow trout fisheries have added an exciting new dimension to Scottish sport. Equally importantly, it has taken the pressure off the brown trout resource to such an extent that over the decades, with more

enlightened policies, brown trout have recovered extremely well and the resource is now being managed with care.

So where can the visiting anglers enjoy casting a fly for this really sporting fish – the now ubiquitous rainbow trout? The answer to that is simple – there are fisheries situated from the north of the country right down to the borders.

The largest concentration of stillwater fisheries is close to the heavily populated Central Belt.

But before you book your day out, it is well worth checking to see if the fishery is a member of the Association of Scottish Stillwater Fisheries, known as ASSF.

Scotland really is the home of world class trout angling in stocked stillwaters and frankly ASSF members provide the pick of the bunch, with member waters – which include all the famous names – well spread throughout Scotland.

They cater for everyone, from the first time angler to the highly skilled specimen hunter. All ASSF fisheries pride themselves on the professional way members run their waters, with the quality of fish and

facilities being second to none: and their very demanding standards preclude some fisheries from membership.

Let's start off then with the big waters.

Right now, one of the premier rainbow waters has to be the lovely **Lake of Menteith**. a veritable jewel set amongst the glorious scenery of the Trossachs.

Last year the Lake experienced one of the best seasons on record with an average weight of almost 2lbs being achieved. And this fishery is reckoned by many, both north and south of the border, to be one of the finest dry fly waters in the UK. And the scenery is stunning.

Over near Kinross, **Loch Leven** offers loch-style sport and if you are lucky enough to connect with one of their superb overwintered rainbows, then you will be privileged to catch a magnificent trout that could go into double figures.

As with the rainbows which grow on vigoroously in the loch, this fishery is still heavily stocked with a large quantity of brown trout each year from the loch's own hatchery, in a determined effort to re-establish a strong population of this native species. On its day the Loch Leven browns can be rewarding.

A new fishing lodge opened in 2001, and 50 boats are available with outboard motors with varying sessions and prices throughout the year.

North Third, on the outskirts of the historic town of Stirling, is set amidst some stunning scenery with the eastern shoreline being dominated by the spectacular crags. The sport here is consistently good from both boat and bank, each season some huge rainbows are caught and a good percentage of the total catch consists of trout each weighing over 3lbs each.

The Kingdom of Fife is well blessed with excellent fisheries with the flagship being **Loch Fitty**, one of the country's oldest established rainbow venues.

Recent developments at this popular fishery have seen the introduction of a Specimen Pool where trout of 3lbs up to double figures can be caught. And a Bait Pool where non fly fishers and youngsters can enjoy catching a trout or two. Fitty has excellent lochside facilities, which include an excellent tackle shop and an extremely good café, which caters ably for the inner man.

One of the things many anglers would like to do is to get to grips with a really big specimen rainbow and a number of Scottish fisheries can offer them that opportunity.

Double figure fish are fairly common these days and most of the fisheries adopt a policy of usually having some biggies swimming around.

But you can shorten the odds considerably by

> "Some anglers are of the opinion that for a fishery to be commercially operated, it generally means artificially created pools and specifically excavated holes in the countryside stuffed full of easily caught trout! *Far from it.*"

visiting some of the smaller outlets that specialise in stocking their waters with good numbers of hefty specimen rainbows.

On the outskirts of Stirling, the **Swanswater Trout Fishery** is fast gaining a reputation for producing some terrific trout and last season alone almost 100 of these big fish came to the anglers' nets. The super thing about Swanswater is the fact that there is a great size range of fish in the water.

And that adds considerably to the excitement at any fishery.

Kingennie Fishings at Broughty Ferry has its own famous Specimen Pool which is entirely stocked with big trout and they too produce substantial numbers of doubles each year.

In the northern regions of the country, pride of place for catching that special fish must go to the bonny **Loch Insch** fishery set in beautiful Aberdeenshire countryside near Colpy.

And considerably further north, at Invergordon,

the highland anglers can get to grips with a big fish at the **Stoneyfield Lochs** fishery.

It can be exciting sport down in the Borders at the **Moffat Trout Fishery**, where anglers not only have a great opportunity of catching specimen trout, but you will able to see them quite clearly swimming about in the gin clear waters.

Stalking your specimen under conditions like this really is the most satisfying way to fish on any small stillwater and I can tell you, it does need a steady nerve.

Markle Fisheries at East Linton has the enviable reputation of producing a consistently high average weight of fish around the 3lb mark. And they too, not surprisingly, produce a high number of very big trout each and every season.

On the big fishery front, **North Third** near Stirling is one of the waters where the opportunity arises to catch double figure fish on a regular basis.

But of all the big waters, **Loch Leven** has the

A Swanswater specimen comes to the net.

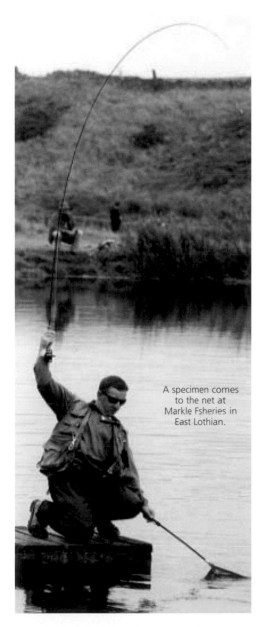

A specimen comes to the net at Markle Fsheries in East Lothian.

or three seasons, these fish pack on weight at a terrific rate and are beautifully proportioned, muscle packed specimens that are an absolute joy.

Some anglers are of the opinion that for a fishery to be commercially operated, it generally means artificially created pools and specifically excavated holes in the countrysides stuffed full of easily caught trout!

Far from it. Here in Scotland, the majority of fisheries being commercially managed are, by and large, natural waters set in extremely attractive surroundings. It would be no exaggeration to describe the scenery at some like Butterstone, Menteith, North Third, Lower Frandy, Glensherrup and Howwood as spectacular.

When it comes to the practicalities of fly fishing, there are also a few misconceptions when it comes to the terminal tackle used to try and tempt rainbow trout so it's maybe time to quash some myths.

No, you don't have to use enormous great lures stripped back at some enormous rate of knots.

It might be stating the obvious but a rainbow is a fish that eats the same diet as any other trout and believe me your catch rate will soar if you lay off the big lures and concentrate a bit more on the more imitative patterns.

Having said that, lures of course do have their day and the most popular top takers include the Damsel, Cat's Whisker, various Fritz patterns, Montana and the Ace of Spades.

But all the fisheries you visit will be more than happy to advise you as to what the best methods are on the day.

Clearly it is quite impossible to mention all the commercially operated fisheries in this short article but any angler visiting Scotland is never going to be more than a relatively short drive away from a fishery which will offer them what they want at a more than reasonable price – enjoy!

According to Mike Heath of Mike's Tackle Shop, Portobello, Edinburgh, stillwater trout fishing now accounts for more anglers than river fishing for trout, salmon and sea trout, coarse fishing and sea angling combined. It is also an ideal introduction to fishing for youngsters, with a real chance of catching fish even as novice anglers. Stillwater fisheries continue to grow, but a good starting point is to choose one of the ASSF member fisheries listed overleaf.

potential to produce not only the largest but possibly the best looking rainbows in the British Isles. The big difference between the Leven rainbows and others is that this is nearest thing to a really wild rainbow trout. Introduced at a relatively small size, over two

ASSF Members List 2002

ALLANDALE TARN FISHERY
Gavieside, West Calder EH55 8PT
Contact Mrs Margo Allan
Tel/Fax: 01506 873073
Email: margo@thefishery.fsnet.co.uk

ARDGOWAN
45 Oxford Avenue, Gourock PA19 1UG
Contact David J Moffat
Tel: 01475 632067/522492

BALLO
26 Penicuik Road, Roslin,
Midlothian EH25 9LH
Contact R Warson, Tel: 0131 440 2047

BOWDEN SPRINGS
Carriber, nr Linlithgow
Contact Mairi Henderson
Tel/Fax: 01506 847269

BURNS TROUT FISHERY
Station House, Station Road,
Tarbolton, Ayrshire KA5 5NT
Contact Tommy Burns, Tel: 01292 541509

BUTTERSTONE LOCH
Butterstone Nr Dunkeld,
Perthshire PA8 0HH
Contact Rick Knight, Tel: 01350 724238
Email: rik-_knight@agilent.com

COLDINGHAM LOCH
West Loch House, Coldingham,
Berwickshire TD14 5QE
Contact Dr Ted Wise, Tel: 018907 71270

DRUMMOND FISHERY
Drummond Fish Farm, Comrie,
Perthshire PA6 2LD
Contact Simon Barnes,
Tel: 01764 670500 Fax: 01764 679480

EASTER BALADO TROUT FISHERY
Easter Balado, nr Kinross
Contact Richard Philp, Kaimeknowe Farm

GLENDEVON
Tel: 01577 862371, Mobile 0780 1547869,
Fax: - 01259 781306
Email: helen@glensherrup.fsbusiness.co.uk

LOCH FAD
Loch Fad Fisheries Ltd,
Loch Fad, Isle of Bute
Contact Alastair McFarlane
Tel: 01700 504871 Fax: 01700 505127

LOCH FITTY
Kingseat, Dunfermline, Fife KY12 0SP
Contact Gerry MacKenzie
Tel: 01383 620666
Email: mackenzie_gerald@hotmail.com

LOWER FRANDY RESERVOIR
Glen Devon, Tayside
Contact Richard Philp, Kaimeknowe Farm,
Glendevon
Tel: 01259 781352, Fax: 01259 781306
Email: helen@glensherrup.fsbusiness.co.uk

GARTMORN DAM
Clackmannan District Council, 29 Primrose,
St Alloa
Contact Jimmy Stewart, Tel: 01259 214319

GLEN OF ROTHES TROUT FISHERY
Glen of Rothes, Rothes,
Morayshire AB38 7AG
Contact Duncan Dunbar-Nasmith
Tel: 01340 831994, Fax: 01340 831626
Email: dmdm@glen-of-rothes.co.uk

GLENSHERRUP TROUT FISHERY
Kaimeknowe Farm, Glendevon, Tayside
Contact Richard Philp
Tel: 01259 781631, Fax: 01259 781306
Email: helen@glensherrup.fsbusiness.co.uk

The thistle, Scotland's traditional emblem. Many of Scotland's stillwater fisheries are set in beautiful countryside and are a haven for wild flowers and wildlife.

HEADSHAW FISHERY
Headshaw Farm, Ashkirk, Nr Selkirk TD7 4NT
Contact Nancy Hunter
Tel: 01750 32233, Fax: 01750 32335

HEATHERYFORD FISHERY
Heatheryford, Kinross KY130NQ
Contact John Cairns
Tel: 01577 864212, Fax: 01577 864920

HOWWOOD FISHERY
Bowfield Road, Howwood, Renfrewshire
PA9 1DG
Contact John Cassells
Tel: 01505 702688/ Fax: 01505 813042
Email: john.cassells@ntlworld.com

INVERAWE FISHERY
Taynuilt, Argyll PA35 IHU
Contact Robert Campbell-Preston
Tel: 01866 822446
Fax: 01866 822274

KILLEARN HOUSE FISHERY
Killearn Home Farm, Killearn,
Glasgow G63 9QH
Contact David Young
Tel/Fax: 01360 550994

KINGENNIE FISHINGS
Kingennie, Broughty Ferry,
Dundee DD5 3RD
Contact Neil Anderson
Tel: 01382 350777, Fax: 01382 350400
Email: kingennie@easynet.co.uk

LAWFIELD FISHERY
Houston Road, Kilmalcolm,
Renfrewshire PA13 4WY.
Contact Billy McFerrin, Tel: 01505 874182

LOCH INSCH
Old Inn Farm, Colpy, Insch,
Aberdeenshire AB52 6TS
Contact Yvonne Mair
Tel/Fax: 01464 841 301

LOCH LEVEN
Loch Leven Fisheries, Kinross Estates Offices,
The Muirs, Kinross KY13 7WF
Contact Willie Wilson, Manager
Tel: 01577 865386/407, Fax: 01577 863180

LOCHORE MEADOWS
Lochore Meadows Country Park, Crosshill,
Lochgelly, Fife KY5 8BA
Contact Mike Gregge, Facilities Manager
Tel: 01592 860086, Fax: 01592 414345

LAKE OF MENTEITH
Gateside Cottage, Port of Menteith,
Stirling FK8 3RD
Contact Quint Glen, Fishery Manager
Tel/Fax: 01877 385648

LINDORES LOCH
The Fishing Hut, Lindores Loch,
by Newburgh, Fife KY14 6JB
Contact Andy Mitchell
Tel: 01337 810488

NEWMILL TROUT FISHERY
Cleghorn, Lanark, ML11 7SL
Contact Dave Buchanan
Tel: 01555 870730, Fax: 01555 870317
Email dave@newmilltrout.com
www.newmilltrout.com

NEWTON FARM LOCH
Wormit, Fife
Contact Katherine Crawford
Tel: 01382 54251, Fax: 01382 540125
Email: newtonhill@lineone.net

NORTH THIRD FISHERY
Greathill House, Stirling FK7 9QS
Contact George Holdsworth
Tel: 01786 471967, Fax: 01786 447388
Email: georgeholdsworth@norththirdtroutfishery.
freeserve.co.uk

ORCHILL LOCH TROUT FISHERY
South Lodge, Orchill, Braco,
Dunblane FK15 9LF
Contact Elizabeth Jackson
Tel/Fax: 01764 682287

PORT-NA-LOCHAN
Fairhaven, Catacol,
Isle of Arran KA27 8HN.
Contact George Bannatyne
Tel: 01770 830237
Email: bannantyne@lineone.net

MARKLE FISHERIES
Markle, East Linton, East Lothian EH40 3EB
Contact David Jon Swift
Tel: 01620 861213, Fax: 01368 865252
Email jon@marklefisheries.co.uk

MIDDLETON TROUT FISHERY
Brisbane, Glen Road, Largs,
Ayrshire, KA30 8SL
Contact Ian McIntyre
Tel: 01475 672095

MORTON FISHERY
Keepers Cottage, Mid Calder,
Livingston EH53 0JT.
Contact Julie Hewat,
Tel: 01506 882293
Email: morton1@easicom.com

PIPERDAM GOLF AND COUNTRY PARK LIMITED
Fowlis, Dundee, DD2 5LP
Contact Murdie Smith
Tel: 01382 581374, Fax: 01382 581102

PITFOUR LAKE
Saplinbrae Sporting Estates,
4 Mid Street,
Buchanhaven,
Peterhead AB42 1NP
Contact Alan Ritchie
Tel: 01771 624448/622300, Fax: 01771 624448

ROTHIEMURCHUS ESTATE

Rothiemurchus Estate, by Aviemore,
Inverness-shire PH22 1QH
Contact Neil Shand, Manager
Tel: 01479 810703, Fax: 01479 810778

SANDYKNOWES FISHERY

Bridge of Earn, Perthshire PH2 9QA
Contact David Brien
Tel: 01738 813033

SPRINGWATER FISHERY

Drumgabs Farm, Dalrymple,
by Ayr, KA6 6AW
Contact Danny Wilson
Tel: 01292 560343/560300/
Fax: 01292 560343

STONEYFIELD LOCH FISHERY

Stoneyfield House, Newmore,
Invergordon IV18 0PG
Contact Jennifer Connell
Tel/Fax: 01349 852632

SWANSWATER FISHERY

Sauchieburn, Stirling FK7 9QB
Contact Alasdair Lohoar
Tel/Fax: 01786 814805
Email: morna@swanswater@virgin.net

WATCH FISHERY

Lonformacus, Duns, Berwickshire
TD11 3PE
Contact Bill Renton
Tel: 01361 890331, Fax: 01361 884542

WAUKMILL FISHERY

New Deer, Turriff, Aberdeenshire
AB53 6UP
Contact George Davidson
Tel: 01771 644357

This page: John Wotherspoon has his
hands full with this specimen jumbo
rainbow.

Opposite: Thomas was only 12 years
old when he took this nice rainbow
from Orchill Loch Trout Fishery and has
caught even better fish since.

Coarse Fishing in Scotland

by *Jim Neilson*

To a lot of anglers (and non anglers), fishing in Scotland means game fishing for salmon, sea trout, brown trout and rainbow trout, with coarse fishing in general, relegated to the domain of the young or unskilled angler.

Being a not so young and reasonably skilled angler (no honestly) I would like to introduce you to a few of the species of coarse fish, which each in their own way can be a rewarding challenge.

Throughout Scotland, a wealth of relatively untapped venues are to be found where you can fish for a diverse variety of species.

THE TENCH
A hard fighting species which has reached weights of over seven pounds in the Forth and Clyde canal, poses a real challenge to the skill of any angler. You will have to use sensibly strong tackle if you ever expect to successfully play and land one of these power houses.

On hooking your first tench be prepared for an arm wrenching battle as it makes repeated lunges for the security of the abundant lily roots or reed stems - not to mention the odd supermarket trolley!

However, with careful playing, your net may soon be graced with a plump tench, whose glistening, gold dusted, green flanks and bright red eyes make it, in my humble opinion, one of the most visually rewarding species you can catch. I would strongly recommend that tench in particular, and most other species in general should never be retained in a keep net, and should in all cases be returned gently to the water.

THE PERCH
Another strikingly beautiful species that can be caught in many rivers and lochs throughout Scotland, with weights of almost four pounds possible

Although not an exceptional fighter, its boldly striped flanks and red fins, coupled with its eagerness to accept a bait, whether a float fished minnow or lo worm, or a small artificial lure, make the perch an attractive and rewarding species, worthy of your attention.

Great care is required when unhooking perch, as they possess sharp dorsal spines and gill covers which can cause injury to the unwary.

THE ROACH

A widely spread species which can be caught on float or leger tackle in many rivers and lochs, on a variety of small baits. Eagerly sought after by match anglers, it can be caught in large numbers and although in general a diminutive species, larger specimens of approaching two pounds can be caught from Loch Lomond in the early spring. With its silvery flanks and orange fins this attractive species is a rewarding fish for any angler.

THE DACE

A small species inhabiting the faster streches of the River Clyde and River Endrick, where it has become established in recent years. It is also present in the lower Tweed.

With an average weight of less than a pound, you can catch them on very light float tackle, sometimes in vast numbers in the early spring. It will also take a fly readily.

With its lightning fast bites, the dace offers you a challenge which will certainly keep you on your toes.

An elongated bright silver fish with pale yellowish fins, this species, although generally small, can none the less provide you with excellent sport.

THE BREAM

A large shoaling species which can be found in a few southern lochs, the most notable being Castle Loch near Lochmaben, and more recently in the River Clyde and River Endrick.

Although reaching a weight of over ten pounds the bream is no hard fighter, its main attractions being its overall size and the fact that it can at times be caught in large numbers.

This somewhat dour fish can, on occasion, steadfastly refuse to take your bait, whether legered or float fished.

However, if the prospect of throwing in many pounds of groundbait and waiting, and waiting, and waiting patiently for a bite attracts you, then bream fishing is for you. You may be rewarded for your patience with a catch of large bream.

Silvery flanked when young, the bream becomes a deep bronze colour as it matures.

GRAYLING

This is a species that inhabits most of the well known salmon rivers throughout Scotland. Although not

actually a coarse species, the grayling receives little of the acclaim given to other game species, being relegated into the category of 'something to catch during the trout closed season', a category to which it most certainly does not belong.

Mostly fished for during the colder months with light line and a small float, the grayling will challenge your angling skills to the limit, with its stubborn refusal to concede one inch. It will test your patience and your skills during the exciting and often prolonged fight. However, if you can control your impatience and play the fish gently but firmly, it may all come right in the end as you slip your net under this fine fish – aptly dubbed 'the lady of the stream' by many enthusiasts, which is yours to admire for a moment, before returning it gently to the river.

An exceptionally beautiful species with turquoise tinted metallic silver flanks and an enormous dorsal fin edged with red, the grayling is a very worthwhile species to catch.

THE CARP

This is one of the two 'big boys' of coarse fishing in Scotland, the other being the pike, which is dealt with elsewhere by Mike Maule. Reaching weights of over twenty pounds, you may fish for them in quite a few well stocked lochs.

As you endeavor to tempt this wary fish (which on many occasions, can refuse to be tempted) you will have to use a more specialised approach and, because of its potential size, heavier tackle when legering your choice of a vast variety of baits,

If you do eventually hook one, be prepared for a very hard fight with powerful long runs by the fish, occasionally deep into the nearest weed bed, leaving you in despair and utter frustration at the thought of losing your prize.

Perch don't come any prettier than this superb near 3 pounder from Balmaha Bay on Loch Lomond. Brandling or lobworm tail are excellent baits.

However, if you eventually manage to land your carp, you will be rewarded not only with a fine fish, but also with the satisfaction that you have caught one of the most elusive fish to be found in Scotland.

THE CHUB

A greedy, sometimes aggressive species that can be found in the River Annan and a few other rivers in Scotland's south west. More recently, the river chub have been introduced into the River Endrick.

Although a large fish, occasionally reaching weights of well over five pounds, it is its elusiveness rather than its fighting ability that is the chub's greatest challenge: its uncanny awareness of your approach makes its capture a far from foregone conclusion.

You may fish for chub with a variety of baits, on either float or leger tackle, and although the bite may be violent in the extreme, it is almost always followed by a few short, halfhearted lunges, before the chub gives up and comes gently to the waiting net.

Chub will also take a fly, particularly a well presented bushy dry fly, pitched under overhanging trees or undercut bank. The sight of a big chub rising slowly to intercept a floating fly, sucking it down with its big mouth and lazy action, can indeed be exciting.

Stockily built, with large, brassy, golden scales and orange fins, the chub is an impressive fish, justly fit to grace any landing net.

THE BARBEL

This 'King of the Coarse Fish' has recently made an appearance in the River Clyde, comprising a few isolated captures.

Although so rare at present as to make fishing for them a daunting, if not completely futile endeavour, the barbel may become established in the years to come, providing future coarse anglers with an opportunity to fish for this astounding species.

If you do decide to try coarse fishing, you are sure to enjoy many noteworthy days and also the pleasure of catching some of the exciting other species which in Scotland tend to be largely ignored in preference to 'a better class of fish'. Tight Lines.

Scotland for Fishing does not condone the unauthorised introduction of species alien to Scottish rivers and lochs – The barbel and crayfish dilemma on the River Clyde is just one example of the appearance of potentially damaging species.

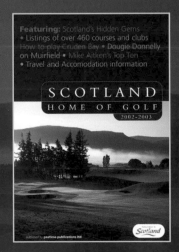

The Lady of Tweedside

Peter Miller on Whiteadder Water

This little Berwickshire river, like it's English sister the Till, is surprisingly undiscovered for a water which hosted Scotland's first formal association of fishermen, The Ellemford Fishing Club, back in pre-Victorian days. This may be because she lives in the shadow of the Tweed, whose estuary she shares at Berwick.

Although there is considerable empirical evidence that the Whiteadder once enjoyed great runs of migratory salmonids, the construction of numerous mills along the banks last century effectively denied access to salmon and seatrout in all but the highest of water. Thus the river became the preserve of trout fisherman and garnered a considerable reputation for wild brown trout among the Borderers.

> "By August many of the pools are almost paved with fish, but they have nocturnal anglers tearing out their hair with little but the occasional tweak on many nights."

About eight years ago, The Tweed Commissioners decided that it was time to open the river as valuable additional spawning ground for the parent system and, through it's practical arm, The Tweed Foundation, instigated a programme of improvement. This largely comprised the removal or passing of the various caulds or wiers to facilitate access to the dozens of miles of wonderful clean headwaters both on the Whiteadder and it's numerous tributaries. The response to this initiative was pretty immediate and within a very few years, the river had an established and improving run of fish.

Most pleasing was the quality of the spring run. As is widely known, the majority of Tweed springers turn left at Boleside and run the Ettrick, but few had appreciated how many took a look at the Whiteadder before even entering the main river.

There's still a lot of work to be done before the situation is as secure as high-seas netting allows, but despite some disappointments during the freak dry conditions of 1999 and 2000, things are looking pretty good. In March stocks of springers build up behind the rather inadequate fish ladder at Canty's Brig, immediately above the tide, and there's some fairly spectacular fishing here until the back end of April. Given water, fish move upriver as temperatures rise and by the beginning of May there are springers in most pools right up to Dyefoot.

Above Dyefoot, no migratory fishing is permitted. Sea trout enter the river in early May, but the main run is reserved for mid July, closely followed by the grilse if they haven't been decimated elsewhere! In common with the rest of the Tweed system, there's a good run in the back-end, but a lot of these fish are coloured, with few fresh fish reaching the upper river.

The headwaters of the main stream are dammed to form the Whiteadder Reservoir, supplying water to Edinburgh some 30 miles distant. The impoundment does cause some additional sensitivity to dry conditions but is largely compensated for by a weekly freshet release if the river is low. Again. there's a lot more work to be done here in connection with the Scottish Environmental Protection Agency but nothing that can't be tackled given a measure of co-operation.

The Whiteadder is a small river, about thirty miles in length and barely thirty yards wide in its lower reaches. Single handed rods are the order of the day and most folk find an intermediate line the most effective in all but the shallowest water. Salmon undoubtedly respond best to very small flies with

"Never forget that the main criteria for fishing all small rivers fall into the usual three categories – stealth, stealth and stealth!."

sizes 12 and 14 giving good results and 10's and 16's in extreme conditions. These are, of course, only guidelines as plenty of fish are caught on larger patterns but many anglers use nothing but small trout singles. Being a small river, fish are very often visible in the lies and far too many anglers fail to realise that this is a reciprocal situation – with depressingly predictable results!

The Whiteadder seatrout is a notoriously fickle creature. By August many of the pools are almost paved with fish, but they have nocturnal anglers tearing out their hair with little but the occassional tweak on many nights. While they provide great daytime sport in high water, the night requires special tactics. As a rule, forget the fish lying in slack water and concentrate on those in the necks and tails. Better still, find a shoal surging around at dusk in a broad but ripply shallow, and offer them something drab and natural like an Invicta or a Greenwell's Glory.

Never forget that the main criterea for fishing all small rivers fall into the usual three categories – stealth, stealth and stealth! This applies almost as much to the salmon as to the seatrout: and it also applies to the wild brown trout, of which there are many throughout the river. Although dilution of the resident stock by their migrating sisters has resulted in a significant reduction in numbers of fish above smolting age, there is still great sport to be had with both dry and wet fly and the Trout Associations have access to the vast majority of the river.

The Whiteadder is a beautiful, unspoilt river in beautiful, unspoilt countryside and its regeneration is a credit to the authorities who have participated.

Ours is a fragile environment so let us hope that it's preservation is as creditable as the efforts so far made to return this stream to its former glory.

Scotland's Legendary Pike

Mike Maule has the lowdown and the hi-tech . . .

Scotland has hundreds of beautiful lochs like Loch Awe which are home, not only to salmon and trout, but to giant pike. There is a growing band of Scottish anglers and dedicated visitors who take the high and low roads to some of the best action-packed sport there is: where the pike are weighed, photographed and returned.

Scotland has its fair share of rivers and lochs, most of which tend to be renowned more for their game fish than coarse fish. Nevertheless the angler who wants something a bit different can, if he looks hard enough, discover that many of these same waters contain that most worthy of adversaries – the pike.

Even the most famous of salmon rivers, the Spey, holds pike, as does the Tay. Getting access to fish can present a problem however. Coarse fishing generally still struggles for recognition, although the situation is improving all the time.

The most famous of pike havens is Loch Lomond, followed closely by Loch Awe and Loch Ken. Much has been written and filmed about the quality of pike in these waters so I do not intend to spend any time describing them here. Having said that the majority of my piking is spent afloat either on Lomond or Awe, so take it as read that these are still Scotland's premier waters.

There are many other waters which can provide excellent sport with numbers of fish often exceeding the magical 20 lb mark. It is not my intention to list them all – that would take a book in itself, so instead I will give the reader a flavour of the opportunities available by region.

THE BORDERS

To the east of the M74 does not tend to be heavily game orientated, but the odd interesting waters do exist. If you feel brave try **The Haining** near Selkirk. I fished this in 1978 and had little or no success.

There were some big perch caught whilst I was there and rumours still abound about some giant pike lurking amongst the ammunition supposedly dumped after the Second World War! A grenade or two might even be louder than some of the latest bite indicators.

Another one is **Castle Loch** near Kirk Yetholm. The farmer used to be quite amenable to the odd pike angler so long as you kept away from the birds.

St Mary's Loch too, near to Moffat is gaining a reputation for some decent fish in this otherwise sparse area for pike: worth a shot though, so long as permission is sought from the local club.

DUMFRIES and GALLOWAY
If the Borders is a desert then this area is the opposite. Partly because of the warmer, wetter climate, coarse fishing is prolific and appreciated as a valuable asset in most part. Where to start though is the problem. If my life depended on catching a pike I would probably go to **Loch Auchenriach** near Sprigholm: I fished it one October from a boat and ran out of bait – nothing big, just great sport.

There is a host of waters here. Some of the more accessible include **Castle Loch** at Lochmaben – well known for its bream – **Loch Rutton**, at Lochfoot, **Mill Loch**, **Woodhall Loch** adjacent to Loch Ken and, of course **Loch Ken** itself.

All of the above have produced very big fish in the past including authenticated 30 pounders.

I sometimes fish the rivers. My favourite is the **River Dee** out of Loch Ken. Much of it is private. However some stretches are ticketed and hold decent pike. An enquiry to the local shops will direct you to where to get the necessary permits.

LOTHIAN
Perhaps surprisingly pike are thin on the ground around here. The local trout waters turn up the odd surprise. One such loch is the picturesque **Linlithgow Loch**. I did well here when we were offered access some time ago. The more persistent may get permission, but don't bank on it! Linlithgow is home to some excellent wild browns as well as rainbow trout.

More accessible is **Roseberry Reservoir**, at least at certain times of year. Stocked with Rainbows the odd really good Pike lurks in the depths. As with most stocked bigger Lochs there is always the possibility of infiltration by Pike.

A good example is **Cobbinshaw** which certainly does hold a good head of decent pike although once again access is difficult.

Perhaps the **Union Canal** which runs through Edinburgh itself holds big Pike. I have heard of the odd double figure fish being caught.

Certainly it holds a good head of perch and roach so there is no reason why pike should not be present in decent numbers.

George Scoular with a 27 lbs 8 oz specimen pike – well worth the wait and the overnight camping.

CENTRAL BELT
The best known coarse venue is the **Forth and Clyde Canal**. It holds prolific roach and perch as well as decent tench, eels and reputedly bream and carp. It most certainly holds big pike – I know because I've caught some crackers, including six 20 pounders!

This is not a water though that you can expect to bag up. It is hard work but rewards will come to those

Linlithgow Loch is primarily a brown trout and rainbow fishery of note, but occasional access for pike fishing is allowed and produced some exceptional pike. Rosebury Reservoir is more accessible for visiting pike anglers.

who are prepared to put in a little bit of effort. Nor are fish confined to one area so it seems. The good fish are caught the whole length, which is not insubstantial, running as it does from Falkirk through to the Clyde at Bowling.

It is also a water of infinite variety encompassing both urban and rural aspects. The depth and breadth also vary in parts being 15 ft deep. Access is both easy and welcoming with no game fish interests being present. Any method works although my best results have always come from free-lined mackerel for some reason.

There are numerous lochs, many of which are worth attention. **Forestburn** near to Glasgow East has produced some decent fish. I would not look much past the Forth and Clyde myself though.

STIRLING AND THE TROSSACHS

Lake of Menteith – what can be said! This is the latest Llangedfed to dedicated pike anglers. Access is restricted to Pike Anglers Club members on a ballot basis at designated days of the year. If your number comes up then take it, as the water produces huge fish and thrives on neglect.

Six thirty-pounders in one day – and none of them mine! *C'est la vie*!

Down to earth and try the **River Forth**: some decent fish and good sport to boot. Same with the

River Teith although beware access.

The Trossachs Lochs hold the odd surprise. **Loch Venacher** and **Loch Achray** both produce pike and even if they don't, its worth the visit for the scenery alone.

Loch Chon holds some good fish although oddly despite looking the part, Lubnaig and Voil do not throw up pike at all. Why this should be beats me as perch are present in numbers in both.

Both lochs are stuffed with char, which make an interesting diversion as well as a tasty meal. Bring to simmer heat in a pan of slightly salted water, add tarragon, dill or coriander, cut the heat and lid the pan. Once cool, serve with a simple green salad!

WEST of SCOTLAND

I include Glasgow here. Being from the East, this area is a mystery to me. I know Lomond like the back of my hand as 90% of my pike fishing these days is on Lomond.

I did promise not to talk about Lomond though. Rumours do leak through to us about the River Clyde throwing up some really big fish. Of their precise whereabouts, I know not!

Also further into Ayrshire, the abode of that legendary Piker 'Golden B' Colquhuon, rumours have it that he does well in **Kilwhinning Loch** or somewhere close by.

'Mike the Pike' Maule has been catching specimen pike for over 20 years and travels the length and breadth of Scotland in search of that elusive record-breaker. This one topped 30 lbs.

HIGHLANDS

Loch Awe springs to mind immediately. This famous Pikery turns up specimens regularly, as well as huge ferox trout and occasional big rainbow: well worth a visit on all accounts.

After that it gets difficult. Taking a swing northwards Pike can be found in many Lochs; in surprisingly cold deep Lochs like **Arkaig**. Through the Great Glen **Lochy** and **Oich** are well worth a try and Northwards still **Cluanie** and **Garry** hold Pike. **Loch Ness** itself holds a few although I have yet to hear of any of size.

Into the Black Isle, the rivers hold a few fish. More famed for Salmon, the **Conan** has the odd toothy critter, but check permission before going near!

More into the Central Highlands now, the **Spey** and its feeder Lochs hold very good fish, especially **Lochs Insch** and **Morlich** as well as the Spey itself.

Moving to the Tay catchment, you should try Lochs **Clunie** and **Marlee**. These are quite rich waters and have produced some big pike in their time and occasional big trout, including a specimen 12 lb brownie that had a taste for Sardines!

The **River Tay** itself holds some very big Pike: beware again access on this game fishing river and seek permission first. Like the **Tweed** and **Spey** these are the preserves of salmon anglers who pay considerable sums for their sport.

Having said that, care and research can yield results. We have had excellent sport at Logierait where some good pike can be caught.

Try the backwater on the south bank just upstream from the railway bridge and the hotel.

In conclusion, the opportunities for pike fishing are numerous for those prepared to spend time and effort looking. Scottish piking is not just about Lomond and Awe.

This has of necessity been a whistle stop tour and is the result of 30 years of accumulated knowledge of piking in Scotland and I know I have only scratched the surface. Hopefully I have whetted the appetite of the more adventurous with more time than I have, to seek out new opportunities.

I have not mentioned either Loch Tay or Loch Leven, the latter in particular with massive potential. Good luck to you if you can build on the efforts of those like Ralston Mac Pherson who have opened up options for us to fish previously exclusive waters.

The Orkney Isles
— not for the faint-hearted

by Stan Headley

As my fishing forays take me further and further from home, I become increasingly convinced that Orkney has the best, readily accessible wild trout fishing in the UK, and possibly anywhere.

Every fly fisherman worthy of his salt has heard of lochs Harray and Swannay, but there are a host of other waters, equally fascinating, but which have had considerably less publicity. Within a couple of hundred yards of my front door is a water which, if located in any other part of the country, would have a queue of waiting anglers, standing by the water's edge. This wonderful water is known as Loch Stenness, or the Stenness loch, to give it its correct title.

Stenness is like a fine wine or artistic masterpiece: it won't appeal to everyone, but for those who appreciate real quality, it must be sampled for its rare and magnificent characteristics. Though sister loch to the famous Harray, they have little in common. Harray is justly famous for its offshore shallows, which renders almost all of its 2,500 acres fishable. Stenness, on the other hand, has very few such shallows and, although it has an area of 1876 acres, productive fishing effort is best restricted to the shorelines. Harray is highly prolific water where the average sized fish weighs just under the pound mark. Stenness, however, does not hold a great 'head' of trout (although impressive runs of sea trout enter the loch throughout the year), but their average size is considerably bigger.

There can't be many trout fisheries where the predominant species has to share its environment

> "Stenness just loves breaking its own rules. Just when it looks like a formula has been arrived at that will cover most eventualities, something comes along to blow all the carefully constructed theories apart."

with cod, coalfish (saithe), pollack (lythe), herring, mullet, garfish and the occasional turbot. All of these marine species have been swept up the short estuary from the Atlantic Ocean and have, to a greater or lesser extent, made a home in the loch's brackish water. Seals are also frequent visitors, to the disgust of many trout fishermen, and the 'inter-tidal zone' is a mass of bladder wrack and mussel shells. Insect forms, which rely on a freshwater habitat, are few and far between, and the major items on the menu are marine copepods, crustaceans and stickleback fry. Insect hatches are not totally absent and decent midge hatches occur from time to time, and I once saw a reasonable caenis hatch take place. But the fact that twice a month, spring tides flood millions of gallons of salty Atlantic water into Stenness should tell even the least experienced fly fisherman that any preconceived notions on how to tackle such a loch may have to be re-assessed.

One of the journalistic tricks frequently employed to describe a water and how it fishes is to use the 'imaginary day' ploy. A typical day on the loch in question is described in detail. You and I are going to fish together and as the imaginary day unfolds I, as the writer, will pack the narrative with all the things likely to happen, name all the popular drifts as we 'fish' them, discuss the flies as they catch fish – and the job is done.

It works very well, usually, and I've resorted to this trick in the past with effect. But it won't work on Stenness. Why? Because, firstly, if I could rake together a typical day, you'd suspect I'd being sniffing gink. And secondly, no two fishing days are remotely similar on this water.

Stenness just loves breaking its own rules. Just when it looks like a formula has been arrived at that will cover most eventualities, something comes along to blow all the carefully constructed theories apart.

For instance, Stenness trout are famed for lying in very shallow water. It is virtually impossible to fish too shallow and the normal technique is to bump the stones and cast to within inches of the margins. In this fashion big, and I mean big, browns are regularly caught, and I'll leave it to your imagination what a thoroughly unchuffed 3 lb. Trout can do in water with this lack of depth. I sometimes think they must lie on their sides like flounders in order to cover their backs.

But they do stack up in deep water – not often it's true – but often enough to force the Stenness regular to try such tactics on difficult and frustrating days when the margins seem deserted. Having said that, it is very unusual to find the best of the browns in deep water, but sea trout of size seem to sometimes prefer the deeper marks, so nothing ventured! Complacency and percentage fishing has no place on Stenness.

Many anglers consider Stenness to be beyond them, and although I do consider it to be Orkney's most challenging loch, it does respond to determination, perseverance and patience. And the rewards can be great (Did I mention that a 29+ lb. Stenness trout was captured on a flounder setline in the early 1900s?). The necessity for a patient approach is best explained by reference to an occasion from my catalogue of memories. A number of us set out to fish the loch one particular day at about 2.00 pm, having agreed to meet up at the Standing Stones Hotel at 8.00 pm that evening. The precise dimensions of the total catch I cannot recall, but I do

"The jury is still out on this one, but if any environment is going to produce a unique trout, then Stenness must be a contender."

remember being surprised to discover in discussion in the bar that the seven best fish (all in the region of 2 to 2.5 lb.) were caught between quarter and half past six. I had two of them. I saw nothing before 6.20 pm.

After 6.30 pm, it takes about 15 minutes to have a cup of tea, a sandwich and light the pipe – draw your own conclusions! The two trout were caught during a 20-minute period three-quarters of the way through a 4-hour stint.

Although Stenness is a prolific sea trout water with almost monthly runs of fish from February to October, real Stenness aficionados would much rather 'tie into' a good brown than a similarly sized sea trout. If there is another water in the British Isles inhabited by both browns and sea trout from which anglers prefer to capture the former, I've never heard of it! That, in a nutshell, sums up the quality of Stenness browns.

Fly selection has never been much of problem, the general rule being that almost anything repulsively garish, glittery and with a dash of fluorescence will work. Most Stenness regulars have 'secret' patterns, which consist of copious quantities of gold, silver, or pearl Lurex, orange or red hackles and bits & pieces of the sort of wild stuff that often remains in fly-tying kits more in hope than expectation. My own favourite patterns, which rarely see the light of day on any other water, are the Silver Cardinal Slick, Magenta Slick and the Dame Edna, the latter having proved indispensable over the last 5 years or so. Added to this small collection I would add Dunkeld, Fluo Soldier Palmer, Orangeman, Orange Zulu and, on occasion, something green. Floaters or intermediate lines are most popular, and on the two occasions when I resorted to a fast-sinking line on an experimental basis, I caught a pollack on the first and a whacking great crab on the second. Failure to catch fish will rarely have anything to do with fly selection or means of presentation, but more likely to be caused by weather conditions, height of water

(remember that the loch level, being influenced by marine tides, goes up and down like a fiddler's elbow) and location.

Although I can recall some very good fish being taken from this loch in very bright and calm conditions, quality Stenness trout are distressingly spooky and, by and large, un-catchable in calm conditions and this may be due to their desire to lie in very shallow water. Sunshine may not be a critical factor but wind speed and direction most certainly are. A good wave blowing on to the shore will stimulate the trout and an angler wading out to the top of his waders and casting back into the shore must expect fish. Obviously boat fishing with an on-shore wind plus the added factor of fish holding in inches of water produces boat-handling problems and visiting anglers would be advised to acquire ghillie. Should the loch level be abnormally high the angler will be wise to keep his options open as regards searching for fish-holding depth. I suspect that fish hold their territory regardless of level fluctuations and may well be found marginally deeper in such conditions, but Stenness browns are rarely at their most co-operative when the level is high and locals expect good fishing when the loch is low or, at least, falling.

All these factors make Stenness a fascinating water, but the story is not finished there: the trout may well be a unique sub-specie. Hamish Stuart, writing in the early '20s, certainly seemed to think so, and Gunther, a taxonomist who classified most of our British freshwater fishes, designated this sub-specie as Salmo trutta orcadensis. Although this system of separating trout into a variety of sub-species fell into disfavour in the latter half of this century, it has recently been vindicated by genetic studies. They have proved that specific environments may well produce adapted strains of trout, which, to a greater or lesser extent, may be considered sub-species. The jury is still out on this one, but if any environment is going to produce a unique trout, then Stenness must be a contender!

They are the most beautifully formed trout that I have come across in my wide travels and, though this may seem like heresy, they are also the sweetest tasting fish I have eaten, no doubt due to their environment and semi-marine diet.

It is common to use the term 'slob' in conjunction with brackish water trout. This is unfortunate as it gives the impression of ugliness and lack of vigour. Nothing could be further from the truth – estuarine/brackish water brown trout are invariably attractive, powerful and commonly above average size. The word 'slob' when used in this conjunction originates from an Irish word meaning estuary marshlands, which is a reference to environment rather than a character description. Another indicator of their possible unique quality is the way they come to a fly. In really wild weather these browns tend to mimic their lesser brethren and slam into the fly with a vigorous slash, but in a lesser wave they come furrowing through the water with a wave on their back. It is a characteristic of this strain of trout that they rarely take a fly that they have not followed for a distance, and to see a big brown sweeping in on a fly in the gin-clear water of Stenness is a major angling thrill.

Stenness is perhaps the least popular Orcadian venue for vacation anglers. This is largely due to logistical problems. Boat-hire is not as easily obtained here as on other lochs, although the Standing Stones Hotel has this facility available to guests and casual visitors, and can arrange ghillies that will put you on the mark. It tends to fish best when inexperienced anglers may be deterred by wind and wave condition. It does not fit the picture of the typical trout water, and many of us are reticent about subjecting our beloved tackle to the corrosive effects of brackish water. One almost needs a brand new mind-set when tackling Stenness but, like the trout themselves, if you can adapt to this environment you will succeed!

FLY PATTERN DRESSINGS

Dame Edna
Hook: Kamasan B170, #10 & 12
Silk: Fluo white thread
Tail: Crimson fluff from base of big hen hackle
Body: Flat pearl tinsel
Wing: White goose/duck
Hackle - Longish crimson hen, tied over the wing

Silver Cardinal Slick
Hook: As above
Silk: Very fine flat silver holographic tinsel
Tail: slim bunch of scarlet rabbit fur
Body: Created in tinsel by the tying in of the wing
Wing: Bunches of scarlet rabbit fur, tied matuka-style down the back of the hook

Magenta Slick
Hook: as above
Silk: Very fine red holographic tinsel
Body: Created in tinsel by the tying in of the wing
Wing: Bunches of magenta rabbit fur, tied matuka-style down the back of the hook

TRAVEL
Most visiting anglers prefer to bring their own transport for increased mobility during their stay. Contact P&O Scottish Ferries at Tel. 01224 572615 or Fax. 01224 574411 for details of car-ferries from Aberdeen or Scrabster.

ACCOMMODATION
The Standing Stones Hotel, on the shores of the loch, offers the angler all the services required for a perfect stay. Recently modernised, the hotel is comfortable, friendly and with a reputation for good food. Scottish Tourist Board – Highly Commended (4 crown). Contact Colin Inness for details on 01856 850449, or Fax: 01856 851262.

FURTHER INFORMATION
Further information on fishing may be obtained from W S Sinclair, The Tackle Shop, 27 John Street, Stromness, Orkney. Tel. 01856 850469

General tourist info may be obtained from the Orkney Tourist Board, 6 Broad Street, Kirkwall, KW15 1NX. Tel: 01856 872856, Fax: 01856 875056.

Scotland for Sea Angling

The Scottish Federation of Sea Anglers (SFSA)

The Scottish Federation of Sea Anglers (SFSA) is recognised by the Scottish Sports Council as the governing body for the sport of Sea Fishing in Scotland.

Secretary/Administrator is Mrs Paula Lees. Paula can be contacted at the SFSA Headquarters, Caledonia House, Edinburgh, Tel/Fax: 0131 317 7192

The SFSA, in association with member clubs, organises a full schedule of sea angling fixtures, competitions and major championships throughout the year, around mainland Scotland and the Western Isles, Orkney and Shetland.

The angling has changed much over the last forty years since the early days of organised Scottish sea angling events, but there are still wonderful opportunities for sports fishermen to test their skills from the shore, dinghy fishing and charter boats.

For many years now, conservation has been very prominent both in Scottish competitions and leisure recreation and considerate anglers return much of their catch carefully to the water, keeping only what they need for the dining table.

With fresh cod and haddock costing more these days than farm salmon, it is a welcome and acceptable bonus to sports fishing, to have delicious fresh fish to eat. It also makes the effort of getting afloat or travelling to your favourite beach or rocky headland extremely cost effective if the fish are biting!

For the individual angler, competitions are a cost-effective way of getting afloat on a professional sea angling charter.

SFSA Competition Venues

Scotland for Fishing takes you on a coastal tour of the main annual competition venues, based on the 2001 fixture list: most will host similar events in 2002.

The SFSA fixture season starts and ends with a New Year shore event and the boat fishing competitions heat up with the April spring fixtures.

January 2002

The **Central Region New Year Open Sweepstake** takes place on January 6th, which hopefully gives everyone enough time to recover from the Hogmany festivities.

Entry Form and further details can be obtained from P Smalls, 119 Jennie Rennies Road, Dunfermline KY11 3BD. Telephone: 01383 733 175 (SAE Please)

The **North East Region (Open) Shore** competition is scheduled for 27th January. Venue is from Carnoustie to Ferryden.

Registration: 7.00am – 8.30am. Fishing: 9.00am – 3.00pm. For further details, contact Stan Eggie. Telephone: 01307 465 355

April

The **SFSA Open Shore Sweep** normally takes place along the shores of Loch Ryan with registration from 9.00am – 9.45am and fishing from 10.30am – 2.30pm

The 4 hour event is normally pegged and can accommodate 70 anglers. Loch Ryan can produce excellent shoreline sport with thornback rays, dogfish, flatfish and codling.

Good conger eels sometimes turn up too. Lug and ragworm can be dug locally. Fish strip baits are also excellent for dogfish, ray and conger. Thornbacks and conger can make a mess of nylon traces, so a bottom snood with wire is sometimes recommended when targeting these fish.

The local SFSA representative is Mr D Neil, 3 Roman Road, Ayr, KA7 3SZ . Telephone: 01292 281 945. When writing for information, please mention Scotland for Fishing and enclose a stamped addressed envelope.

May

Erskine (Open) Shore Sweepstake. Normally around mid-month and a 6 hour free-range event which can produce codling, flatfish and occasional ray and conger.

Ragworm and lug are both good baits, but fresh peeler crab is hard to beat and often produces the best catches. If you want to target dogfish, both LSD's (lesser-spotted dogfish) and spurdogs can be caught, try fresh mackerel or herring strip.

Details of the 2002 event can be obtained from Mr D Neil, 3 Roman Road, Ayr KA7 3SZ

Telephone: 01292 281 945 (SAE Please)

The **Orkney Tourist Board Trophy** is another event which normally takes place in May in the Orkney Isles out from the Mainland town of Stromness on Scapa Flow.

Venue is Stromness but depending on the weather, boats can fish inside Scapa Flow around Graemsay Island and beyond, or head out through Hoy Sound for the Pentland Firth.

This is superb, big fish country and one of the first venues for common skate and porbeagle shark. The legendary Les Moncrieff shared a catch of 5 common skate with Mike Shepley in June 1968, the first-ever recorded on rod and line in Scotland. That other great sporting fish, the elusive halibut is also home to the tide rips and races off the Orkney Isles. The first British Rod-caught Record for the species was taken way back in 1967 by Jack Scott, on the same day that Mike Shepley smashed the then ling record with a fish which more than doubled the record at 33 lbs. The following year, the then Provost of Stromness, Bunt Knight landed an

A beautiful red gurnard, one of three gurnard species found in Scottish waters. They are generaslly found inshore in relatively shallow waters up to 10 fathoms (20 metres) and will readily take a small fish strip bait, lug or ragworm. You can find wrasse, rock codling, coalfish and pollack on the same ground.

enormous halibut of 163 lbs. while fishing for haddock – a new European and British rod-caught record.

It's not surprising that the EFSA European Championships have been awarded to Orkney in 2003. Local SFSA contact for the spring event is John Geddes, Quarryfield, Orphir, Orkney KW17 2RF, Telephone: 01856 811 311 (SAE Please).

The **SFSA Home Nations Boat International** in 2001 was fished out from Arbroath on the Firth of Forth in late May, an excellent time normally for the spring runs of codling into the firth. Unlike the Clyde, shellfish baits and worm/ mussel cocktails work better than rag or lugworm, Mussel can be notoriously difficult to keep on the hook, and red wool bound round the bait helps keep this tasty morsel on long enough to secure a hook-up. Catches are predominantly codling, but better cod to double figures occasionally turn up, as well as coalies, sea scorpions, wrasse, small ling and flatfish.

The **Alistair Craig Memorial (Open) Shore Festival** normally takes place in late May and is a shore-fished event, from Erskine Bridge (Old Kilpartick) to Rosneath Point. Good flatfish and codling shoreline this and the event encourages youngsters to participate. There is an extensive junior prize table, senior cash prizes and the impressive Alistair Craig Trophy to the top SFSA

Club Member. An added bonus is the free entry for juniors accompanied by an adult entry.

Entry Forms and details of the 2002 event can be obtained from John Syme, 3 Thornhill Way, Carnbroe, Coatbridge ML5 4UD, Telephone: 01236 602723. When writing for information, please mention *Scotland for Fishing* and enclose a stamped addressed envelope.

June

Last season, the **Scottish Individual & Team (Open) Shore Championships** took place early in June, with registration at the Riverside Drive Venue in Dundee. This is normally a roving competition and can produce some good shoreline flatfish and codling from beaches and rocky points.

While mussel/ worm cocktails work well, they don't cast successfully and ragworm, peeler crab and lugworm are preferred baits, and good for flounders, dabs and codling.

The SFSA liason and organiser for last year's competition can advise visitors about this competition and the fishing along the Firth of Tay Contact I Hardie for further information, 51 Suttieside Road, Forfar DD8 3EL, Telephone: 01307 466 042 (Stamped addressed envelope please.)

Another June event is the **Peever Open Shore Championship** fished out from Kirkcudbright. Registration is normally at the Gordon House Hotel with fishing from 10.00am – 4.00pm. Pre-booking is available and information can be obtained from organiser and SFSA contact Keith Marshall, 64 Millflats, Kirkcudbright DG6 4ER Telephone: 01557 331 761 (SAE Please)

Another popular Orkney Islands event for the **Orkney Tourist Board Trophy** takes place out from Stromness each June. This coincides with the build up of inshore stocks and can also produce some big 'barn door' common skate. These slow-growing fish are generally released alive to the water after tagging and measuring.

Good ling and codling can be taken off St John's Head in Hoy Sound. Drift fishing is the preferred method and feathering with or without bait will also attract coalfish and pollack. Haddock fishing used to be good, but these fish are far more elusive these days.

Further details are available from John Geddes, Quarryfield, Orphir, Orkney KW17 2RF. Telephone: 01856 811 311 (SAE Please)

Pittenweem has been the popular venue for the **EFSA (Scotland) European Cod Championships** for many years now, and generally produces excellent sport with light tackle drift fishing a short distance offshore. Mixed cocktail baits, mussel, rag, lugworm and peeler crab if available are all excellent baits.

The event offers 2 man and 4 man teams plus Sweep and Super Pool with some excellent cash and tackle prizes. For further details contact Ian MacGregor, 35 Nevis Park, Inverness IV3 8RX, Telephone: 01463 223 621. When writing for information, please mention *Scotland for Fishing* and enclose a stamped addressed envelope.

July
Another great month for fishing in the Orkney isles and the July **Tourist Board Trophy** is normally fished out from Stromness, targetting common skate, raysa and dogfish in Scapa Flow, the reef pollack, or cod and ling drift fishing the grounds off St John's Head. Depending on the weather, boats can go further afield along the Pentland Firth coast of the Island of Hoy or south out of Hoy Sound. Other species include coalfish, haddock, wrasse and flatfish.The mackerel shoals are generally plentiful at this time of year, and fresh mackerel strip is hard to beat for most species. Whole coalfish fillet is also an excellent bait for common skate.

Details and entry forms can be obtained from John Geddes, Quarryfield, Orphir, Orkney KW17 2RF. Telephone: 01856 811 311 (SAE Please)

LADS Club SAC Open Shore Festival is an open event which usually takes place from the Borrowhead Holiday Village, Isle of Whithorn.

A roving competition, the venue covers the Innerwell Fishery to Portwilliam. No Lesser Spotted Dogfish are weighed in, which indicates just how common this species is. Don't use fish strip baits and you are less likely to target them. Fresh lugworm and peeler crab will attract somegood pollack (lythe) from rocky outcrops,

coalfish, wrasse and flatties, the latter from sandy venues. Surprisingly good rock codling and cod can also come to hand. The Solway Firth and Mull of Galloway host some of Scotland's biggest bass - and these can turn up on surf beaches and rocky outcrops adjacent to estuaries and beaches. They feed on white ragworm, rag, lugworm and especially sandeels and other small fish. Bait up accordingly to target them!

Details of fishing in the area can be obtained from Frank McCrone, 30 Downs Place, Heathhall, Dumfries DG1 3RF. Telephone: 01387 265 856 (SAE Please)

The **East Fife Summer Open** is another roving competition which covers the shoreline from Elie to St Andrews, both towns probably better known for their superb championship golf courses.

East Fife offers splendid opportunities for a family holiday, and for the angler, excellent stillwater fisheries nearby such as Loch Fitty (Kingseat) and Loch Leven (Kinross) among many other excellent rainbow and brown trout fisheries offering bank and boat fishing.

For information on sea angling, particularly for the roving shore fishing event, please contact Rose Brown, 93 Windsor Road, Falkirk FK1 5DB. Telephone: 01324 626 568 (SAE Please)

The **SFSA Interclub Knockout Shore Final** (Closed event) in 2001 was fished out from the Isle of Whithorn. Entry details for Isle of Whitehorn based events for 2002 can be obtained from Mr J Williamson, 33 Ross Street, Ayr KA8 9PL. Telephone: 01292 618 719

Also in July, the **P&O Ferries Festival** keeps holiday anglers happy in Orkney. Stromness is again the port of call and John Geddes, Quarryfield, Orphir KW17 2RF can advise visitors of competition details. Telephone: 01856 811 311 (SAE Please)

Orkney offers anglers excellent wild brown trout fishing in many lochs and sea trout sport from the shoreline. The excellent choice of hotels includes the

Stromness Hotel for the sea angling events and Merkister Hotel (Loch Harray) and Stenness Hotel (Loch Stenness) as your base for superb wild brown trout fishing. You can also check full details of Orkney hotels in our hotel directory.

Peterhead hosts an annual Scottish Week, and the **Scottish Week (Open) Shore** competition is popular with visiting anglers as well as the local experts. Codling, coalfish, pollack (lythe) and flatfish are the predominant species. Contact Mr J Maskame, 74 Ravenscraig Road, Peterhead, AB42 1RA for more details. Telephone: 01779 490 666 (SAE Please)

Another island venue and the first seasonal competition visit to the Western Isles is for the annual **Western Isles (Open) Championships**, normally fished out from Carloway, Isle of Lewis. This well established event is run annually by Stornoway SAC at a venue described with relish as 'where anglers can be assured of quality fish, great variety of species and excellent hospitality.'

The editor Mike Shepley has personally experienced Stornoway SAC's first class club facilities and the superb fishing on many occasions over more than 20 years, including two EFSA European Championships:

"I can guarantee that visitors who make the trip, whether by sea on CalMac or fly inbound to Stornoway on the regular scheduled flights, are assured a warm welcome. The problem is balancing the fishing offshore with the refreshments the night before!"

Stornoway has the distinction of also holding the Scottish Record for that rare visitor, the blue shark: porbeagle are more common.

More details from C J Buchanan, 15 Killegray Court, Stornoway, Isle of Lewis. Telephone: 01851 706 525 (SAE Please). Anglers should note that the Isle of Lewis has excellent loch fly fishing for wild brown trout, and good runs of salmon and sea trout throughout the summer months.

The **Isle of Skye (Open) Boat Competition** is another venue where sea anglers are assured of good sport and good company. And judging by local SFSA representative's address, golf is also on the menu. Add to that the Stoer lochs and reasonably priced and accessible sea trout and salmon fishing on spate rivers and lochans, Skye has plenty to offer as well as some of the most stunning and majestic scenery in Scotland.

The sea angling festival dates are confirmed well

ahead of the event but the venue is generally not decided until the availability of boats can be confirmed, normally one week prior to the competition. Details of the annual event can be obtained from John McInnes, 'Golf View', Kilmuir, Dunvegan, Isle of Skye. Telephone: 01470 521 724 (SAE Please).

August

One of the busiest months in the SFSA festival calendar with the **SFSA Interclub Junior Knockout Shore Final**. This closed event was fished last season at Society Point, Abercorn, South Queensferry on the south shores of the Firth of Forth. Very much 'flattie' country, the catches are mainly of flounders and dabs: ragworm, lug and peeler crab are all excellent baits, and long distance casting is not necessary. The Forth can produce some nice school bass, and peeler or sandeels or fish strip baits to imitate them [fresh mackerel strip makes an excellent substitute] will give you a chance of success with these tasty fish. In recent seasons, chicken turbot have also been taken by shore anglers along the Firth of Forth and again, these handsome flatfish prefer a fish strip bait or peeler crab to worms.

Further details can be obtained from P Smalls, 119 Jennie Rennies Road, Dunfermline KY11 3BD. Telephone: 01383 733 175

The August **Orkney Tourist Board Trophy** is featured out from Stromness and details as before can be obtained from John Geddes, Quarryfield, Orphir, Orkney, KW17 2RF

Telephone: 01856 811 311 (SAE Please). In addition to the splendid trout fishing which Orkney has to offer, already mentioned previously, there is some excellent sea angling from the shoreline, which includes fly and bait fishing for sea trout. There are numerous sandy beaches which offer first class sport with flounders and dabs as well as occasional plaice. Spinning and bait fishing from the Churchill Barriers connecting the islands can also give the intrepid angler sport with pollack (lythe), coalfish, codling and flatfish. Sea trout can also taken from February 25th when the season opens throughout the summer and early autumn.

One of the most popular shoreline venues for sea angling in Scotland is the Firth of Clyde and its associated sea lochs. August offers an annual opportunity for club and competition anglers to participate in one of Scotland's major shore events, the **Inverclyde (Open) Shore Championships**. The fishing takes place from Largs

Burn to Custom House Quay, Greenock, with plenty of hot spots from which to choose. Harbour marks can produce codling and some surprisingly good conger eels. The shoreline is rocky and you can lose quite a lot of terminal tackle, but if you are targetting the better cod, it's often necessary to get in amongst the tangle. Ragworm and lugworm are both excellent baits, but the elusive peeler crab is the supreme bait for codling and wrasse.

Sandy marks also offer good flatfish and 2lbs plus flounders are not uncommon. Fish strip baits will also attract lesser spotted dogfish and occasional spurdogs as well as conger eels and thornback ray. The attractively marked cuckoo ray is not uncommon in the Firth of Clyde, although as with the conger, most activity is nocturnal, so they are a rare catch during day-time competitions.

Registration is always at the Ashton Car Park, Gourock and fishing normally coincides with the last of the ebb and the first few hours of the incoming tide which generally produces the best of the catches. Mackerel are taken in good numbers from the shoreline all along this part of the Firth of Clyde, but are restricted during the competitions. Fresh mackerel make an excellent cut-strip bait and are also great fried freshly filleted in oatmeal!

More information on the competition and dates for 2002 can be obtained from D Neil, 3 Roman Road, Ayr KA7 3SZ. Telephone: 01292 281 945.

The **Highlands of Scotland, Small Boats Championships** is fished in August from a number of venues and is one of several small boat events around the Scottish coast, where anglers can enter their own dinghy or smaller craft. Strict safety rules of course apply.

Details of this event can be obtained from Scottish Internationalist, Hamish Holmes, Inglewood, Braal Road, Halkirk, Caithness, Tel: 01847 831 985 (SAE Please).

The **Mary Mass Small Boats Competition** is organised by Irvine Water Sports Club, with fishing taking place inshore, drift fishing over rough ground. Codling are the main target species normally, although good shoals of spurdogfish can turn up. Softer ground offers some nice flatfish, including specimen sized plaice.

Details from C Higgins, 31 Druid Drive, Kilwinning KA13 7BB. Telephone: 01294 557 078

The **Stan Pyke Trophy** is Orkney's second contribution to the August festival calendar. Stromness is again the venue and details and entry forms are available from John Geddes, Quarryfield, Orphir, Orkney KW17 2RF. Telephone: 01856 811 311 (SAE Please)

The **Western Isles Cod Festival** is again centred on Carloway, Isle of Lewis and drift fishing with baited feathers, Mr Twisters, Regills and other spoons and lures all do the trick. Sometimes the problem is to stay on target with the cod, as spurdogs, coalfish and pollack can get in the way at times!

Details are available from C J Buchanan, 15 Killegray Court, Stornoway HS1 2UJ. Telephone: 01851 706 525.

Millport on the Isle of Cumbrae is but a short ferry ride from Gourock, Ardrossan or Fairlie and hosts an **All Nighter Sea Angling Competition** with registration at the Royal George Hotel, Millport from early evening and fishing from 9 pm through to breakfast time next day.

Look out for some good congers at night and a chance of occasional thornback and even cuckoo ray if you are lucky. Dogfish, codling, coalfish, pollack, wrasse and flatfish will make up the bulk of the rest of the catches

September
The **Scottish Light Line Championships** in 2001 took place out from Scrabster in Caithness, port of call and departure for Mainland Orkney, visible across the Pentland Firth.

Thurso Bay and Dunnet Head are famous for superb sea angling, whether you head east for Dunnet and beyond, or head west towards Dounreay. Previous Scottish, British and European records have been taken out from Scrabster, including ling, pollack, halibut and porbeagle shark.

The light line championships do not target the 'big-game' species such as halibut and porbeagle, but they have been known to turn up, as well as giant 'barn-door' common skate, although they are less frequently hooked than in Orkney waters.

For further details on the light line championships, contact A J Mackenzie, 6 Teal Avenue, Inverness IV2 3TB. Telephone: 01463 230 227 (SAE Please)

The **Clyde & Western Region Pegged (Open) Shore Sweep** also incorporates the **Junior Open Shore Championships**. There is an excellent prize list and sweeps with junior tackle prizes amounting to over £ 1000. Junior entry is free when accompanied by a participating adult.

Fishing is from Greenock Esplanade and is a restricted peg match, with catches mainly codling, flatfish, coalfish and wrasse. Further details are available from Chad J Wright, 41 Maple Avenue, Dumbarton G82 5HT.

Telephone: 01389 605426

Catch the right tide and September is an excellent month for flatfish. No surprise then that the organisers stage the popular **Scottish (Open) Flounder Championships** at Port Edgar, South Queensferry during this month. Ragworm, lugworm and peeler all work well, and expect good flounders to better 2lbs, dabs and, if you're lucky, occasional plaice from this vast sandy shoreline. Bait can be dug at low tide, but Mike's Tackle Shop of Portobello, Edinburgh can always provide bait, tackle and excellent friendly advice. Telephone: 0131 657 3258

The **Caithness (Open) Boat Competition** choses Scrabster for its venue and anglers are fishing with experienced local skippers who know the grounds well. Specimen pollack, excellent cod and ling, coalfish until your arms drop at times, whiting and haddock if you are lucky. And beware the elusive but predatory porbeagle shark and legendary halibut which stalk the endge of the tide races off Dunnet Head and Holborn Head. Further details from Scottish Internationalist, Hamish Holmes, Inglewood, Braal Road, Halkirk, Caithness. Hamish is also no beginner when it comes to salmon and wild brown trout either and is always happy to point visiting anglers in the right direction. You can reach Hamish by telephone on 01847 831 985, or if writing, please don't forget to enclose a stamped addressed envelope.

For shore fishing in and around Thurso Bay, look no further than Scrabster Harbour for flatfish, codling and excellent conger eels.The Scottish Record shore-caught conger of 45 lbs came from the inside harbour wall.

Try the giant slab rocks below Holborn Lighthouse for pollack, rock cod, coalfish and wrasse. But do take care, and use a floatation jacket for security and never fish alone, as the tidal surge can be dangerous in rough weather.

There are plenty of other shoreline marks including the majestic surf beach spanning Dunnet Bay, with excellent night time sport with flatfish, dogfish, congers and surprisingly so far north, bass. The little bay at Myrkle will also delight the shore angler with specimen flounders on the flood tide.

Back on the Firth of Clyde, the **Predators Cash For Kids Charity Sweepstake** is venued at Old Kilpatrick & Bowling. This is normally a pegged match with 20 pegs at Bowling and 40 at Old Kilpatrick. There are cash prizes and all juniors accompanied by participating adults fish for free.

Details: David Waters, 82 Edinbegg Avenue, Rutherglen, Glasgow G42 0EW. Telephone: 0141 569 9608

The penultimate event in a very busy Orkney sea angling festival calander last year was the prestigious **Scottish (Open) Boat Championships**. This event was fished in conjunction with the **Orkney (Open) Boat Championships** out from Stromness.

The Orkney Islands S.A.A, now in its 36th year, once again presented these major championships, with generous prizes, good organisation and excellent fishing for which Orkney is justly famous. And no greater recognition of this, than that Orkney has been awarded the EFSA European Championships in 2003.

October

It should come as no surprise to those that know Orkney that their annual **Ling Competition** takes place in October on some of the best ling grounds in the North Sea. The combination of tides and rough, kelpy ground off St John's Head and the Old Man of Hoy are ideal hunting ground for big ling – and indeed big pollack.

Expect some good cod too, and the writer once witnessed a huge halibut follow a hooked cod close to the surface, before turning and disappearing back to the depths.

Main target species is of course ling which peak in October and November, and best method drifting over these skerries, is to use a fresh mackerel strip or whole small squid on a flowing trace. Ling have sharp teeth, so a wire trace is adviseable if not compulsory.

A sink and draw action, feeling for the bottom and the troughs, will minimise tackle loss, and attract the ling to the bait. when a ling takes, it is a surprisingly gentle but forceful pull: dip the rod tip into the take and then strike hard, continuing to keep the pressure on and hopefully ensure your prize ling doesn't find the kelp.

The **SFSA Inter Club Knockout Boat Final** took place last year at Scrabster in Caithness and is a closed event, open only to member clubs of the Scottish Federation of Sea Anglers.

For the holiday angler and visitor, charter boats operate out from Scrabster throughout the year and winter can produce excellent sport with cod, pollack and big coalfish. The mighty porbeagle shark are present throughout the year, especially off the two headlands in Thurso Bay, but Dunnet Head to Dunnet Bay produces particularly spectacular sport with these giants, which seems to peak in mid-February each year. Many of these huge shark are tagged and released nowadays by sporting anglers, although they can fetch a good price at market. It can be cold and rough, but the dedicated anglers who target these tough fighters, wouldn't have it any other way.

There are excellent hotels in Thurso and the Upper Deck in Scrabster serves some of the freshest haddock and best steaks north of Inverness. Caithness offers the holiday fisherman unlimited wild brown trout fishing on many lochs, with excellent value-for-money salmon and sea trout too. Golfers can find an excellent links course at Reay and both Thurso and Wick have first class courses open to visitors.

October also sees the annual **Ayr (Open) Shore Sweepstake** fished at a popular and easily accessible venue, the Troon Ballast Bank. This is a short boundary roving event offering good sport on rough ground for codling, dogfish, pollack and wrasse.

The **South Ayrshire Masters** takes place on **Prestwick and Newton Beaches** and is regarded as Scotland's largest pegged angling event with top class takle prizes and large cash prizes.

Registration is at the Prestwick Sailing Club and flatfish, codling and dogfish feature prominently in the catches from both beaches.

Information on this part of the Ayrshire coastline and both 2002 events can be obtained from Jim Williamson, 33 Ross Street, Ayr KA8 9PL. Telephone: 01292 618 719

Another closed competition for SFSA members only is the annual **SFSA Inter-region Challenge Cup** fished at various venues on the Fife coast. This event epitomises the strong club based competitive spirit of the Scottish Federation of Sea Anglers. and details can be obtained from SFSA, Caledonia House, South Gyle, Edinburgh EH12 9DQ. Telephone: 0131 317 7192

The **Clyde Specimen Hunters (Open) Shore Festival** from Erskine Bridge (Old Kirkpatrich) to Roseneath point is another popular shore-based event, with codling, dogfish and flatfish the main target species.

For the 2002 competition, please contact John Syme, 3 Thornhill Way, Carnbroe, Coatbridge ML5 4UD. Telephone: 01236 602723

The **West of Scotland Region (Open) Shore Championship** venue is Ayr, Custom House Quay. Details for the 2002 event are available from Pat McGoogan, 17 Central Avenue, Ardrossan KA22 7DZ. Telephone: 01294 461 280.

November
Caithness (Open) Shore Competition

This competition is fished on various Caithness Beaches. The surf can be prodigious on Dunnet Beach and powerful rods and grip leads are sometime needed to hold the bait amongst the fish. Lighter tackle is often all that is need for the flatfish, which run close inshore on the shallow tables between the waves, where they suck up the worms, shellfish and crabs dislodged by the waves. Bass can also be on the menu as well as dogfish.

Hamish Holmes, Inglewood, Braal Road, Halkirk, Caithness has the details for 2002. Telephone: 01847 831 985 (SAE Please)

The **East of Scotland Open Shore Festival** also incorporates the **Scottish Winter (Open) Shore Championships**

In 2001, this event was staged out from Dysart in Fife. The Scottish Winter Shore Championships was again run in conjunction with the East of Scotland Open Shore Festival, which is organised by Central Region.

Details of forthcoming events for the 2002 season can be obtained from S Taggart, 120 Croft Crescent, Markinch, KY7 6ES. Telephone: 01592 759 170 (SAE Please).

December
The **St Serfs SAC Xmas (Open) Shore Competition** offers you the chance of festive fish on the menu along with your traditional Christmas turkey.

For further details and entry forms, please contact George Harris, 4 Colquhoun Avenue, Pitcairn, Glenrothes KY7 6FH. Tel: 01592 620211 Tel/Fax: 0131 317 7192.

Sea Angling on Arran

by Mike Prichard

I love islands! As I look back at my sea fishing career, if you can call it that, I find that many if not most of my more successful moments were when fishing off or around an island. That isn't remarkable when you look at the attraction that islands have for both humans and fish.

Coming from an island race, albeit a bit mixed in race and country of origin, I think it natural that people from the British Isles feel comfortable on a bit of land stuck out in an ocean. Fish, on the other hand, are aware that an island gives them many favourable places to live.

These can be territories that present good feeding opportunities, places of safety and resting places out from the tidal stream as it sweeps around an island. In short, I'd rather fish around an island than on an open seabed!

I've been thinking over the best of these island situations: The Blaskets, at the end of the Dingle Peninsula, The Aran Islands, out from Galway Bay, The Orkneys, The Isle of Wight, The Channel Isles and last, but not least, The Isle of Arran. It

was a great favourite for me. Times have changed and the Island doesn't produce as it once did. Much of the problem has come about because the scallops have disappeared. These shellfish gathered in huge beds along the Scottish West Coast. Arran was fortunate in having a vast quantity of scallops present in Lamlash Bay. It was a haven for haddock fishermen.

I must admit that I preferred to fish outside of the Holy Isle. Here there are patches of roughish ground that attracted haddock, cod and, of course, the pollack. One mark, 'Jamieson's Knoll', was a particular favourite. It's a small pinnacle that rises up from broken ground, probably an extension of the sharply-rising cliffs of the island's outer face. In those days the problem was to pinpoint good marks. We had no video sounders, giving a graphic display of what was under the keel. I had a primitive sounder with a revolving blip on the screen. It gave an indication of depth and would pick up rising rocks from the seabed.

With a few months use, one could actually trace beds of kelp and see a difference between a hard or soft seabed.

The late and great Dennis Burgess who for many years ran self-hire angling boats out of Brodick and Lamlash on the Isle of Arran.

On the top of the pinnacle there were pollack – not massive fish but large enough to put a graceful curve into a 12lb class rod. Below, on the side of the Knoll I once caught a ling, a fish of about 10lb. It was the only ling that I ever had from the Firth of Clyde!

Dennis Burgess, who at one time ran the Arran Sea Angling Centre in Brodick, and I used to fish from a 16 feet clinker dinghy along the seaward side of the Holy Isle. Fishing this way, from a small boat, gives a better contact with the weight and the seabed.

Sometimes we fished the bottom with a haddock rig, designed by Neil McLean. It worked superbly.

Neil told me regularly that I was losing haddock because of striking too early. His argument was that this species feeds very carefully on the open scallops. Neil said that he thought the fish sucked the live scallop from its shell and we could expect the fish to take out hookbaits in the same, carefully, sucked fashion. A massive strike would only result in tearing the bait out of the haddock's mouth!

The Arran Haddock Rig, a sort of leger/paternoster rig worked on the basis that the fish pulled the hookbait against the weight of the sinker. The angler didn't react until he felt a positive pull. This demanded considerable discipline but it worked and our haddock catches improved considerably.

Fishing for pollack was different. We sometimes fished a long flowing trace in a slackish tide, allowing the hookbait to swim in the current above the inshore kelpbeds. At other times trolling was a productive style, towing a Redgill or Mevagissey lure behind a slowly moving dinghy. If we wanted larger pollack, we had to go down to the south end of Arran, to Pladda and the reef area around the island lighthouse.

Our codfishing could be almost anywhere but one mark sticks in my mind. By the creamery at Sliddery, there was a track that ran down to a rocky shore. We could launch our dinghy here and motor out to offshore reefs about a mile or so.

There wasn't much water over the reef but between the spurs, in the sandy patches, there were always cod to be found feeding.

Perhaps they had scallop and mussel beds as a sort of larder, because the reefs gave superb protection in rough weather to the fish that resided in the location.

As I said at the beginning, for me the best and most interesting fishing was always around an island.

We didn't throw an anchor over the side to await the arrival of fish, but we hunted for them.

Using our knowledge of where the food resource was located and how the fish lived in the habitat, we were invariably able to find the fish – and catch them!.

Mike Prichard is a regular contributor to **www.rod-and-line.net** and author of many notable books on angling, including Collins Encyclopedia of Fishing in the British Isles.

Arran for game fishing too!

Arran has often been described as Scotland in miniature and so it's not surprising that with its mountains and glens, it also has a number of rivers. They are basically spate streams and you have to be there at the right time if you hope to catch salmon and sea trout. They do, however, offer delightful fishing in spectacular scenery, and you will not have to pay a king's ransom for the privilege of casting a fly. This is light tackle country and all you need is a trout fly rod and plenty of backing.

The rivers are very much spate streams and the ideal time to be fishing is as the waters are dropping off after a spate. Sea trout and salmon run from late June through the summer and given sufficient water, sport can be good with grilse averaging 5-6lbs and sea trout about 2lbs.

Autumn can produce consistent sport, but fish start to colour up after August and discretion should be used when deciding whether a fish should be kept or returned with care to the water.

Brodick and Lamlash both have excellent golf courses. Port Na Lochan is a small put and take fishery stocked with rainbow trout averaging from 1.5 lbs with the chance of much better fish. Bait and fly are both allowed and tickets are available from the Kinloch Hotel.

Machrie Water fishes best after a spate and produces around 60 salmon and 40 sea trout each season. Small flies and single handed rod is all you require.

And of course water!

Permits are available for the Machrie Water from the River Bailiff (01770) 840241.

Loch Leven

KINROSS-SHIRE

Loch Leven is undoubtedly Scotland's most famous loch, other than perhaps Loch Ness and its elusive monster. The silvery strain of Loch Leven brown trout are a sporting and culinary delight, now joined in recent seasons by equally handsome, grown-on rainbows.

It is a fly only fishery with no bank fishing. As a Nature Reserve, the birdlife is also an added bonus to the spectacular scenery and sport. Fifty years ago, the clinker-style boats required two boatmen on the oars. They were the backbone of the fishery and had a canny knack of knowing where the fish would be rising.

Outboards have replaced the boatmen know, but the trout still have an infuriating habit of restricting their activity to relatively small areas of this huge loch. The loch has its own hatchery and strips brown trout from the two main feeder burns. The young trout are in due course released into the loch.

The owner Sir David Montgomery introduced rainbow trout some years ago, amidst controversy and with mixed response from regular anglers. The decision was made because of the decline in the natural brown trout and sport in general. The rainbows are grown on and released at around 12-16 ounces in weight. Once in the loch, they have proved to be avid feeders and double figure specimens have already been caught. The 2001 season ended on an interesting note however, with relatively few rainbows coming to the net.

Club competitions are very popular on the loch, but fishery manager Willie Wilson has expressed concern that quite a number of small brown trout, although above the minimum size, do get weighed in, and this is undoubtedly affecting the overall average weight of the browns. Increased minimum weights are definitely on the cards for 2002.

Traditional casts for Loch Leven often meant 4 flies, not 3, and small doubles were very much in favour. There was something wrong if your cast didn't include a Greenwell's Glory (with yellow butt), an Invicta or Woodcock and Mixed, Burleigh and perhaps a Kingfisher Butcher or Silver Butcher on the bob. The modern Loch Leven angler will add to the traditional loch-style flies, an assortment of small buzzers, nymphs and dry flies, including hoppers and sedge patterns. Add to that an assembly of mini-lures and fry imitators in the autumn and you will be well prepared for both rainbows and resident browns.

One traditional fly, which has stood the test of time, particularly when trout are on the tiny perch fry, is the peacock-herled Alexandra. It will take surface feeding rainbows and browns. Ask Bill Findlay: he fished with an old Alexandra which had graced his fly box for 20 years and caught a 9 lbs. 13 oz rainbow during a September competition in 2001 with Dundee East End AC.

- Loch Leven has 48 boats available, but they are often booked well in advance for both day time and evening sessions. There is a good selection of flies available for sale and excellent bar snacks.

- Day boats cost £45 for three rods from the start of the season through to 9th May with modest increases peaking at £51 from the beginning of June through to 19th July for day boats. There are reductions for evening boats and part-day boats when available.

River Tay, Dunkeld

PERTHSHIRE

By the time the mighty River Tay reaches Dunkeld and Birnham, it has some of the finest holding pools for salmon on the system. And if any pedigree for such a famous angling area was required, a Dunkeld on the tail of your cast and a Loch Ordy, with its ginger and white hackles, on the bob, must surely confirm it status as a great fly fishing area.

Between Logierait and the broad reaches of Dunkeld, beats such as Kinnaird and Dalguise are also famous for large salmon, many of them running in July. Of course autumn also produces its big fish and a lady angler harling the main pool above Dunkeld Bridge described a cock salmon as being: "…as large as an alligator". "Never mind," retorted the boatman, "I'll just shift the boat a wee bit and let him swim past!" Fishing here can be wading from the bank or harling the big pools from one of the boats. Brown trout and grayling fishing is also excellent. The Dunkeld Hilton has its own beats offering two miles of private fishing, experienced ghillie/boatman and an excellent rod room and drying facilities.

Immediately below Dunkeld, Upper and Lower Newtyle are amongst the first beats on the river to produce spring fish, often on opening day. As well as salmon, there is also restricted access here for brown trout and grayling.

The River Braan joins the Tay on the right bank above Dunkeld and also offers good value sport

> "A Dunkeld on the tail of your cast and a Loch Ordy, with its ginger and white hackles, on the bob, must surely confirm its status as a great fly fishing area."

for trout. Several lochs lie on Atholl Estate to the north of the town, including Loch Ordie, which gives its name to a famous dapping fly. Loch of Butterstone, another mixed fishery, Loch of the Lowes, home to the osprey and Loch Clunie, which can produce specimen pike and big browns, all lie to the east.

If you want to see the British Record rod-caught salmon, visit Perth Museum and look at Miss Georgina Ballantine's huge 64 lbs. specimen, landed on the 7th October, 1922, hooked on Lower Murthly and landed below Caputh Bridge some hours later.

• Hilton Dunkeld House Hotel: Up to six rods on two miles of private fishing. Some tackle, flies and lures available for sale. Packed lunches to order, or dine in this elegant country-house hotel. Tel: (01350) 728370 or Fax: (01350) 728959. E-mail: dunkeld.park@lineone.net

- The Royal Dunkeld Hotel: A former coaching inn on the main street, now a 3 star hotel offering an informal atmosphere and good food. Fishing can be arranged on the river and local lochs. D.B&B 3 nights from £140 pp (sharing) Tel: (01350) 727322 or Fax: (01350) 728989.
- Perth & District Angling Association issue tickets for brown trout and grayling on various beats on the Tay including Kinnaird and Newtyle. £3 per day, fly only. Tickets for the River Tay and River Braan available from Kettles, Atholl Street, Dunkeld, Tel: (01350) 727556.
  Tickets also from P.D.Malloch, 259 Old High Street, Perth. Tel (01738) 632316
- Butterstone Loch: rainbows and brown trout. Fly fishing only. Day session 0900 – 1700 Evenings: 17.30-dusk. Single angler £18 – 6 trout, 2 anglers: £29 – 12 trout, 3 anglers £35 – 18 trout. R. Knight, Lochend Cottage, Butterstone Loch.Tel: (01350) 724238.
- Tourist Information: The Cross, Dunkeld PH8 OAN. Tel & Fax: (01350) 727688.

Whiteadder

BERWICKSHIRE

The Berwick & District Angling Association

manages several miles of the lower river just upstream of its confluence with the River Tweed.

Formerly an excellent brown trout stream, recent seasons have seen increasing and improving runs of sea trout, salmon and grilse.

The club has an excellent web page which can be found at: www.whiteadder.co.uk

The website gives information on ticket charges and fishing availability.

When the conditions are favourable the River Whiteadder offers reasonable, value for money salmon and sea trout fishing, although the association is traditionally brown trout-orientated.

Anglers are expected to return all hen fish in the autumn and any coloured fish after the beginning of September.

Sea trout can be taken during daylight hours, particularly after a spate while the river still retains a little colour. They are notoriously difficult (like Tweed sea trout) after dark, although last light and early morning offer a great chance of a fish or two. Salmon taking times also peak pre-breakfast and late evening, particularly in the summer months.

Brown trout fishing is best in late spring and early summer, with good dry fly sport on the warmer evenings.

- Association Secretary Dave Cowan can be contacted on 01289 306985.
- Middle and upper reaches of the Whiteadder can be fished for brown trout through the Whiteadder Angling Association. Some excellent salmon fishing from late May onwards and sea trout from mid-June, is available through Peter Miller on 07989 652497.

River Tay, Logierait

PERTHSHIRE

My first visits to Logierait go back more than 30 years. In those days, a keen angler, Jim McFarlane and his wife ran the local hotel and there was always a warm welcome, as well as access to some of the best fishing on Middle Tay, whether you were a keen trout angler, or after salmon.

Fly fishing for brown trout and grayling is still excellent and salmon are taken steadily throughout the season, peaking in autumn. I used to head off downstream towards the confluence with the Tummel if looking for trout, or upstream for salmon. Immediately above the hotel, harling was popular, but with plenty of accessible fly water for wading from the bank.

My favourite is still the Church Pool where the fish one day showed me just how effective fly fishing can be,

There were four other rods fishing and the Pool and head stream had been fished hard with an assortment of ironmongery - and in those days, worm and prawn. I didn't really think I had much chance of success: bright sunshine, warm July temperatures and a low river.

I had switched to my trout rod and a number 10 single-hooked lure with two silver bead eyes - a fore-runner of the hugely popular goldheads used so much these days on stillwater fisheries. I was looking really for a hungry trout that might be more interested in minnows than flies. I had had fewer than a dozen casts right up in the head stream, when a strong pull converted into a salmon of some 16lbs which threw itself clear of the water in a headlong run off downstream. Alas the 6 lbs. cast couldn't take the strain and I was too slow to follow. What was interesting was that the fish - a cock salmon of some 16 lbs. - was quite coloured and obviously a resident for some time in the pool. And it must have seen countless lures, spinners, plugs et al since arriving from the firth.

Perhaps all the activity earlier in the day had unsettled it - even moved it out of its normal lie and up into fast, shallow water. It could be that with high water temperatures and low river, it was already in the fast, streamy water for more oxygen and the other fishers had simply not started their efforts high enough.

The lessons are simple: Don't always expect to fish large lures for large fish. Always consider the conditions and where the fish could be resting.

Don't think because a water is hard-fished or recently covered by other anglers, that you can't be successful. Oh and if you DO think there might be salmon about and you have permission to fish for them, make sure your tackle is adequate to bring them to the net!

- Flies for salmon: Ally's Shrimp, Willie Gunn, Munro, Silver Stoat, Hairy Mary, Blue Charm, and Tosh.
- Flies (Trout): Greenwell, Pheasant Tail nymph, Partridge and Orange, Partridge and Yellow, Black Spider, Iron Blue, Olives.
- Spinning: Zebra Toby, blue and silver devon or red and gold devon. Mini-Rapalas also do well. Note: PRAWNS & SHRIMPS are strictly banned on the Tay system, including its tributaries and lochs.

Caption; 44lbs salmon from Kinnaird Beat

Loch Watten

CAITHNESS

Caithness is blessed with a bewildering number of lochs and lochans, readily accessible to holiday anglers and locals alike. Fisheries such as the Reay lochs, Loch Watten, Loch St John, Calder and Toffingal all hold brown trout of varying proportions and quality. Those overlying marl and limestone outcrops have a correspondingly higher pH and produce correspondingly bigger, pink-fleshed trout, which can sometimes exceed 3lbs and very much larger. A mild breeze and a gentle wave will normally produce a basket of fine trout to any fly fisher of a modest ability.

Loch Watten is for many anglers, the Queen of the Caithness lochs and probably the most productive and consistent. The brown trout average close the pound, and are beautifully presented, silvery fish with pink flesh. Most regulars to the loch keep a brace for the table and return the others to grow on.

This is not a loch for large catches however, and a couple of brace is normal for a session. And expect a few missed takes as well: the trout can be fickle and difficult at times.

Traditional loch-style flies, worked on the drift is the best way to interest the trout: best in recent seasons was a fine fish of 4lbs 8 oz. The Loch Watten is for many anglers, the Queen of the Caithness lochs and probably the most

productive and consistent. The brown trout average is close to the pound, and are beautifully presented, silvery fish with pink flesh. Most regulars to the loch keep a few for the table and return the others to grow on.

This is not a loch for large catches however, and a couple of brace is normal for a session. And expect a few missed takes as well: the trout can be fickle and difficult at times.

Traditional loch-style flies, worked on the drift is the best way to interest the trout: largest in recent seasons was a fine fish of 4lbs 8 oz.

The shallow drifts produce the better sport, with the small, grassy island in factor's Bay, one of the best casts. Look for trout hard in to the margins and in a wave, the fish will often come to the bob fly with a splash. This activity requires a patient response, allowing the fish to turn before setting the hook. Use a Soldier Palmer, Black Pennel, Ke-he or Invicta and wait for the explosive action!

• Hugo Ross Fishing Tackle Shop, 56 High Street, Wick (Tel: 01955 604200) has boats on a number of lochs including Loch Watten. And the Brown Trout Hotel, Station Road, Watten KW1 5YN is right on the doorstep. Tel: 01955 621354. Your fishing hosts are Ian and Margaret MacKenzie.

The Reay Lochs at sundown – an ideal time for trout whichever Caithness loch you choose to cover with a team of flies.

Lochcarron

WESTER ROSS

How to get there: Lochcarron is situated on the northern shores of Loch Carron. Take the A9 from Inverness towards Dingwall and Kessock Bridge. At the Tore roundabout take the A835 for Ullapool, then the A890 Kyle of Lochalsh road.

From Fort William Take the A82 through Spean Bridge. Keep left following the A82 to Invergarry. Once there, go left onto the A87 to Glen Moriston. Later, take left onto the A87 to Dornie. After 1.5 miles go right onto the A890 and then A896 to Lochcarron.

About 8 miles south of Shieldaig you will find Couldoran on Lochcarron Estate. A necklace of pearl lochs runs through the heart of the estate, offering excellent wild brown trout fishing and occasional salmon.

The smaller lochans produce numerous, smaller, free-rising trout, which are ideal for beginners, while the larger waters hold much bigger fish, including ferox. The Estate brown trout record, a ferox, was caught in 1998 and weighed 15lbs 4oz. Fishing is by fly only on all estate waters and is available to guests staying on the estate and resident locally.

Fisheries offering sport locally include the River and Loch Carron, River Bhuidheach, River Attadale, Loch Coultrie and Loch an Iasaich.

The rivers fish best after a spate. Boat and bank fishing on lochs is particularly productive where burns enter the lochs. Popular and effective flies include Black Pennell, Loch Ordy, Soldier Palmer, Invicta, Grouse and Claret, Grouse and Mixed, Kingfisher Butcher and Silver Butcher. In a good wave, fish a Black or Blue Zulu on the bob. More anglers these days also find excellent sport with the dry fly, particularly 'daddy' imitations such as claret and olive hoppers.

Sea fishing is available a short drive away at Loch Kishorn. Pollack, coalfish, codling, ling and conger as well as thornback ray and common skate can be taken, as well as the ubiquitous mackerel in summer months.

There is also an excellent 9-hole golf course (Lochcarron Golf Club, tel. 01520 766211), where visitors are welcome and club hire is available.

Anglers are well catered for at the Lochcarron Hotel, which is an ideal base from which to sample the excellent wild brown trout fishing of Ross-shire's hill lochs. Fishing can be arranged through the hotel, as well as stalking and rough shooting.

Lochboisdale

SOUTH UIST

Situated at the southern end of South Uist, the Lochboisdale Hotel is truly a fishermen's haven, offering countless opportunities for wonder wild brown trout fishing in the machair lochs. Salmon and sea trout run the interlinked lochs and streams from late May.

Amongst many gems Mill Loch, Upper Loch Kildonan, Lower Loch Bornish and Loch Grogary shouldn't be missed. While a minimum size of 12 ounces operates on Grogary, many anglers nowadays return most of their catch to the water. Trout average better than a pound but can run to over 3 lbs.

Bornish also favours the Black Penal and bank fishing is safe and rewarding, with browns similar in size and scope to Grogary.

Upper Kildonan offers excellent boat and bank sport, with tout averaging around 12 ounces. Concentrate around the islands and feeder burn.

Mill Loch fishes surprisingly well with a northerly wind from both boat and bank with plenty of brownies in the 1-1.5 lbs. range. The latter part of the season offers good sport too with salmon and late-run sea trout.

- Flies: Black Pennell, Black or Blue Zulus, Soldier Palmer, Bibio for the bob. Peter Ross, Red Invicta, Kingfisher or Hardy's Gold Butcher, Grouse and Claret, Grouse and Green for a traditional lochstyle cast. Dry fly can also be rewarding including mayfly, hoppers and 'Daddy' imitations. John Kennedy is the local expert – he has written a book on the local lochs – and can recommend some self-tied and designed patterns when the fish are proving canny.

SEA ANGLING

There is some excellent shore fishing for flatfish and dogfish from the silver-wite sands. And offshore dinghy sport with codling, pollack (lythe), coalfish, mackerel, ling and occasional haddock. You can also unexpectedly hit the big time with the elusive halibut and porbeagle shark over the rough round and 100 lbs plus common skate on the softer banks. The hotel can advise on getting afloat for saltwater sport.

For special angling packages and rates for 2002, contact Lochboisdale Hotel Tel. (01878) 700 332.

Lochboisdale Hotel offers superb fishing on a variety of machair brown trout lochs and excellent salmon and sea trout fishing in some of the most unspoilt and scenic countryside anywhere in Britain.

The Shetland Isles, once famous for splendid sea trout fishing in the saltwater voes, still hold their secrets. For the angler, it is a magical place with literally hundreds of lochs from which to choose: and unlike many parts of Scotland, spinning is allowed on many of them as well as traditional fly fishing.

Shetland Islands Tourism has published an excellent guide, which highlights over 100 of Shetlands more than 400 lochs and lochans, the majority either owned or rented by the Shetland Anglers Association. On many boats are available for hire and all are accessible for a modest permit fee. And during the 'simmer dim', you can fish virtually 'round the clock'.

To select just a few is virtually impossible, but here is the 'Editor's half dozen', covering from the very south near Sumburgh Head to the very north of the islands.

Spiggie
No spinning allowed on this fine loch, which holds both brown trout and sea trout. No outboards are allowed on this loch either although boats are available, as it is an RSPB Reserve – so make sure you have your binoculars as well as your fly rod.

Trebister
A fine loch which offers sport with brown trout, for spinfishers as well as with fly. The loch is well stocked with excellent browns by the SAA.

Beosetter
This is really a group of 4 lochs set close together, which produce beautifully conditioned and prettily marked brown trout. Fly fishing and spinning are both allowed. Keep what you need for supper and put the others back.

Girlsta
Girlsta is the only Shetland loch with char present. And not surprisingly, where there are char, the ferox aren't far behind. Look out for surprises and big fish, but it can be dour.

Swabie Water/ Hadd/many Crooks/ Sandy Water
You can fish 26 lochs in a day here, if you have the energy and inclination. It's a long walk but well worth the effort, across the magnificent Arctic tundra terrain. And you can spin if you are so inclined. The trout move so well to the fly, that that would be my first choice here.

Cliff
A modest fishery to make up the Editor's 'half dozen', but the browns are beautifully presented and there are always a few sea trout towards the end of the season too, to give you a surprise. Unst Angling Club control this loch and there is a boat for hire. Both fly fishing and spinning are allowed.

For a copy of the splendid angling guide, write to **SHETLAND ISLANDS TOURISM**, Market Cross, Lerwick, Shetland ZE1 0LU, enclosing a stamped addressed envelope as a courtesy.

For other inquiries, tel: 01595 69 3434 fax: 01595 69 5807 or e-mail: shetland.tourism@zetnet.co.uk. Their excellent website is at **www.visitshetland.com**

River Clyde

STRATHCLYDE

The River Clyde, from its source close to the infant Tweed and Annan in the Southern Uplands, drains more than 3800 sq., kms. (1,480 sq. miles) on its run to the Firth of Clyde.

The river is famous for its own 'Clyde-style' trout flies, sparsely-tied spiders on size 16s, 18s and even 20s. And is equally famous for its quality brown trout and grayling. In recent years the average weight of grayling has been smaller, but they are plentiful and offer good sport during the winter months. Trout fishing follows the statutory season and is open from March 15th through to October 6th, both dates inclusive. And nowadays, the river has increasingly good runs of salmon and sea trout.

Glasgow's Coat of Arms, which dates back to 1866, depicts two salmon and there were significant runs of migratory fish at that time. Significantly, the Coat of Arms is emblazoned on the Great Western Road Bridge over the Kelvin, which has now seen the return of these fish to the Clyde and its tributaries.

Clydesdale is an important farming and orchard region and home to the famous Clydesdale horses. While fishing was restricted due to the foot & mouth epidemic in 2001, this also allowed the river and its stock of fish an extended 'close season', which must auger well for 2002.

As well as 'Clyde-style' spiders, locals also fish the gadger – the nymph of the stonefly.

This deadly bait is freelined down the riffles and streams and often takes the better fish, which can run to better than 2 lbs.

Expect a brace of pounders in your basket on a good day. Typical Clyde fish are beautifully marked and a pound fish will be around 15 inches in length. Many serious regulars now practice catch-and-release and this has definitely helped the average weight of the brownies.

The United Clyde Angling Protective Association controls much of the Clyde and its tributaries, upstream of Motherwell Bridge to Daer Reservoir – some 40 miles of the river – and visitors can buy day or season tickets offering some of the best-value deals in the country. Tickets are available from various tackle dealers and sports shops in Glasgow and Lanarkshire.

The association stocks the river annually, and fishing is divided into three sections, the Upper, Middle and Lower Reaches. Permits charges may be revised for 2002 from existing charges of £20 (annual), £5 (day ticket). OAP can fish for free and there are juvenile concessions.

Motherwell and Lanark (Lanarkshire). United Clyde APA has brown trout and grayling fishing on both the Clyde and its tributary, the River Douglas. Permits are available from local tackle shops

Lamington AIA has approximately 9 miles of water from Thankerton Boat Bridge to

The Clyde at Thankerton.

Roberton Burn mouth. This stretch is regularly stocked with 9-10 inch brown trout and offers safe wading.

Season ticket £20, weekly ticket £15, day ticket £5. Grayling season, 7 Oct – 14 Mar: Season ticket £5 and day tickets £2. Permit charges may change for 2002.

Permits are available from Hon Sec., Shieldhill Tackle shop: Bryden Newsagent, High Street, Biggar. and O'Hara, Grocers, Mill Rd, Thankerton.

Concessions for OAP and juniors. No Sunday fishing. United Clyde APA controls the fishings below Thankerton.

The River Clyde between Abington and Crawford is readily accessible from the M74. This stretch offers superb fly fishing for brown trout and grayling and is controlled by United Clyde APA, with other association water at Crawford and Elvanford.

East Kilbride Angling Club leases water on the River Calder, located in South Lanarkshire some 10 miles SE of Glasgow. The trout fishing extends from Auldhouse to the River Clyde at Daldowie.

Tackle shops:
- Country Sports, 27 Neilston Road, Paisley Renfrewshire PA2 6LY. Tel: 0141 889 5535 (Robert Watt).
- The Rod & Gun Rack, 145 Merry Street, Motherwell.
- Lanarkshire ML1 1JP. Tel: 01698 265777. (Alex Cargill)
- Glasgow Angling Centre, 6 Claythorn Street, Gallowgate, Glasgow. Tel: 0141 552 1447 (Paul Devlin) Glasgow.
- Cafaro Bros., Renfrew Chambers, 140 Renfield Street, Glasgow G2 3AU. Tel: 0141 332 6224 (Pat & Jim McKendry).

Loch Ailish

SUTHERLAND

Tucked away in the hills of the Benmore Forest lies the most perfect of trout lochs. Your surroundings are as wild and magnificent as the lochs occupants and if trout heaven exists on the north west coast of Scotland, without question it exists here.

The fish are sleek golden creatures, butter fat and full of spunk. They are exceptionally well fed dining on a fine diet of shrimp, mayfly and caddis along with a good cross section of other goodies like midge, stickleback, stonefly and olive. Ailsh provides an ideal environment for trout with its clear slightly alkaline water.

The loch is laced with weed beds, gravel shores and rocky ledges and is a mile long and not particularly deep. Despite the nearby mountains which should indicate a deep loch, 24ft is the maximum depth of Loch Ailsh with plenty of shallow margins. The entire loch shouts brown trout at you and indeed, there are some very fine fish present.

This is probably the premier water of the parish of Assynt in North West Sutherland in terms of relatively abundant stocks of quality sized trout: the average is 10-12 ounces, but there are much bigger on offer. It's isolated and remote but that only adds to its grandeur and considerable scenic attraction.

Fly fishing by boat is the norm and this is THE place to practise the art of traditional loch style. There's no room for sunk line lure bashing here, its all about working the top dropper quickly through the waves. A team of two or three well versed wets normally does the business, Kate McLaren, Soldier Palmer and Clan Chief make a good beginning. Trout rise well all over the loch but anywhere off the little bays, promontories and islands is good.

Floating lines, 4lb nylon and a light 10-11ft rod is normally all that's required. On Loch Ailsh a short line cast toward the shore and retrieved with medium to fast pace is the preferred method, though if there's a good hatch of mayfly or sedge in calm weather, its worth fishing a big dry either singly or on the top dropper. Whatever method, trout hit your flies with a savageness which belies their size. In amongst the 'average' fish, there are some magnificent trout of more than 2lb. Loch Ailsh is certainly challenging, but it is rarely dour. Fish when a hatch is on and you will almost always find the trout responsive.

- If you want to fish Loch Ailish and the brown trout hill lochs above Loch Ailish:
- Contact the Assynt Angling Club for further details. Inver Lodge Hotel can arrange boats Tel.(01571) 844496 and non-hotel residents can expect to pay around £15 for a boat and £5 for a bank rod. The hill lochs are bank fishing only.
- Lesley Crawford offers guiding in Caithness and Sutherland and can be contacted by e-mail at: lesley@crawford40.freeserve.co.uk

Lyne Water & Manor Water

SELKIRKSHIRE

These two gems hold superb brown trout and grayling for the young enthusiast and beginner. You can almost jump across these streams in places and the average trout you will catch will barely make the span of your fingers, but they are plucky fighters and rise keenly to the fly. Many a youngster has started his fly fishing ambitions casting a wet spider or a dry fly on the lovely pools, riffles and glides.

Controlled by the Peebles Trout Fishing Association, the Manor Water joins Tweed on the right bank just downstream of Manor Bridge. As with the Lyne Water, it is an important spawning tributary for salmon. It is steeper and rockier than Lyne and a good walk upstream will keep you fit.

Lyne Water is gentler and follows the Tweed Valley and fishes best from West Linton downstream, past Blyth Bridge, 'Five Mile Brig' and 'Four Mile Brig' before joining Tweed just below Lyne Station. Great fly fishing water in miniature, and with some excellent wild brown trout better than a pound and grayling twice that size.

Grey Hen and Rusty, Tupps, Iron Blue, March Brown and Greenwell Spider are all great dry flies to use.

Spiders fished downstream and across will also give you fine sport: Black Spider, Olive Quill, Partridge and Yellow or Dark Partridge and Orange.

- Nearest accommodation is in Peebles and permits are available from the local tackle shop. Also, combine a visit to these two streams with loch fishing including the beautiful St Mary's Loch or salmon fishing on Ettrick and Yarrow.
- Tweeddale Tackle, 1 Bridgegate, Peebles Tel. (01721) 720979

Manor Bridge on the upper River Tweed, with the Manor Water joining the main river on the right bank below the bridge. The pool where it joins the parent river is an excellent autumn pool for salmon.

River Don, Monymusk

ABERDEENSHIRE

Mention Aberdeenshire to most anglers and their thoughts might understandably turn to Royal Deeside and that noblest of salmon rivers, the majestic Dee. But it is its near neighbour to the north, the River Don, which offers locals and visitors alike the chance of salmon and sea trout, and outstanding brown trout fishing as well.

The infant stream rises in the Grampian Mountains above Cock Bridge and for much of its initial journey downstream to Alford is Highland in appearance, cutting through steep wooded hillsides, gathering pace and girth from its upper tributaries draining from the slopes of the Ladder Hills.

Below Alford, the countryside is more gentle and the landscape softer – Inverurie down to Kintore and below sees an altogether different character – meadows and meandres. And wonderful wild brown trout water.

Salmon fishing has seen a considerable improvement from the days of industrial pollution and the old cruives and dykes have been breached: efficient passes for migratory fish now offer safe and clear passage upstream.

The Don District Salmon Fishery Board operates a hatchery coping with some 750,000 eggs annually.

Young fry are introduced to a number of feeder burns each spring.

Day tickets are available to visitors on a number of beats and hotels also offer fishing to guests on their own beats. The Aberdeen and District Angling Association has access to the river at Inverurie, Kemnay and Kintore.

For dry fly fishing in late spring, May and June, small parachute patterns (14s, 16s) are popular, including March Brown, Greenwell's, Iron Blue, Tupps, Olive Quill and Black Spider.

Later in the year, sedge patterns including Cinnamon and Gold, and Claret and Olive Hoppers work well. When fish aren't rising, small gold head nymphs, buzzers and Pheasant-tail nymph are all worth a cast.

- The Grant Arms Hotel, Monymusk offers some of the best brown trout water on the river, with dry fly coming into its own in late May and June.
- Other hotels offering salmon and trout fishing on the Don include Colquhonnie Hotel, Strathdon, Glenkindie Arms Hotel, Glenkindie, Haughton Arms Hotel, Alford, Forbes Arms Hotel, Bridge of Alford, Kemnay House, Kemnay and Kintore Arms Hotel at Kintore.

Loch Awe

ARGYLLSHIRE

Loch Awe has always been famous for its large trout, not least since the Ferox 85 Group focussed their attentions on the loch. Founder member Ron Greer, in his excellent book 'Ferox Trout and Arctic Charr' holds that the disputed 39.5 lbs. specimen landed in 1866 by W. Muir is still worthy of record. The British Record for wild brown trout was indeed smashed and ratified in 1997 by a ferox of 25 lbs. 6 oz, measuring 96.5 cms.

Barrhead schoolteacher, Ken Oliver's superb new record taken from Loch Awe on July 13th, 2000, broke the magic 30 lbs. threshold by eight ounces – yet another British Record from the loch.

The provocative introduction of rainbow trout cages and the inevitable escapees changed the ecology of the loch forever. Some of Scotland's largest pike got even larger as the stocks of escapee rainbows got smaller. Not to be outdone of course, the rainbows themselves piled on the weight, and double figure specimens were regularly taken. Fewer now, rainbow trout are something of a tired novelty, and most serious fly fishers have returned to the excellent traditional loch-style drifting for much more modest but hard-fighting wild brown trout.

Whether your interest lies in the specimen ferox trout, wild brown trout, specimen pike, or even the rainbows, boats are readily available for visiting anglers at very reasonable rates.

The Loch Awe Improvement Association controls angling on the loch and with a Protection Order firmly in place, previous illegal activities have been reduced to a minimum. In spite of its length, around 23 miles long and 'dog-legged', this expansive water is hugely popular and heavily fished and the LAIA requests visiting anglers to park with consideration and please take their litter with them. That way, we can all enjoy a splendid loch, which on its day can produce fish of which most of us only dream. Salmon are also taken trolling on the loch.

Loch Avich at a higher altitude is reached from Dalavich via the Kilmelford road (A816) and produces hard fighting brown trout, slightly smaller in average than Loch Awe, but with enough 2 lbs. plus fish to make sport interesting. A 7.5 lbs. brown trout was one of the best in recent years. The lively River Avich runs for some 1.5 miles and can also produce good sport with fly and worm.

Lochgilphead and District Angling Club control a number of hillside lochs. Boat fishing only on Loch Coillie-Bharr, Barnsluasgan and Loch Linnhe. The club has access to a number of Forestry Commission lochs, including Loch Glashan and Black Mill Loch, all of which hold good brown trout. The River Add is a good spate stream and holds salmon.

- Permits for all lochs and stretches of the Add from: Archie McGill, Fyne Tackle, 22 Argyll St., Lochgilphead, Argyll. Tel: 01546 606878
- Boat Hire for Loch Awe and Loch Avich: Lochaweside Marine, 11 Dalvich by Taynuilt, Argyll PA35 1HN. Tel: 01866 844 209
- Loch Awe Boats at Arbrecknish, Tel: 01866 833 256. This boat facility covers the north end of the loch and the islands. Salmon permits are also available.
- Day and weekly permits are issued from Loch Awe Stores, Dalmally, Tel: 01838 200 200, and local hotels.

Coldingham Loch

BERWICKSHIRE

This delightful fishery is only 22 acres in extent, but has a well-deserved reputation for the quality of its brown trout and rainbows. The pretty little boathouse on the far side of the loch stands sentinel over some of the best drifts and there is also excellent bank fishing. Numbers of both boat and bank rods are restricted, to ensure that all anglers have plenty of room.

> "You can catch trout literally anywhere in the loch, but don't expect them to be easy: that's all part of the delight in spending a day on Coldingham Loch."

Coldingham was one of the first lochs in Scotland to be stocked with rainbow trout, more than 50 years ago, and the quality of the fish is unsurpassed. The fish are grown on initially in their own holding lochan before transfer to the main loch. The fishery has a reputation for being dour, but the rainbows you catch will be full-finned and fickle. The brown trout are magnificent, deeply coloured and marked specimens which can if you are lucky, better 5 lbs. and more.

Unless there is a breeze, don't go too large in fly sizes: 12s and 14s are the norm and many regular anglers fish small 16s, buzzers and spiders or even dry flies, size 18 and 20. Summer evenings can produce prodigious hatches of caenis and if the trout are ignoring small imitative patterns, a Whickham's Fancy, Black Pennel or Soldier Palmer on the bob, will often bring a solid, splashy rise. These trout often take the imitation as a sedge, slapping at it, to drown the morsel before turning and supping it down at leisure. Strike too quickly and you miss the fish, or even worse, occasionally by the tail.

Visiting anglers new to the loch, will always find staff extremely helpful, whether in pointing out favourite drifts or weed-fringed corners in one of the bays. You can catch trout literally anywhere in the loch, but don't expect them to be easy: that's all part of the delight in spending a day on Coldingham Loch.

The loch is open from March 15 to October 31, with brown trout fishing closing on October 6. For bookings and details of charges for 2002, telephone: 01890 771270. Enjoy the birdlife – waterfowl and woodland birds are joined here by marine species, as the loch nestles close to the cliff edge overlooking the coastal waters of the Firth of Forth. There's some great sea angling from rocky headlands, beaches and by boat.

Loch Fitty

FIFE

On the B912, 3 miles Northeast of Dunfermline, Loch Fitty is truly a loch for all seasons – a specimen bay open all the year round with separate coarse and bait fisheries offering variety. Loch Fitty itself totals some 160 acres, and is regularly stocked with healthy fully-finned rainbows. Fishing is traditional loch style or at anchor, with full bank and boat options. The season's early start in February is usually rewarded with great weather and great fishing. Over-wintered rainbows often run to double figures. By late spring and throughout the rest of the season, dry fly, buzzers and hoppers prevail.

CHARGES FOR 2002
- Specimen Bay, 9.00 am – Dusk, £24 for 2 trout for any 4 hours. No Catch & Release
- Main Loch, 10.00 am – Dusk, Bank £17 Day Session; £14 Eve Session
- Boat: £19 per rod, Day Session, £16 per rod, Eve Session
- East Bay – Bait, 9.00 am – Dusk: £13 per rod for any 5 hours for 4 trout
- Concessions for retired and out of work, Tuesdays and Thursdays. Adult and Junior anyday
- No. of boats: 30
- Acreage: 160 acres+ coarse, specimen and bait fisheries
- Rainbows: 1.5 lbs – 15 lbs. Browns and Steelheads. Specimen Bay 3 lbs to double figures.
- Best flies: Morning Glory, Whickhams, Buzzers, Daddy-Longlegs, Mini-Lures
- Favourite methods: Drift or anchor, bank

River Annan

DUMFRIESSHIRE

This pastoral river flows majestically into the Solway Firth through the town of Annan and is famous for its salmon and sea trout.

Less well known is the quality of its wild brown trout and specimen-sized grayling and chub. Dry fly fishing offers splendid sport from early spring throughout the summer months. Resident expert Brian Gibson regularly catches big browns from the Annan, including a matching brace of four pound brown trout caught at Woodhead Scaur on the Upper Beat of the Upper Annandale Angling Association, both on his own tying of a dry Greenwell tied spent, size 14. He followed that catch a couple of seasons ago with a specimen close to 6 lbs. and another near three pounder, taken from Poldean and Kirn. There are also some excellent grayling to be taken in this area. The Chub lurk in the deeper glides near Hoddom Castle and will readily suck down a bushy Whickhams or 'Daddy' cast under the trees.

Most anglers' attention however will be salmon and sea trout. Spring fishing has tailed off in recent seasons, but the big Solway Greybacks still feature in autumn catches, and 20 lbs. plus fish are always a real possibility. Sea trout fishing can be excellent, peaking in June and July. Recent seasons have also seen good numbers of herling (finnock) or smaller sea trout.

Just about anything you wish to know about the river can be obtained from Andy Dickson, who is Secretary and Treasurer of the Upper Annandale Angling Association. Andy is also involved in the National Sea Trout Festival, which has produced some spectacular fishing in recent years.

There is an excellent choice of hotels in the area, including the Warmanbie Hotel, which offers its own private stretch of salmon and sea trout water. The hotel can also arrange fishing on the nearby River Nith and River Eden, on the English side of the Border.

- Warmanbie Hotel, Annan, Dumfriesshire DG12 5LL. Tel/Fax: 01461 204015 e-mail: info@warmanbie.co.uk
- Andy Dickson, Secretary/Treasurer, Upper Annandale Angling Association, Braehead, Woodfoot, Moffat, Dumfriesshire. DG10 9PL e-mail AndyD@uaaa.softnet.co.uk Or adickson@madasafish.com
- UAAA site: www.soft.net.uk/uaaa/upper Annanline site www.soft.net.uk/uaaa www.warmanbie.co.uk National Sea Trout Festival, www.seatroutfestival.com

Helsmdale

SUTHERLAND

Think of a place where you can catch salmon on a fly, fish for sea trout and finnock at night, catch wild loch brown trout drifting in a boat or wading the bank as golden-bellied brown trout splash at your team of flies, or go sea angling from the harbour for pollack, codling and ling.

The chances are you are in Helmsdale. This picturesque east coast fishing village is at the mouth of the famous River Helmsdale and yet visitors can fish the town water for a fraction of the cost of most Scottish salmon fishing. There is even an excellent 9 hole golf course.

Fishing on the river, one of the earliest in Scotland, starts on January 11th with a traditional opening ceremony, sponsored by the Bridge Hotel Tackle Shop, Dunrobin Street, Helmsdale. The angler catching the first fish off the river is presented with a special salmon fly rod and magnum of champagne.

Day tickets for the town water can be purchased at the Bridge Hotel tackle shop, which also stocks an excellent selection of local flies for both salmon and trout as well as an extensive range of rods, reels, waders and country clothing.

Helmsdale town water fishes particularly well throughout the summer and autumn, and fishing the income tide for sea trout and finnock can be excellent.

As with so many rivers where there is heavy demand, it pays to fish late and early and the tickets reflect this. Permits allow anglers on from 9 am until 9 am the following morning. Times are strictly adhered to and the fishery is well patrolled by river watchers. Fly only is allowed and there are restrictions on maximum fly size and no treble hooks. You must purchase a ticket before you go on the water.

There are some excellent trout lochs of varying sizes, with plenty of boats available from Badenloch Estate. A few of the lochs produce occasional salmon.

Brown trout average about 3 to the pound, but with plenty of larger fish: and they are free rising. Traditional loch-style works best with a team of 3 wet flies. A bushy offering dibbled on the bob (top dropper), such as a blue or black Zulu, Soldier Palmer or Loch Ordy will often bring the trout up, particularly in a good wave. Add an Invicta or a butcher on the tail for some explosive action!

In calmer conditions, dry fly is always worth a try: hoppers or small dapping flies tweaked slowly or anything sedgy, particularly on warm June and July evenings almost guarantee a lively response from the wild brownies.

For 2002, a unique opportunity to fish the River Helmsdale has been made possible by the proprietor of the Bridge Hotel and Tackle Shop, in conjunction with the Helmsdale River Board.

For the first time in its history, the main river is being opened to visitors on Friday 11th and Saturday 12th January, to celebrate the opening of the season. Fishing is free of charge to anglers staying for one or more nights in Helmsdale. Bookings and pre-registration can be made at the Bridge Hotel and Tackle Shop.

A special opening ceremony in Helmsdale has been arranged on the Friday before anglers go to the beats on the river. Ghillies and angling experts will be on hand to assist with visitors. The main beats on this fly-only river are amongst the finest in Europe.

The town club water also offers excellent sport throughout the year with finnock, sea trout and salmon.

Accommodation at the Bridge Hotel in en-suite rooms is £50 per night single and £95 per night

Permits, clothing, waders and tackle for river, loch and sea angling, including rods, reels and a selection of local and popular flies can be obtained from the Bridge Hotel Tackle Shop, Tel. (01431) 821102 Fax: (01431) 821103. For reservations, contact the Bridge Hotel, Tel. 01431 821100 Fax: (01431) 821101.

double, exclusive of breakfast. Being a sporting hotel, a la carte breakfast service is available on a 24 hour basis – ideal in the summer months when you might want to fish sea trout into the dusk, or be out on the hill before sunrise.

A Willie Gunn variant, originally named by Rob Wilson after Willie Gunn the Brora ghillie, who in testing the original fly, caught several fish at his first attempt. It's a deadly Scottish salmon fly, either tied as here Waddington style, or as a small double for summer use. Paul Young is the angler.

Loch Lomond

ARGYLE

Bill McEwan, who wrote the definitive angling book on Loch Lomond, called it The Big Loch. And so it is, not only in geographical size but for its wonderful sport. The western shoreline gives easy access but for solitude, cross the loch.

Lying some 20 miles north-west of Glasgow, boat fishing on the drift or trolling is the most productive method for salmon and sea trout;. Loch Lomond however also has some excellent brown trout and they can be large, although average is around 8-10 ounces. The northern shores and around any of the islands and bays are your best spots. Traditional loch style flies do the business, and attractor patterns such as Dunkeld, Silver Invicta and Kingfisher Butcher can also raise salmon and sea trout. Salmon flies include Loch Ordy, White-tipped Turkey, Hairy Mary and Silver Stoat.

Zebra Tony, natural sprat (gold or silver) and Rapalas are all popular for trolling on the loch. Dapping is also productive given a good breeze and a wave on the loch.

Lomond is also home to some of the largest pike in Britain, and most specimen hunters carefully release their fish to the water. (See Mike Maule's article on pike fishing).

Live baiting in the past has brought its problems: no longer acceptable as a form of pike fishing, released bait fish have established themselves, and coarse anglers can now catch a wide variety of species, some like the dace and chub, usually more at home in a river. Loch Lomond produces specimen roach and perch and the lower River Endrick also offers excellent sport with coarse fish. Gudgeon and ruffe are also present and anglers have even taken carp and goldfish!

> "The Big Loch . . . not only in geographical size but for its wonderful sport . . ."

It is the excellent specimen sea trout and salmon throughout the season which attract most anglers to the loch. The biggest fish are the spring salmon, followed by grilse from mid-June, followed by sea trout. Double figure sea trout are always a possiblity on this fishery.

The Loch Lomond Angling Improvement Association manages the fishing on the loch and River Leven. Approximately 5 miles of fishing is available on the River Leven from the loch downstream, with 23 named pools. Access is also available on the River Endrick, although much of the fishing is privately controlled. The lower reaches offer good coarse fishing.

Recent years have seen numbers of farm salmon entering the system and although welcome by some local anglers, they undoubtedly affect the runs of wild salmon, grilse and sea trout.

- No Sunday fishing for salmon and sea trout.
- Boats and outboards are available all year

round depending upon water levels to hire from MacFarlane & Son, Boatyard, Balmaha. They can also provide permits. Call to book – Tel. (01360) 870214 Also Cullen Boat Hire Tel. (03014) 244 In conjunction with the Ranger Service, the LLAIA has produced a useful angling map, price £5.

- LLAIA is managed by: Clements Chartered Accountants, 379, Hamilton Rd, Glasgow G71 7SG. Tel: (0141) 781 1545

HOTELS:
- Ardlui Hotel, Arrochar, Dunbartonshire Tel: (01301) 704 243
- Balloch Hotel, Balloch. Tel: (01389) 75 25 79
- Inverbeg Caravan Park, Luss, Dumbartonshire Tel: (01436) 860 267
- Inverbeg Inn, Luss, Dunbartonshire Tel: (01436) 860 678
- Rowardennan Hotel, Drymen Tel: (01360) 870 273
- Tarbet Hotel, Tarbet. Tel: (01301) 702 228

Ettrick & Yarrow

SELKIRKSHIRE

Ettrick has wonderful scenery and splendid fishing, whether you fish the hill lochs, the burns or Ettrick and Yarrow, the twin tributaries of the Tweed that between them support most of the spring-run salmon entering the river.

The wild brown trout of these streams offer excellent sport throughout the season, beginning with hatches of March Browns in the spring. The average fish may not be much more than half a pound, but there are plenty of bigger fish and superb dry fly fishing. Dusk and early morning normally are prime time on Tweed and its tributaries.

The salmon pools of Ettrick and Yarrow can generally be covered with a single-handed rod, although the autumn can produce some large fish, and normal double-handed fly rods are generally preferred. Many of the fish are coloured up in the autumn and anglers release them carefully back to the river.

St Mary's Loch up in the hills is a scenic alternative to the rivers, with good bank access and boat fishing available on a day ticket basis.

- Gamescleugh Fishery in Ettrick Valley offers good value rainbow trout fishing with bank sport producing fish from 1.5 lbs. upwards. Montana, Pheasant tail and Damsel nymphs do well and small buzzers, particularly so in the evenings. Sink-tip lines and mini lures such as Ace of Spades, Green and Orange Fritz all have their day. Dry fly and hoppers can also do well in the warmer evenings.

- Clearburn Loch at Tushielaw holds a good stock of wild brown trout and fishing is free to residents at Tushielaw Inn, which also offers excellent accommodation and good value packages for anglers.

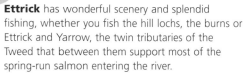

Roy Bridge

INVERNESS-SHIRE

Great fishing country this and some of the finest scenery in Scotland. Lochs abound with wild brown trout, ranging from plump, spotted, half pounders to large ferox, which can better more than 10 lbs. There are also some large pike in the deeper, weed-fringed lochs.

Loch Laggan has easy access throughout the length of its north bank from the A86 Spean Bridge to Kingussie Road and offers good bank and boat fishing. The loch is 12 miles long and is really two lochs, Loch Moy and Loch Laggan, which linked when the water was raised by the construction of the huge dam to the west end of the system. When the water is low, the original bed of the river can be seen and often produces the best sport.

Traditional wet flies work well and include a Black Pennell or Soldier Palmer on the bob when there's a good wave. The trout can be dour at times, but perseverance will normally bring you a good basket of fish, ranging from half a pound to better than a pound. Trolling produces occasional ferox and large pike.

Loch Lochy, which links with the Caledonian Canal is nine miles in length and up to 500 feet deep. Home to brown trout and more recently, rainbow trout escapees, fishing is free and unusually in this part of Scotland, Sunday fishing is also allowed. Char also inhabit the loch and as elsewhere, this results in ferox, a strain of brown trout, which feed almost exclusively on fish, mainly char. Brown trout up to 1.5 – 2 lbs. can be taken from the many bays. Look for sport where burns run into the loch. The main feeder is the River Arkaig, and angling is prohibited at the mouth of this stream. Bait fishing is allowed, but no set lines. Always be considerate and take your rubbish with you. There is easy access from the main road throughout its length and the scenery is splendid.

Most of the local rivers depend on spates to produce good sport in the summer months. Much of the salmon fishing is preserved, but rods can be arranged through The Inn at Roy Bridge. The River Spean is an excellent highland stream, with rocky runs and deep holding pools, but the going can be difficult on some reaches and agility is important. Fly fishing and spinning are both allowed.

The River Roy is a major tributary of the River Spean, which it joins below Roy Bridge. The salmon arrive in mid June and there is normally a good stock of fish from late July, depending on water conditions. Limited day tickets are available on both rivers.

- James Coutts of Fishing Scotland runs regular courses throughout the summer for trout anglers, and will be offering salmon fishing from the spring of 2002. Tel: (01397) 712 812
- Comfortable and homely accommodation is available at The Inn at Roy Bridge, Inverness-shire PH31 4AG, Tel: (01397) 712 253

Tomdoun & Loch Garry

INVERNESS-SHIRE

If you follow the Great Glen south-westward past Loch Ness and its Monster, you climb gently until you reach Loch Oich and Invergarry. Salmon, which entered the River Ness on the east coast at Inverness, pass through Loch Oich and take a right to join the River Garry. By the time they travel through Loch Garry and Inchlaggan past Tomdoun and the Upper River Garry, they are only a handful of miles away from saltwater again, this time on the west coast, at beautiful Kinloch Hourn. The main salmon fishing is on the lower Garry and Loch Oich. But if you are looking for some of the largest wild brown trout in Scotland, then you have to stop at Tomdoun.

As you climb above Loch Garry, take the little road turning left off the A87 and you can follow the lochside all the way to Tomdoun. When the main loch level was raised as part of the hydro-electric scheme, the upper River Garry was flooded and now forms a separate, shallower loch, Inchlaggan, which offers superb fly fishing for wild, hard-fighting brown trout. The scenery and wildlife are stunning.

Ferox have grown large in Garry and neighbouring Loch Quoich further up the glen and they undoubtedly feed on the Arctic char, which are present in both lochs. A previous British Record brown trout, weighing 18 lbs. 2 oz, was taken here. And if you have a taste for big trout, then Tomdoun Hotel is the ideal base for your expedition.

The number of cased specimens, which adorn the walls of this fine old coaching inn, reflects the quality of the fishing. Tomdoun Hotel has fishing on the Upper River Garry exclusively for guests, and boats available on Inchlaggan, Loch Garry and Loch Quoich. Salmon are taken occasionally from the river and also by anglers trolling for ferox, but it is the wild brown trout that reigns supreme. The upper river opens into a series of lochans and large pools. Excellent fly hatches occur in the late spring and throughout the summer and dry fly can offer exceptional sport, with brown trout averaging around 12 ounces, but with plenty of pounders and much bigger to bend the rod. Two and three pound trout are regularly taken on the fly.

A cast of traditional wet flies fished down and across also does well, particularly where the lochans feed back into the river. Look for the bigger fish behind the rocks, which fringe the weedy gravel. Greenwell, Black Pennell, Grouse and Claret, Invicta and Soldier Palmer all do equally well on the river and drifting the loch.

Loch Quoich also holds very large ferox and trolling produces the bigger trout. Fly fishing will give the keen angler good baskets of dark, golden coloured brown trout averaging around the 12 ounce mark. Many of the big trout are taken early in the season, with fly fishing for both loch and river browns peaking in late May, through June and July. Add to that the delight of summer evenings and excellent natural hatches of flies to bring the trout and the char to the surface, you couldn't ask for better fishing or better surroundings. But don't forget the midge repellent!

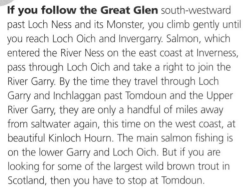

Fishing for all seasons

In Scotland, there is no statutory close season for either rainbow trout or coarse fish. The statutory season for brown trout is from March 15 to October 6 inclusive. For conservation reasons, many clubs, associations and hotel beats have slightly shorter seasons, normally opening on April 1 and ending September 30.

On mixed fisheries where rainbows and browns are present, many stillwater fisheries are open all year round, weather permitting, but only for rainbows.

Shortening of seasons for conservation also applies to certain salmon rivers. The Aberdeenshire Dee has delayed the start (normally February 1) for a number of years, although reverting back again in 2002. Spinning will be allowed on some beats, but restricted to a single hook (not a treble) until April 15. Catch and release is encouraged.

Sea trout being migratory fish are always classified along with salmon and written permission is always required before going onto the water. Sea trout rarely run Scottish rivers until well into April, although there are exceptions, with runs peaking in late May through June and July. This makes for exciting summer fishing for visitors and many an angler fishing late into the dusk or up with the dawn, connects with a summer salmon or grilse.

The sleek lady of the stream, the grayling, while often associated with coarse species because of its seasonal activity, is a salmonid and can be found in many of Scotland's game rivers. Local conditions apply, although there are many rivers which allow winter fishing for grayling. The Earn, a major tributary of the River Tay as well as the Clyde and Tweed, offer splendid grayling fishing with fly and bait. Less well-known are the specimen grayling to be found in the Solway rivers Nith and Annan.

As a special treat for salmon anglers this year, the Helmsdale River Board agreed to open the lower river on the first two days of the season on January 11th and 12th for free salmon fishing for visitors who were staying in Helmsdale and have pre-registered at the Bridge Hotel and Tackle Shop. More than 120 anglers fished the opening two days and enjoyed the official opening and weekend celebrations. Fishing on the River Helmsdale is strictly fly only and rods enjoyed unique access to the main beats 1-6 up the the falls which divide the river.

Springers seldom go over the falls until the temperatures rise in April. Given mild, open conditions, prospects for an early fish are always excellent and the two day opening festival offered a unique opportunity to cast a fly over such famous pools as Upper and Lower Torrish, which gave their name to an equally famous fly pattern. In excess of 2000 salmon were landed from this exclusive andprolific river in 2001. Day and weekly visitor tickets for the Helmsdale town water are available throughout the season from the Bridge Hotel and Tackle Shop, Dunrobin Street, Helmsdale, Sutherland.

The following are the statutory open seasons for fishing for Salmon in Scotland:

RIVER	ROD SEASON	RIVER	ROD SEASON
Add	Feb 16 - Oct 31	Fyne	Feb 16 - Oct 31
Aline	Feb 11 - Oct 31	Girvan	Feb 25 - Oct 31
Allan	Mar15 - Oct 31	Gruinard & Little Gruinard	Feb 11 - Oct 31
Alness	Feb 11 - Oct 15	Halladale	Jan 12 - Sep 30
Annan	Feb 26 - Nov 15	Helmsdale	Jan 11 - Sep 30
Applecross	Feb 25 - Nov 15	Hope	Jan 12 - Sep 30
Awe	Feb 12 - Oct 15	Inver	Feb 11 - Oct 31
Ayr	Feb 11 - Oct 31	Irvine	Feb 25 - Nov 15
Beauly	Feb 11 - Oct 15	Kannaird	Feb 11 - Oct 31
Berriedale	Feb 11 - Oct 31	Kirkaig	Feb 11 - Oct 31
Bervie	Feb 25 - Oct 31	Kishorn	Feb 11 - Oct 31
Bladnoch	Feb 11 - Oct 31	Laxford	Feb 11 - Oct 31
Borgie	Jan 12 - Sep 30	Lochy	Feb 11 - Oct 31
Broom	Feb 11 - Oct 31	Lomond (Clyde)	Feb 12 - Oct 31
Brora	Feb 1 - Oct 15	Moidart	Feb 11 - Oct 31
Carron (E. Ross)	Jan 11 - Sep 30	Morar	Feb 11 - Oct 31
Carron (W. Ross)	Feb 11 - Oct 31	Nairn	Feb 12 - Oct 30
Conon	Jan 26 - Sep 30	Naver	Jan 12 - Sep 30
Cree	Mar 1 - Oct 14	Ness	Jan 15 - Oct 15
Creed	Feb 11 - Oct 16	Nith	Feb 26 - Nov 30
Croe	Feb 11 - Oct 31	Orchy	Feb 12 - Oct 15
Dee (Aberdeenshire)	Mar 1 - Sep 30	Oykel	Jan 11 - Sep 30
Dee (Kirkcudbrightshire)	Feb 11 - Oct 31	Shiel	Feb 11 - Oct 31
Deveron	Feb 12 - Oct 31	Shin	Jan 11 - Sep 30
Dionard	Feb 11 - Oct 31	Spey	Feb 12 - Sep 30
Don	Feb 12 - Oct 31	Stinchar	Feb 24 - Oct 31
Doon	Feb 11 - Oct 31	Strathy	Jan 12 - Sep 30
Dunbeath	Feb 11 - Oct 15	Tay	Jan 15 - Oct 15
Eachaig	Feb 16 - Oct 31	Teith	Feb 1 - Oct 31
Earn	Feb 1 - Oct 31	Thurso	Jan 11 - Oct 5
Esk (North & South)	Feb 16 - Oct 31	Torridon	Feb11 - Oct 31
Ewe	Feb 11 - Oct 31	Tweed	Feb 1 - Nov 30
Findhorn	Feb 12 - Sep 30	Ugie	Feb 16 - Oct 31
Fleet (Kirkcudbrightshire)	Feb 25 - Oct 31	Ullapool	Feb 11 - Oct 31
Fleet (Sutherland)	Feb 25 - Oct 31	Wick	Feb 11 - Oct 31
Forss	Feb 11 - Oct 31	Ythan	Feb 12 - Oct 15
Forth	Feb 1 - Oct 31		

The Editor would welcome feedback from readers of Scotland for Fishing on any hotels, guests houses or self-catering accomodation, which they would recommend as being specifically helpful to anglers. We would also appreciate any comments or suggestions regarding specific ommissions or information which you would like to see included in future editions of this guide.

It is inevitable that errors do occur from time to time, particularly with charges for fishing and accomodation and contact names and phone numbers. Your help is invaluable to ensure we keep these to a minimum and all comments will be acknowledged and very much appreciated.

Any amendments to the directory can be made at our editor's website which you can find at:
www.rod-and-line.net

		PAGES
Borders		72 – 77
Dumfries and Galloway		78 – 83
Forth and Lomond		84 – 92
Great Glen and Skye		93 – 98
North East and Speyside		99 – 107

		PAGES
Orkney and Shetland		108 – 110
North of Scotland		111 – 126
Strathclyde		127 – 138
Tayside		139 – 152
Western Isles		153 – 156

The Borders

ACREKNOWE RESERVOIR
Location • Hawick
Species • brown trout and rainbow trout
Permit • The Pet Shop, 1 Union Street, Hawick, Roxburghshire, Tel: 01450 373 543 (£7 per day – includes other waters. For further information contact The Secretary, Hawick Angling Club, 6 Sandbed, Hawick, Roxburghshire, Tel: 01450 373 771. Fly only. One boat available. 2 rainbow and 4 brown trout bag limit).

ALEMOOR LOCH
Location • Hawick
Species • pike, perch and brown trout
Permit • The Pet Shop, 1 Union Street, Hawick, Roxburghshire, Tel: 01450 373 543 (£7 per day – includes other waters. For further information contact The Secretary, Hawick Angling Club, 6 Sandbed, Hawick, Roxburghshire, Tel: 01450 373 771).

BLACKADDER
Location • Berwickshire
Species • brown trout
Permit • D Cowan, Hon Secretary, Berwick & District Angling Association, 129 Etal Road, Tweedmouth, Berwick-upon-Tweed, Tel: 01289 306 985 (Appox. £1 per day).
  • T Waldie, 26 East High Street, Greenlaw, Berwickshire, Tel: 01361 810 542 (Price as above).
  • Game Fare, 12 Marygate, Berwick-upon-Tweed, Tel: 01289 305 119 (Price as above).
  • Cdr. Baker, Millburn House, Duns, Berwickshire, Tel: 01361 883 086 (Price as above).
  • R Welsh & Sons, 28 Castle Street, Duns, Berwickshire, Tel: 01361 883 466 (Price as above).
  • R B Harrower, Blackadder Mount, Duns, Berwickshire, Tel: 01890 818 264 (Price as above).
  • R Carruthers, Bridgend House, 36 West High Street, Greenlaw, Berwickshire, Tel: 01361 810 270 (Price as above).

CLEARBURN LOCH
Location • Tushielaw
Species • wild trout
Permit • Gordon Harrison, Tushielaw Inn, by Selkirk, Tel: 01750 62205 (£15 per rod per day, including the use of a boat. Trout fishing is free to Tushielaw Inn residents. Boat fishing only).

COLDINGHAM LOCH
Location • Coldingham
Species • brown trout and rainbow trout
Permit • Douglas and Kirsty Aitken, Westloch House Estate, Coldingham, Berwickshire TD14 5QE, Tel: (018907) 71270, Fax: (0189017) 71991 (Day session £17 per rod, bag limit 4 fish. Evenings £14 per rod, bag limit 3 fish. Boat costs £4 per rod during the day, and £3 per rod in evenings. Self catering cottages also available for rent. Advance booking is essential).

ETTRICK
Location • Tushielaw/Selkirk
Species • salmon, sea trout and brown trout
Permit • The Factor, Buccleuch Estates, Bowhill, Selkirk TD7 5ES, Tel: 01750 207 53 (Salmon fishing costs from £20-£40 per day depending on dates. Trout fishing is £5 per rod per day).
  • Steve Osbourne, Tushielaw Inn, by Selkirk, Tel: 01750 622 05 (Prices as above. Trout fishing is free to Tushielaw Inn residents).

ETTRICK & YARROW
Location • Selkirk
        • Gala Water
Species • salmon and sea trout
Permit • Selkirk: The Factor, Buccleuch Estates, Bowhill, Selkirk TD7 5ES, Tel: 01750 207 53 (Salmon fishing costs from £20 – £40 per day depending on dates. 13 miles of double bank fishing).
  • P & E Scott, Newsagents, 2 High Street, Selkirk, Tel: 01750 207 49 (Prices as above).
  • Gordon Harrison, Tushielaw Inn, by Selkirk, Tel: 01750 62205 (Trout fishing is free to guests at the Inn).

- Ettrickshaws Hotel, Ettrickbridge, Selkirk, Tel: 01750 522 29 (Trout fishing is free to hotel guests).
- Gala Water: Galashiels Angling Association per J & A Turnbull, 30 Bank Street, Galashiels, Tel: 01896 753 191 (Visitor permits from £22 per rod per day).
- Kingsknowe Hotel, Galashiels, Tel: 01896 758 375 (Prices as above).

FRUID RESERVOIR
Location • Tweedsmuir
Species • brown trout
Permit • Crook Inn, Tweedsmuir, Broughton by Biggar, Tel: 01899 880 272 (Bank fishing only. £6 per rod per day).

GAMESCLEUCH TROUT FISHERY
Location • Ettrick
Species • trout. Fly fishing on 4 acres of water.
Permit • Ettrick, Selkirk TD7 5HX. Call 01750 6225/ for details. Tuition and rod hire available.

HEADSHAW FISHERY
Location • near Ashkirk, Selkirk
Species • rainbow trout, brown trout. Boat and bank fishing on 17 acre loch.
Permit • Headshaw Farm, Ashkirk, or fishery manager, Tel: 01450 376 809, mobile: 0374 287762. (£15 boat rod, 2 rods permited. Bank: full and sporting tickets, reductions for OAPs and disabled anglers. Limit 3 rainbows and 2 browns, then catch and release).

KAILZIE FISHINGS
Location • near Peebles, 2.5 miles east on B7062
Species • rainbow trout and brown trout on 2 acre lochan.
Permit • Day ticket £20 (5 fish then catch and release), reduced prices for 4 hour session. Disabled access, tuition and rod hire. Tea room and gardens open to October 31. Salmon, sea trout and wild brown trout fishing on nearby Kailzie fishings on River Tweed by appointment. (Prices under review).

LEADER WATER
Location • Leaderfoot
Species • brown trout
Permit • Tibbie Sheil's Inn, Yarrows, by Selkirk, Tel: 01750 42231 (Boat and bank fishing on St Mary's Loch, bank fishing only on Loch of the Lowes. A boat seat for disabled anglers is available through the Keeper (prior booking). Fly fishing £5 per rod, bait fishing £8 per rod).

LINDEAN RESERVOIR
Location • Selkirk
Species • brown trout and rainbow trout. Boat fishing on 35 acre loch.
Permit • P & E Scott, High Street, Selkirk, Tel: 01750 207 49 (£14 per boat per day with 3 rods. There is a boat limit of 12 fish).
• Tibbie Sheil's Inn, Yarrows, by Selkirk, Tel: 01750 42231 (Boat and bank fishing on St Mary's Loch, limit as above. Boat fishing 3 rods, prices under review.

LOCH OF THE LOWES/ST MARY'S LOCH
Location • Selkirk/Moffat
Species • brown trout, pike and perch
Permit • Tibbie Sheil's Inn, Yarrows, by Selkirk, Tel: 01750 42231 (Boat and bank fishing on St Mary's Loch, bank fishing only on Loch of the Lowes. A boat seat for disabled anglers is available through the keeper (prior booking). Fly fishing £5 per rod, bait fishing £8 per rod. Boat hire £20 per day – 3 man boat).
• Henry Brown, The Keeper, Henderland East Cottage, Cappercleuch, St Mary's, Yarrow, Selkirk, Tel: 01750 422 43

LYNE WATER AND MANOR WATER
Location • Peebleshire
Species • brown trout & grayling
Permit • Peebles Trout Fishing Association, Tweeddale Tackle, 1 Bridgegate, Peebles, Tel: 01721 720979

MEGGET RESERVOIR
Location • Selkirk/Moffat
Species • brown trout
Permit • Tibbie Sheil's Inn, Yarrows, by Selkirk, Tel: 01750 42231 (£6 bank permit, £15 weekday boat, £20 weekend boat – 2 anglers. Prices under review for 2002).

MOFFAT FISHERY
Location • Moffat
Species • rainbow trout
Permit • The Secretary, Hawick Angling Club, 6 Sandbed, Hawick, Roxburghshire, Tel: 01450 373 771 (£20 per rod per day for salmon. Trout fishing £4 per rod per day. Monday to Friday only).

PORTMORE LOCH

Location • Eddlestone/Peebleshire
Species • brown trout and rainbow trout
Permit • Portmore opens Saturday 30th March, 2002.
Steve McGreachie, Tel: 01968 675684,
Fax: 01968 674337, mobile: 0374 127467,
• Ticket prices shown are a guide only. Please
check with the fishery for 2002 season
charges.
Bank fishing – day sessions (4 fish limit) £ 17
Bank fishing – evening session (4 fish limit)
£16
Bank – sporting ticket (catch & release) £ 11
Boats – 2 rods – day & evening sessions (10
fish limit) £ 36
Discounts available for boats, Monday -
Wednesday
Website: www.portmore.co.uk
• Mike's Tackle Shop, Portobello High Street,
Edinburgh, tel: 0131 657 3258

TALLA RESERVOIR

Location • Tweedsmuir
Species • brown trout
Permit • Tweedside Tackle, Bridge Street, Kelso,
Tel: 01573 225 306/Fax: 223 343
(Season ticket £20, week £10, day £5.
Concessions for juniors and OAP's).

TEVIOT

Location • Hawick/Kelso
Species • salmon, sea trout, brown trout & grayling
Permit • Intersport, The Square, Kelso,
Tel: 01573 223 381 (Trout season ticket £20,
week £10, day £5. Concessions for juniors
and OAP's. Salmon tickets, price on
application).

TEVIOT & TWEED

Location • Hawick/Kelso
Species • salmon, sea trout and brown trout
Permit • James Leeming, ARICS, Tweed Salmon Fishing
Agent, Stichill House, Kelso,
Tel: 01573 470 280/Fax: 01573 470 259/
freephone: 0800 387 675 (Prices for the
Middle River can cost from £1,000 per
rod per week, and vacancies are rare.
Excellent fishing can be obtained elsewhere
for £25 – £60 during spring and summer.
Autumn prices are in the region of £60-£600
per rod per day (weekly lets preferred).
• Euan McCorquodale, Crossflat Farm,
St Boswells, Tel: 01835 823 700 (Permits for
Lower Mertoun and Maxton, prices vary
according to dates and location).

TWEED

Location • Kelso
Species • salmon, sea trout and brown trout
Permit • Ted Hunter, Angler's Choice, 23 Market
Square, Melrose, Tel/Fax: 01896 823 0701
(Permits for Dryrange and Leaderfoot Water,
prices vary according to dates and location).
• Douglas and Angus Estates, per Tweedside
Tackle, 36/38 Bridge Street, Kelso, Tel:
01573 225 306/Fax: 01573 223 343
(Permits for Birgham Dub, prices vary
according to dates and location).
• Mrs Jane Douglas-Home, The Lees,
Coldstream, Tel/Fax: 01890 882 706 (Permits
for The Lees, prices vary according to dates
and location).
• James Leeming, ARICS, Tweed Salmon Fishing
Agent, Stichill House, Kelso,
Tel: 01573 470 280/Fax: 01573 470 259/
freephone: 0800 387 675 (various beats and
charges depending on season and location)

TWEEDALE MILLENNIUM FISHERY

Location • Nr Gifford, East Lothian
Species • rainbow trout, blue trout, brown trout.
Famous for 20 lbs. plus specimen rainbows
and browns.
Permit • On the water or Tel. 0131 440 3749

WATCH RESERVOIR

Location • Longformacus, by Duns
Species • brown trout & rainbow trout
Permit • F Renton, Watch Reservoir,
Longformacus, Duns, Berwickshire,
Tel: 01361 890 331/ 01289 306 028. Also
mobile: 0860 868 144 Fax: 01361 890 331.
(Day ticket £16 with 6 fish bag limit. Evenings
£13 with 4 fish limit. Boat costs £5 per
session. Charges under review for 2002.
Catch & release using barbless hooks after
bag limit. Telephone bookings advised
for boats).

WEST WATER RESERVOIR

Location • West Linton
Species • wild brown trout
Permit • East of Scotland Water, 55 Buckstone
Terrace,Edinburgh, Tel: 0131 445 6462
(Boat for 2 anglers, £14. You will need keys
to access parking and the boathouse.
Keys available from J & R Bell, Newsagent,
Raemartin Square, West Linton,
West Lothian, Tel: 01968 660 407

WHITEADDER

Location • Lower River, Berwick
Species • salmon, sea trout and brown trout
Permit • D Cowan, Hon Secretary, Berwick & District
Angling Association, 129 Etal Road,
Tweedmouth, Berwick- upon-Tweed,
Tel: 01289 306 985 (Cost is in the region of
£10 – £20 per day per rod, depending on
time of year. Best after heavy rain for salmon
and sea trout. Good brown trout fishing.
• Game Fare, 12 Marygate, Berwick-upon-
Tweed, Tel: 01289 305 119 (Costs as above).

Location • Middle & upper river, Berwickshire
Species • brown trout only
Permit • Whiteadder Angling Association
• R Welsh & Sons, 28 Castle Street, Duns,
Berwickshire, tel: 01361 883 466 (Season
tickets under review).
• RB Harrower, Blackadder Mount, Duns,
Berwickshire, tel: 01890 818 264 (Prices
under review).
• R Carruthers, Bridgend House, 36 West High
Street, Greenlaw, Berwickshire,
Tel: 01361 810 270 (Prices under review).

Location • Abbey Saint Bathans
Species • Salmon, sea trout and brown trout
7 miles of productive private beats offering
excellent salmon fishing from late May
through to end of October, and sea trout
from late June. Dedicated lodge and riverside
self-catering accommodation.
Charges • £299 per person for a three night stay and
£599 for a seven night stay assuming shared
room and beat, inclusive of fishing. All
rooms en-suite and prices full-board. Single-
room supplement 10%, but no supplement
during late June, July and early August.
Contact Peter Miller, tel. 01361 890 311
e-mail: whiteadderfishing@yahoo.co.uk

WHITEADDER RESERVOIR

Location • Berwickshire, Near Cranshaws on B6355
Species • brown trout, 193 acres, boat & bank fishing,
good wading, stocked fish up to 2 lbs plus
wild brown trout.
Permit • Goblin Ha Hotel, Gifford, East Lothian,
Tel: 01620 810 244 (Prices under review).
• Mrs E Graham, Cranshaws Smiddy,
Cranshaws, Duns, Berwickshire,
Tel: 01361 890 277 (Prices under review).
• The Water Keeper's House, Hungry Snout,
Whiteadder Reservoir, East Lothian,
Tel: 01361 890 362 (Prices under review).

ALLANTON INN
Berwickshire.
Tel: (01890) 818260

Well located in Border country for fishing on lower **Tweed** and **River Whiteadder**. Rods available for salmon and sea trout from £25 per day, August, September, October. Special package 3 days DBB £120.

CROOK INN
Tweedsmuir, Broughton, by Biggar.
Tel: (01899) 880272

Upper **River Tweed** and tributaries, fishing for salmon (mainly autumn and late summer) and good fly fishing for wild river brown trout. £8 per day for trout fly fishing and £30 upwards for salmon fishing depending on the season.

ETTRICKSHAWS HOTEL
Ettrickbridge, Selkirk. Tel: (01750) 52229

Well-positioned for upper **Tweed**, **Ettrick** and **Yarrow**. Salmon fishing mainly late summer and autumn.

Good trout fishing on rivers and adjacent lochs. Access to Selkirk & District Angling Association water on Ettrick offering salmon fishing at £22 per day. Only 4 rods available, so advance booking necessary. Trout fishing from £5 per day.

GEORGE HOTEL
Walkerburn. Tel: (01896) 8703360

Salmon fishing available from september to November from £50 per day.

GOBLIN HA' HOTEL
Main St, Gifford   **SEE AD ON PAGE 59**
Tel: (01620) 810 244, Fax: (01620) 810 718
www.goblin-ha-hotel.com

Family-run hotel at the foot of the Lammermuirs.

HORSESHOE INN
Eddleston, By Peebles.
Tel: (01721) 730225/730306

Handy for **Portmore Loch** and **River Eddleston**, with upper **Tweed**, **Lyne Water** and **Manor Water** only a short scenic drive over the hills.

Portmore is stocked with rainbows and also produces good browns, particularly in the evenings when the sedge are up in late June. Peebles Angling Improvement Association and Peebles Trout Fishing Association stocks the River Tweed and tributaries with brown trout. Salmon fishing restricted mainly to autumn months. Association and private beats available. The Horshoe Inn has access to nine, 2 rod beats on the Tweed from £35 per rod per day to weekly lets from £80 to £110 per rod. Trout fishing charges around £8 per day.

KINGSKNOWE HOTEL
Galashiels.
Tel: (01896) 7558375

Middle and upper **Tweed** association water for salmon, sea trout and brown trout. Good brown trout fishing on hill lochs and Tweed tributaries such as **Gala** and **Leader Water**. Excellent centre for touring this attractive area and Border country. Trout fishing from around £5 per day. Salmon fishing from £15 per day to £50 and more for private beats in the autumn.

PHILIPBURN COUNTRY HOUSE HOTEL
Selkirk
Tel: (01750) 20747. www.philipburnhousehotel.co.uk

Hotel fishing breaks in this country house hotel and restaurant and self catering lodges, offering access to beats on the upper **River Tweed**.

Rod storage, drying and changing rooms, freezer facilities. Rod and wader hire, ghillies arranged. Lets on prime lower beats can also be arranged throughout the season February 1 to November 30. Rates on application.

THE ROXBURGHE HOTEL
Roxburghshire.
Tel: (01573) 450331

Owned by the Duke of Roxburgh, and with its own rainbow trout fishery and golf course. Rods fishing the Duke's beats on the **River Tweed** stay here. Prices on application.

TIBBIE SHIEL'S INN
Yarrows by Selkirk.
Fishing bookings only: Tel: (01750) 42231

Good base for trout fishing on **St Mary's Loch**, **Megget Reservoir**, **Megget Water**, upper **River Tweed** and tributaries **Yarrow** and **Ettrick**. Other hill lochs offer inexpensive but good sport with wild brown trout. Bait fishing allowed on St Mary's Loch. £5-£8 per day. Boats £20 per day for 3 rods, booked through the keeper (01750) 42243.

TILLMOUTH PARK HOTEL
Cornhill-on-Tweed, Northumberland TD12 4UU.
Tel: (01890) 882255.
Fax: (01890) 882540

A 'Border Raider' which may be excused in a guide to Scotland's fishing, as Tillmouth has some excellent beats on the lower **Tweed** and on its major English tributary the **River Till**. Excellent big sea trout in season and first class autumn salmon sport, although fish are taken throughout the season. Not cheap, but good value for money in this comfortable hotel, with fine dining and equally good cellar. Prices on application.

TRAQUAIR ARMS HOTEL

Innerleithen, EH44 6PD.
Tel: (01896) 830229
Fax: (01896) 830260

Good anglers' hotel, well positioned for middle and Upper **Tweed** with salmon fishing available on association and private beats. Also **River Ettrick** and **Yarrow Water**. The short Traquair private beat on the right bank above Innerleithen Bridge can produce excellent sport with salmon in the autumn. Good wild brown trout and grayling in season. Prices on application vary with beat and time of season.

TUSHIELAW INN

By Selkirk.   **SEE AD ON PAGE 66**
Tel: (01750) 62205

Fishing arranged on Buccleugh Estates waters on the **River Ettrick**, a major upper tributary along with the Yarrow of the **River Tweed**. Salmon are present from late spring, but main runs are in the autumn, which can produce excellent sport given rain. Many of the fish can be coloured and discretion should be used and all hen fish returned in late season where practical. Small hairwing flies, single handed rods and intermediate lines except in high water conditions, when double handed rods and sink tip can be used in conjunction with tubes or Waddingtons from 1.5 – 2 inches. Good accessible trout fishing on the river, managed by Selkirk Angling Association as well as excellent boat fishing on **Clearburn Loch**. Salmon rods from £ 20- £40 per day depending on season and trout fishing from £5 per day. Clearburn loch is boat only and costs £15 per rod per day including boat.

TWEED VALLEY HOTEL

Walkerburn EH43 6AA.
Tel: (01896) 870636
Fax: (01896) 870639
Email: 101325.2515@comupserve.com

Excellent fishing hotel and up market accommodation, with good food and well stocked bar. Another ideal base for middle and upper **Tweed**, offering a choice of association and private beats for salmon and sea trout. Good brown trout and grayling fishing also available. Loch trout fishing and splendid visitor golf nearby on the excellent course in Peebles overlooking the River Tweed.

Peebles sits astride the lovely River Tweed in its upper reaches. The small tributaries Eddleston, Manor and Lyne water are all excellent trout streams, offering challenging fly fishing for young and experienced anglers. The Tweed offers inexpensive association and town water fishing here for trout, salmon and sea trout.

Dumfries & Galloway

ANNAN

Location • Annandale

Species • salmon, sea trout, brown trout & grayling

Permit • Sport & Tackle Shop, 52 High Street, Lockerbie, Dumfriesshire DG11 2AA, Tel: 01576 202 400 (February – August cost £8 per rod per day, thereafter £45 per rod per week, Monday to Friday).
- The Factor, Annandale Estate, Estate Office, St Ann's, Lockerbie, Dumfriesshire, DG11 1HQ, Tel: 01576 470 317 (Prices as above).
- Jardine Hall & Millhouse Fishings, Anthony Steel, Kirkwood, Lockerbie, Dumfriesshire DG11 1DH, Tel: 01576 510 200 (Prices as above).
- McJerrow & Stevenson, 55 High Street, Lockerbie, Dumfriesshire DG11 2JJ, Tel: 01576 202 123 (Prices as above).
- G M Thomson and Co, 35 Buccleuch Street, Dumfries DG1 2AB, Tel: 01387 252 689 (Season tickets only on Dryfeholm Water at around £120 per rod).
- Mrs K Ratcliffe, Jay-Ar, Prestonhouse Road, Hightae, Lockerbie, Dumfriesshire DG11 1JR, Tel: 01387 810 220 (£8 per day and up to £150 per week depending on dates and location).

BLADNOCH

Location • Kirkcudbright

Species • salmon, sea trout, brown trout and pike

Permit • Newton Stewart & District Angling Association, per Galloway Guns & Tackle, 36a Arthur Street, Newton Stewart DG8 6DE, Tel: 01671 403 404 (£5 – £25 per rod per day depending upon dates. Book well in advance).
- David Canning, Torwood House Hotel, Glenluce, Newton Stewart, Tel: 01581 300 469 (Prices as above).
- A Brown, Three Lochs Holiday Park, Kirkcowan, Newton Stewart, Wigtownshire, Tel: 01671 830 304 (Prices as above).
- Jonathan Haley, Mochrum Park Sporting Holidays, Riverview Cottage, Spittal Bridge, nr Kirkcowan, Wigtownshire DG8 0DG, Tel: 01671 830 471/01422 822 148 (Prices as above).

- Peter McDougal, Corsemalzie Hotel, Port William, Newton Stewart, Wigtownshire DB8 9RL, Tel: 01988 860 254/ Fax: 01988 860 213 (Prices as above).
- Peter McLaughlan, Bladnoch Inn, Bladnoch, Wigtown, Tel: 01988 402 200 (Prices as above).
- Galloway Sporting Agents, Wyncherry Yard, North Corar, Newton Stewart, Galloway DG8 8EJ, Tel: 01850 733 670/ 01860 553 584, Fax: 01532 813 056 (Prices as above).
- Sue and Gary Pope, Church End, 6 Main Street, Kirkcowan, Wigtownshire, Tel: 01671 830 246 (Prices as above).
- Creebridge Hotel, Newton Stewart, Galloway, Tel: 01671 402 121 (Prices as above).

CLATTERINGSHAWS LOCH

Location • Newton Stewart/New Galloway

Species • brown trout, pike and perch

Permit • Newton Stewart & District Angling Association, per Galloway Guns & Tackle, 36a Arthur Street, Newton Stewart DG8 6DE, Tel: 01671 403 404 (£3 – £6.50 depending on dates).
- Merrick Camp Site, Glentrool Village, Newton Stewart, Kirkcudbright, Tel: 01671 840 280 (Prices as above).

CREE

Location • Newton Stewart/Girvan

Species • salmon, sea trout, herling, brown trout and pike

Permit • Newton Stewart & District Angling Association, per Galloway Guns & Tackle, 36a Arthur Street, Newton Stewart DG8 6DE, Tel: 01671 403 404 (Costs from £15 per rod per day, to £800 per week for a 3 rod beat in October. Also Water of Minnoch and Penkiln Burn).
- Jonathan Haley, Mochrum Park Sporting Holidays, Riverview Cottage, Spittal Bridge, nr Kirkcowan, Wigtownshire DG8 0DG, Tel: 01671 830 471/01422 822 148 (Prices as above).
- Galloway Sporting Agents, Wyncherry Yard, North Corar, Newton Stewart, Galloway DG8 8EJ, Tel: 01850 733 670/

01860 553 584/Fax: 01532 813 056
(Prices as above).
- G M Thomson & Co, 10 Victoria Street,
  Newton Stewart DG8 6NH,
  Tel: 01671 402 887/Fax: 01671 402 650
  (Prices as above).
- Jonathan Bradburn, Bargaly House, Newton
  Stewart, Wigtownshire DG8 7BH,
  Tel: 01671 402 392 (Prices as above).

DALBEATTIE RESERVOIR
Location • Dalbeattie/Castle Douglas
Species • brown trout and rainbow trout
Permit • M McCowan & Son, 43 High Street,
Dalbeattie, Kirkcudbrightshire,
Tel: 01556 610 270 (Boat and bank fishing.
No wading except to reach the small island at
the north end. Boats are not allowed to fish
north of the island. £14 per rod, boats £5
extra (2 rods fishing). No outboard motors.
Call for further information on the Dalbeattie
Angling Association Waters).
- J Moran, 12 Church Cresent, Dalbeattie,
  Kirkcudbright, Tel: 01556 502 292 (Prices as
  above).

FYNNTALLOCH LOCH
Location • Newton Stewart/Pinwherry
Species • rainbow trout
Permit • Newton Stewart & District Angling
Association, per Galloway Guns & Tackle, 36a
Arthur Street, Newton Stewart DG8 6DE,
Tel: 01671 403 404 (Bank fishing only. £15
per rod per day. 2 fish bag limit).

GLENKILN RESERVOIR
Location • Shawhead
Species • brown trout and rainbow trout
Permit • Customer Services, South West of Scotland
Water, Marchmont House, Moffat Road,
Dumfries DG1 1PW, Tel: 01387 250 000
(£2.75 per rod per day, £3 for boat hire.
£1.50 after 6pm. OAP's and under 16's free
when accompanied by an adult).

JERRICHO LOCH
Location • Dumfries/Beattock
Species • rainbow trout, brook trout and brown trout
Situated 3 miles north of Dumfries on the
A701 Dumfries – Moffat road, this 10 acre
fishery offers bank fishing for rainbow, brook
and brown trout, average weight 1.5 – 2 lbs.
Permit • David McMillan, Fishing Tackle Shop, 6 Friars'
Vennel, Dumfries DG1 2RN,

Tel: 01387 252 075 (£15 per day, 4 fish limit.
Bank fishing only).
- Patties of Dumfries, 109 Queensberry Street,
  Dumfries, Tel: 01387 252 891 (Prices as
  above).
- R M Currie, Glenclova Caravan Park,
  Amisfield, Dumfries, Tel: 01387 710 447
  (Prices as above. Easy disabled access. Good
  facilities with tackle shop and kitchen).

KEN
Location • East Bank
St John's Town Dalry/Castle Douglas
Species • pike, brown trout, rainbow trout, artic char,
also the occasional salmon and sea trout
Permit • Kenmure Arms Hotel, High Street, New
Galloway DG7 3RL, Tel: 01644 420 240
(From £2 per rod per day. Boat hire £30 per
day, 2 rods fishing).

Location • West Bank
New Galloway/Kirkcudbright
Species • pike, brown trout, rainbow trout, artic char,
also the occasional salmon and sea trout
Permit • Kenmure Arms Hotel, High Street, New
Galloway DG7 3RL, Tel: 01644 420 240
(From £2 per rod per day. Boat hire £30 per
day, 2 rods fishing).

KETTLETON RESERVOIR
Location • Morton Mains
Species • rainbow trout, some wild trout
Permit • Mid Nithsdale Angling Association, 110
Drumlanrig Street, Thornhill, Dumfriesshire,
Tel: 01848 330 555 (Bank fishing only. £15
per rod per day. 4 fish limit for rainbow trout,
thereafter use barbless hooks. No limit on
brown trout).

KIRKCHRIST FISHINGS
Location • Newton Stewart
Species • rainbow trout
Permit • Newton Stewart & District Angling
Association, per Galloway Guns & Tackle, 36a
Arthur Street, Newton Stewart DG8 6DE,
Tel: 01671 403 404 (Bank fishing only. Worm
fishing allowed after the 1st June. Bag limit
of 4 fish per rod. £12 per rod per day).

KIRRIEREOCH LOCH
Location • Glentrool Village
Species • brown trout
Permit • Merrick Camp Site, Glentrool Village, Newton
Stewart, Kirkcudbright, Tel: 01671 840 280
(Bank fishing only. Worm fishing allowed

after the 1st June. Bag limit of 4 fish per rod. £12 per rod per day).

- George Graham, The Old School, Hagg-on-Esk, Canonbie, Dumfriesshire DG14 0XE, Tel: 01387 371 416 (All Waters ticket [Esk & Liddle Associaton Waters] £61 – £119 per rod per week. Day tickets may be available from £7 – £38 per rod).

LIDDLE

Location • Saughtree

Species • salmon, sea trout, brown trout, finnock (young sea trout)

Permit • Stevenson & Johnstone WS, Bank of Scotland Buildings, Langholm, Dumfriesshire DG13 0AD, Tel: 01387 380 428 (All Waters ticket [Esk & Liddle Associaton Waters] £61 – £119 per rod per week. Day tickets may be available from £7 – £38 per rod).

- Caldons Campsite, Bregrennan, Newton Stewart, Wigtownshire, Tel: 01671 840 218 (£3 for adults, £1.50 for under 16s).

LILLIES LOCH

Location • Newton Stewart/New Galloway

Species • brown trout

Permit • Forestry Commision, Creebridge, Newton Stewart, Wigtownshire, Tel: 01671 402 420 (£3 for adults, £1.50 for under 16s).

- Forestry Commision, 21 King Street, Castle Douglas, Kirkcudbrightshire, Tel: 01556 503 626 (Prices as above).
- Talnotry Caravan Park, Newton Stewart, Wigtownshire, Tel: 01671 40217 (Prices as above).
- Clatteringshaws Forest Wildlife Centre, New Galloway, Ayrshire, Tel: 01644 2285 (Prices as above).
- Caldons Campsite, Bregrennan, Newton Stewart, Wigtownshire, Tel: 01671 840 218 (£6.50 per rod per day, under 16s £3 per rod per day).

LOCH DEE

Location • Newton Stewart/New Galloway

Species • brown trout

Permit • Forestry Commision, Creebridge, Newton Stewart, Wigtownshire, Tel: 01671 402 420 (£6.50 per rod per day, under 16s £3 per rod per day).

- Forestry Commision, 21 King Street, Castle Douglas, Kirkcudbrightshire,

Tel: 01556 503 626 (£6.50 per rod per day, under 16s £3 per rod per day).

- Talnotry Caravan Park, Newton Stewart, Wigtownshire, Tel: 01671 402 170 (Prices as above).
- Clatteringshaws Forest Wildlife Centre, New Galloway, Ayrshire, Tel: 01644 2285 (Prices as above).
- Kirrieoughtree Visitor Centre, Tel: 01671 402 165 (Prices as above).
- John Crofts, Blawbrae, Ettrick, Thornhill, Dumfriesshire DG3 5HL, Tel: 01848 330 154 (£15 per day, 4 fish limit. Boat £10 per session, 2 rods fishing).

LOCH ETTRICK

Location • Kirkpatrick

Species • rainbow trout and brown trout

Permit • Closeburn Post Office, Closeburn, by Thornhill, Dumfriesshire, Tel: 01848 331 230 (£15 per day, 4 fish limit. Boat £10 per session, 2 rods fishing.

- Tommy's Sport Shop, 178 King Street, Castle Douglas, Tel: 01556 502 851 (£25 per day for boat with 2 rods. Bag limit of 8 fish. Boat fishing only).

LOCH ROAN

Location • Walbutt

Species • brown trout and rainbow trout

Permit • Anthony Steel, Kirkwood, Lockerbie, Dumfriesshire DG11 1DH, Tel: 01576 510 212 (Permits from £5 upwards depending upon where and when).

MILK

Location • Hoddom Mill

Species • trout

Permit • The Factor, Buccleuch Estates Ltd. Drumlanrig Mains, Thornhill, Dumfriesshire DG4 3AG, Tel: 01848 600 283 Fax: 01848 600 244 (Boat and bank fishing, no wading. 2/3 rods £40 +VAT, per day. 3 trout per rod per day. Also fishing on Starburn Loch and Statehouse Loch at £30.50 +VAT and £12.50 +VAT).

MORTON CASTLE LOCH

Location • Drumshinock

Species • rainbow trout and wild brown trout

Permit • David McMillan, Tackle Shop, 6 Friars Vennel, Dumfries DG1 2RN, Tel: 01387 252 075 (£15 – £30 per rod per day depending on dates).

NITH

Location • Dumfries
Species • salmon, sea trout, grilse, brown trout and grayling
Permit • Dumfries & Galloway Council, Housing Services, High Street, Dumfries DG1 2AD, Tel: 01387 253 166 (£15 – £30 per rod per day depending on dates).
• Newton Stewart & District Angling Association, per Galloway Guns & Tackle, 36a Arthur Street, Newton Stewart DG8 6DE, Tel: 01671 403 404 (Boat and bank fishing. £15 per rod per day, boat hire £8 per day. 2 fish per rod bag limit).

OCHILTREE LOCH

Location • Newton Stewart/Pinwherry
M McCowan & Son, 43 High Street, Dalbeattie, Kirkcudbrightshire, Tel: 01556 610 270 (£15 per rod per day. Visitor tickets not available on Saturdays).

URR

Location • Kippford Sands/Dalbeattie
Species • brown trout, rainbow trout, pike and perch
Permit • Tommy's Sport Shop, 178 King Street, Castle Douglas, Tel: 01556 502 851 (£15 per rod per day. Visitor tickets not available on Saturdays).
• J Haley, Mochrum Park Sporting Holidays, Riverside Cottage, Spittal Bridge, nr Kirkcowan, Wigtownshire, Tel: 01671 813 471 (Prices as above).
• Cowan's Law, Moscow tel.01560 700 666 (Prices as above).

Beautiful Luce Bay on the Solway Firth, a wonderful shoreline for bird watching, particularly waders and geese. The extensive sands offer the beach angler sport with flatfish and bass. The Scottish record came from Luce Bay.

AE INN
Parkgate, Dumfries DG1 3NE
Tel: (01387) 860222

Convenient for **Loch Barony**, an attractive put and take fishery, stocked with rainbows and brown trout average weight 1lb 12oz and up to 5 lbs. Bank only fishing in this pleasant, wooded fishery within the gronds of Barony Agricultural College, with excellent facilities for disabled anglers. Damsel nymphs and lures work well, but try light tackle dry fly and small nymphs and you will find the larger fish as co-operative as the 'stockies'. Charges, please apply to the Ae Inn.

BARON'S CRAIG HOTEL
Rockcliffe, By Dalbeattie, Dumfries & Galloway DG5 4QF
Tel: (01556) 630225
Fax: (01556) 630328
Email: info@baronscraighotel.co.uk,
www.baronscraighotel.co.uk

Baron's Craig is the ideal base for touring Dumfries and Galloway and enjoying the wildlife, scenery and angling. Bird watching on the **Solway Firth**. Salmon, sea trout and browns on lochs and rivers. Rockcliffe produced a winter shore caught SFSA Record cod of 28 lbs. Catches from beaches include flatfish and bass.
   Sea trout, salmon and trout fishing by arrangement through the hotel, from £5 per day for brown trout and from £20 per day for salmon and sea trout.

CALLY HOUSE HOTEL
Gatehouse of Fleet, Kirkcudbright
Tel: (01557) 814341

Fine country house hotel in its own extensive gardens, convenient to **Water of Fleet** and its two major tributaries, brown trout lochs and the Solway shoreline, noted for sea angling and its bird life.
   The hotel has its own 6 acre stocked fishery, **Lake Cally** within the grounds, offering excellent fly fishing for brown trout, average weight 1lb up to 3lbs. No bank fishing, but the boat fishing produces good results to traditional flies, buzzers and small nymphs, particularly early and late in the day. Fishing is reserved exclusively for hotel guests.

CORSEMALZIE HOUSE HOTEL
Port William, Newton Stewart DG8 9RL
Tel: (01988) 860254 Fax: (01988) 860213

Good base for game and coarse fishing in the area, including **River Bladnoch** with good salmon fishing. Its two tributaries **Tarf Water** and **Malzie Burn**, offer more than 5 miles of good fly fishing for brown trout.
   The Bladenoch produces a good number of salmon each season and fair sea trout fishing. The river produces large fish in the autumn, known in the Solway rivers as 'grey backs'. There are excellent wild brown trout in the system. **River Cree** also produces good salmon and sea trout fishing.
   23 acre **Loch Glugston** offers stocked rainbows to 6lbs and wild brown trout. Traditional loch style fishing produces best results, or buzzer and small nymph patterns.
   For coarse anglers there are some excellent double-figure pike both here and nearby Kirkcudbrightshire **River Dee** as well as in some of the lochs. Other coarse species in the area include, perch, bream, roach and carp. No bank fishing: boat fishing for trout costs £16 per rod per day.

CREEBRIDGE HOTEL
Newton Stewart, Galloway
Tel: (01671 402121

Salmon fishing on rivers **Cree** and **Bladnoch**. **Upper Bladnoch** and **Water of Tarf** offer good trout fishing. Trout fishing around £5 per day. Salmon fishing from £15-£25 per day per rod.

CROSS KEYS HOTEL
Canonbie, Dumfrieshire
Tel: (013873) 7125
Fax: (013873) 71878

Overlooking Border **Esk**. Good salmon and sea trout fishing available. Also good coarse fishing on lochs for bream, roach, perch and specimen pike. Prices on application from the hotel.

DALSTON HOUSE HOTEL
5 Laurieknowe, Dumfries
Tel: (01387) 254422

Family run hotel with personal, friendly service, good food and comfortable bar. Mealtimes to suit anglers. Centrally located for salmon trout and sea trout fishing on **River Nith** and nearby **Annan** and smaller rivers. Good loch fishing for brown trout and excellent coarse fisheries including bream, roach, perch and pike. Shore and boat sea angling on the **Solway Firth**. Special angling packages can be arranged. Prices on application to hotel.

FRIARS CARSE COUNTRY HOUSE HOTEL

Auldgirth, Dumfriesshire DG2 OSA
Tel: (01387) 740388 Fax: (01387) 740550
Email: fc@pofr.co.uk

Friars Carse is a fine Scottish Baronial Hall dating back to the 13th century. The poet Robert Burns was reputedly a regular visitor. Set in 45 acres, the hotel offers private fishing on a mile of single bank fishing on the **River Nith** for sea trout and salmon, accommodating up to 10 rods. Ghillie available and guest tuition.

Auldgirth is central to the best of the salmon and sea trout fishings on the River Nith, which has one of the latest seasons in Scotland (November 30) along with Tweed. Excellent sea trout fishing in June and July and good back-end sport, with some large autumn salmon, known locally as 'grey backs'. Charges from £15-£50 per day per rod depending on season, with priority given to hotel guests.

KENMURE ARMS HOTEL

High Street, New Galloway DG7 3RL
Tel: (01644) 420240

Excellent facilities for anglers, good food, well stocked bar. Freezer and drying facilities. **Loch Ken** has suffered in recent years from lowering pH values and acidity from afforestation, but still produces good brown trout fishing, averaging around 14oz. with some much bigger specimens. The loch is also famous for its specimen-sized pike and 'doubles' are regularly taken, including fish in excess of 20lbs. Occasional salmon and sea trout.

Trout and coarse fishing also available on **Stroan Loch**, **Mossdale** and **Earlstoun Loch**. Mossdale Loch is stocked with both rainbows and brown trout and restricted to boat fishing only. Earlston is strictly fly-only boat fishing with restricted access to the banks other than at the boathouse.

MURRAY ARMS HOTEL

Gatehouse-of-Fleet, DG7 2HY
Tel: (01557) 814207, Fax (01557) 814370

Nearby **River Fleet** and tributaries offers reasonable, inexpensive salmon fishing and there are also some good hill lochs for brown trout. Commercial forestry plantations have affected this fishery, causing erosion and pool displacement and the river is prone to flash floods. The **Solway** is also excellent for shoreline fishing for bass, flatfish and cod from the rocks, including a chance of bigger winter fish.

Solway tides are fast and can be dangerous, so take care, especially when going onto sandbanks at low tide, which can be muddy and soft. Salmon and trout fishing from £8-£20 per day per rod.

NORTHFIELD HOUSE

Annan, Dumfriesshire
Tel: (01461) 202064

Situated adjacent to the Newbie Beats and below the Newbie cauld, Northfield House has its own short single bank stretch of the **River Annan**, which can produce excellent results on fly, particularly in early and late autumn. A new bridge over the river has created an excellent pool which consistently produces fish. Spacious well-appointed self catering flat in this Georgian mansion offers the ideal base with special inclusive rates for salmon and sea trout fishing.

RED HOUSE HOTEL

Wamphray, Moffat, Dumfriesshire DG10 9NF
Tel: (01576) 470214

Convenient for **River Annan**, offering improving runs of sea trout and good late summer and autumn salmon fishing. Excellent brown trout and specimen grayling are taken from the Annan and Nith each season. Chub are also present in the Annan, especially in Hoddom Castle reaches. Charges vary from £ 10-£30 per day per rod.

TRIGONY HOUSE HOTEL

Dumfriesshire
Tel: (01848) 331211
www.trigonyhotel.co.uk

Edwardian Country House set in 4 acres of wooded parkland. Excellent food featuring 'Taste of Scotland' and local produce. Trigony House Hotel has access to 3 miles of salmon and sea trout fishing on the **River Nith**. Special fishing breaks available: details and costs from the hotel.

WARMANBIE HOTEL AND RESTAURANT

Annan, Dumfriesshire DG12 5LL
Tel: (01461) 204015

Great fishing hotel in a Georgian mansion on the banks of the **River Annan**, with its own beats available exclusively to guests. Every amenity coupled with a fine restaurant and good cellar. What more could an angler ask for, except perhaps cooperative fish? Good brown trout and grayling fishing on the river and tributaries. Excellent and improving runs of sea trout, and particularly good autumn fishing for salmon. Access also to other beats can be arranged. Charges: prices range from around £5-£50 per day per rod.

Forth & Lomond

ALLAN WATER
Location • Bridge of Allan
Species • salmon, sea trout and brown trout
Permit • Country Pursuits, 46 Henderson St., Bridge of Allan, Tel: 01786 834 495 (£5 per day March – June £15 per day July – October. No Sunday fishing.)

ALLANDALE TARN FISHERIES
Location • Polbeth
Species • brown trout and rainbow trout, including blue trout and golden trout
Permit • Allandale Tarn Fishery, Gavieside, West Calder EH558PT, Tel/Fax: 01506 873 073 (Day ticket £15 for 5 fish, half day £10 for 3 fish, evenings £13 for 4 fish. Various other options. Email margo@thefisheryfsnet.co.uk).

ALMOND
Location • West Lothian
Species • salmon, sea trout and brown trout. Enters the Firth of Forth at Cramond Village. Fishes best on a dropping spate. Fly & bait fishing allowed.
Permit • Country Life, 229 Balgreen Road, Edinburgh, Tel: 0131 337 6230 (£5 per rod per day). Enters the Firth of Forth at Cramond Village. Fishes best on a dropping spate. Bait fishing allowed as well as fly fishing.

ALMOND (PERTHSHIRE)
Location • Glen Almond/Dunan
Species • salmon, sea trout and brown trout
Permit • The Factor, Mansfield Estates, Scone Palace, Perth, Tel: 01738 552 308 (salmon, from £10 per rod per day; trout fishing, £3 per rod per day).
• Mr MacKenzie, Auchnafree Lodge, Amulree, Perthshire, Tel: 01350 725 233 (Permits for brown trout on upper river only).
• T Muirhead, Corriemuckloch, Amulree, Perthshire, Tel: 01350 725 206 (Permits for brown trout on upper river only).
• Abercairny Estate, Estate Office, by Crieff, Perthshire, Tel: 01764 652 706 (Salmon fishing at £15 per rod per day).

BALLO RESERVOIR
Location • Auchtermuchty
Species • rainbow trout
Permit • Craufurdland Fishery, Fenwick tel. 01560 600 569

BANGOUR TROUT FISHERY
Location • Dechmont
Species • rainbow trout/ brown trout
Permit • Fairlie Moor, Largs, tel. 0790 427 3665/ 0790 422 6090

BEECRAIGS RESERVOIR
Location • Linlithgow/Beecraigs
Species • rainbow trout, brook trout and brown trout This is very popular big fish water, with double figure specimens taken regularly throughout the season. Fly fishing only. Mini lures, buzzers and nymphs take the bigger fish.
Permit • Beecraigs Country Park, Linlithgow, West Lothian EH49 6PL, Tel: 01506 844 516 (£38 per boat (under review), 2 rods, 12 fish per boat limit. Night sessions from May – August. Book well in advance).

BONALY RESERVOIR
Location • Edinburgh/Bonaly road
Species • brown trout and rainbow trout
Permit • No charges. Permission not required. Bank fishing only. Brown trout average 8 oz, rainbows larger.

BOWDEN SPRINGS FISHERY
Location • Linlithgow/Armadale
Species • brown trout, rainbow trout and blue trout. This popular two-lake fishery is well stocked and regularly produces big specimens.
Permit • Tony Coulson, Bowden Springs Trout Fishery, Carriber, Linlithgow EH49 6QE, Tel: 01506 847 269 (Day ticket 8 hours, £17 for 4 fish. Advance booking essential. May be hired for exclusive use, prices on application. Fish average 2lb).

CAMERON RESERVOIR
Location • St Andrews/Upper Largo
Species • brown trout, occassional sea trout
Permit • The Fishing Hut, Cameron Reservoir,
St Andrews, Fife, Tel: 01334 476 347
(Bank fishing £12 per rod per day,
boat fishing £33 for 3 rods, no outboards.
6 fish per rod).

CARRON
Location • Auchtermuchty Denny/Fintry
Species • brown trout
Permit • James McGhee, Tel: 01324 815 178
(The River Carron is generally reserved for
Association members, but day tickets may be
available at £8 per day).

CARRON VALLEY RESERVOIR
Location • Denny/Fintry
Species • brown trout
Permit • East of Scotland Water, Woodlands,
St Ninnian's Road, Stirling FK8 2HB,
Tel: 01786 458 705/01324 823 698
(Boat fishing only. £14 for boat with 2 rods.
Outboard hire £8).

COCKSBURN RESERVOIR
Location • Bridge of Allan
Species • trout
Permit • Country Pursuits, 46 Henderson St.,
Bridge of Allan Tel: 01786 834 495
(Adults £15. 2 person boat. No bank fishing).

DEVON
Location • Alva/Yetts o'Muckart/Rumbling
Bridge/Glendevon
Species • salmon, sea trout and brown trout
Permit • Ronald Breingan, 33 Redwell Place, Alloa,
Clackmanan FK10 2BT, Tel: 01259 215 185
(£6 per rod per day).
• Scobie Sports, Primrose Street, Alloa,
Clackmanan, Tel: 01259 722 661
(Prices as above).
• D W Black, The Hobby & Model Shop,
10-12 New row, Dunfermline,
Tel: 01383 722 582 (Prices as above).
• The Inn, Muckhart, Tel: 01259 781 324
(Prices as above).

EASTER BALADO FISHERY
Location • Kinross
Species • rainbow trout and brown trout
Permit • Helen Philp, Tel: 07801 547 869
(call for details).

EDEN
Location • Fife
Species • salmon, sea trout and brown trout
Delightful small salmon and sea trout stream,
which can produce excellent sport with fly
and worm on a dropping spate.
Permit • George Wilson, Franks Army Store, 10
Olympia Arcade, Kirkcaldy, Fife,
Tel: 01592 640 402 (Prices under review).
• J Gow & Sons, 12 Union Street, Dundee,
Tel: 01382 225 427 (Prices as above).
• J Wilson & Sons, Ironmongers, 169 South
Street, St Andrews, Fife, Tel: 01334 472 477
(Prices as above).
• J A Stewart, 31 Ladywynd, Cupar, Fife,
Tel: 01334 652 202 (Prices as above).

ENDRICK
Location • Balmaha (Loch Lomond)
Species • salmon and sea trout
This excellent stream can offer superb sport
in the late summer and autumn, particularly
after a spate. Catch and release encouraged.
Loch Lomond sea trout can run better than
7lbs.The lower reaches offer good coarse
fishing, including dace, perch and roach.
Permit • Loch Lomond Angling Improvement
Association. Inquiries for membership to Hon.
Sec, PO Box 3559, Glasgow.

ESK
Location • Dalkeith/Musselburgh
Species • salmon, sea trout and brown trout.
This once badly polluted stream now
supports good runs of migratory fish and the
river is well stocked with brown trout.
Permit • Mike's Tackle Shop, 46 Portobello High
Street, Edinburgh EH15 1DA. Tel: 0131 657
3258 (salmon and sea trout fishing £8 per
rod per day, trout fishing £4 per rod per day).
• James Dickson, 3 Haddington Road,
Mussleburgh, Tel: 0131 665 0211
(Prices as above).
• Musselburgh Pet Centre, 81 High Street,
Musselburgh, Tel: 0131 665 4777
(Prices as above).
• A & P Supplies, 24 The Square, Penicuik,
Tel: 01968 678 700 (Prices as above).

FORTH
Location • Aberfoyle
Species • salmon, sea trout and brown trout
Permit • Angling Centre, Stirling, Tel: 01786 430400
• Hooked on Scotland Ltd, 74 Port Street,
Stirling, Tel: 01786 446 564 (call for details).

- Forest Enterprise, Aberfoyle
  Tel: 01877 382 383 (1 February – 31 October
  £5.50 sea trout 1 February – 15 October £3
  brown trout 5 March – 6 October £3.00
  Juniors – £1.50 salmon season ticket – £30.
  No concessions. No Sunday fishing).

FRUIN
Location • Dumbarton/Crinlarich
Species • salmon, sea trout and brown trout
Permit • Loch Lomond Angling Improvement
Association. Inquiries for membership to Hon.
Sec, PO Box 3559, Glasgow.
- Michael Brady, Chairman, LLAIA,
  Tel: 0141 423 2873.

GARTMORN DAM FISHERY
Location • Near Alloa/Stirling
Species • brown trout and rainbow trout
Disabled anglers Wheelyboat available.
Permit • Clackmannan District Council, Leisure Services
Department, Spiers Centre, 29 Primrose
Street, Alloa, Tel: 01259 213 131/214 319
(Day tickets, boat fishing £24, bank fishing
f7. 5 fish per rod per session).
- Gartmorn Dam Visitors Centre, by Alloa,
  Tel: 01259 214 319 (Prices as above).

GLADHOUSE RESERVOIR
Location • Howgate/Temple
Species • brown trout
Permit • East ot Scotland Water, Comiston Springs,
55 Buckstone Terrace, Edinburgh,
Tel: 0131 445 6462 (Boat with 2 rods £16,
boat fishing only).

GLENCORSE RESERVOIR
Location • Flotterstone
Species • brook trout, brown trout and rainbow trout
Permit • East of Scotland Water, Comiston Springs,
55 Buckstone Terrace, Edinburgh,
Tel: 0131 445 6462 (Boat fishing only. £26
boat with 2 rods).

GLENQUEY RESERVOIR
Location • Flotterstone, Midlothian
Species • brown trout
Permit • Yetts o'Muckhart Post Office, Clackmannan,
Tel: 01259 781 322 (£9 per rod per day. Fly
fishing only).
- McCutcheons Newsagent, Dollar,
  Tel: 01259 742 517 (Prices as above).
- The Inn, Muckhart, Tel: 01259 781 324
  (Prices as above).

HARLAW RESERVOIR
Location • Balerno and Currie.
Close to Thriepmuir Reservoir. Boat and bank
fishing, using traditional loch flies. Margins
can be soft and difficult, so wading requires
caution, particularly at the north-west corner.
Species • brown trout and rainbow trout
Permit • A Fleming, 42 Main Street, Balerno,
Edinburgh, Tel: 0131 449 3833 (Day tickets
from 7am onwards, buy on the day you
intend to fish. £8 for adults, £6 for juniors
and OAPs. Wading is unsafe).

HARPERRIG RESERVOIR
Location • Edinburgh/Lanark
Species • brown trout
Permit • Cairns Farm, Tel: 01506 881 510
(£7 per rod per day, boat hire £8. Boat with 2
anglers £22. Bank and boat fishing).

HILLEND RESERVOIR
Location • Blackridge/Caldercruix
Species • brown trout & rainbow trout (1999), perch
and pike
Permit • Cafaro Bros., 34 Dundas Street, Glasgow,
tel: 0141 332 6224. (£5 per rod per day bank
fishing, occasional visitor boats f10 per
session.
- J Potter, Secretary Ardrie & District AC,
  12 Sharp Avenue, Kirkwood, Coatbridge
  ML5 5RT, tel: 01236 425576.)
- Grants of Airdrie, 120 Stirling Street, Airdrie,
  tel: 01236 755532.

HOPES RESERVOIR
Location • Gifford/Longyester
Species • brown trout
Delightfully situated hill loch with wild,
free-rising brown trout averaging 8-12
ounces. Traditional loch-style cast, drifting
close to shoreline.
Permit • Goblin Ha' Hotel, Gifford,
Tel: 01620 810 244. (Boat with 2 anglers
£25 (under review). No bank fishing. Collect
keys from the Water Manager's House).

LAKE OF MENTEITH
Location • Port of Menteith
Species • rainbow trout and brown trout
Permit • Lake of Menteith Fisheries Ltd., Port of
Menteith, Stirling FK8 3RD,
Tel: 01877 385 664 (Boat fishing only. Prices
under review. Various other options. Disabled
seats available).

LENY

Location • Callander
Species • brown trout, chance of salmon, sea trout
Permit • James Bayne, 76 Main St., Callander
Tel: 01877 330 218 (£15 per day. No Sunday fishing. From Loch Lubnaig to the falls (1 mile) £4 per rod per day).

LEVEN

Location • Windygates/Kinross
Species • brown trout, occasional salmon and sea trout
Permit • Kirkcaldy Tourist Information Centre, Tel: 01592 267 775 (£5 per rod per day).
• The River Leven Trust, The Sluice House, Kinross, Tel: 01592 840 225 (Prices as above).

LINDORES LOCH

Location • Newburgh/Cupar
Species • rainbow trout and pike
Permit • The Peir, Lindores Loch, Tel: 01337 810 488 (Boat fishing only. Single rod £16 – 5 fish, 2 rods £32 – 10 fish, 3 rods £36 – 15 fish per boat).

LINLITHGOW LOCH

Location • Linlithgow
Species • brown trout and rainbow trout
Permit • Forth Area Federation of Anglers, PO Box 7, Linlithgow, West Lothian, mobile Tel: 0831 288 921. Also try: 01506 671 753 and 01506 844 170. (Full day £32 with 16 fish limit per boat, 2 rods fishing. Bank fishing £10.50 (9am – 4.15pm), 4 fish per rod limit. Also day and evening sessions. Concessions for OAPs and juniors).
• Lochside Tackle, 254 High Street, Linlithgow, West Lothian EH48 7ES, Tel: 01506 671477 (prices as above).

LOCH ACHRAY

Location • Callander/Trossachs
Species • brown trout, sea trout, salmon, pike and perch
Permit • Loch Achry Hotel, The Trossachs, by Callander, Tel: 01877 376 229 (£7 per rod per day).
• Visitor Centre, David Marshall Lodge, Queen Elizabeth Forest Park, Aberfoyle, Tel: 01877 382 258 (£7 per rod per day, permits for Loch Drunkie and Lochan Reodhte also available at £3 per rod).
• Trossachs Fishings, Mr. M. Meikle Tel: 0850 558 869 (day) 01786 841 692 (evening) (£27 plus £2.50 license fee, boat fishing only).

LOCH ARD

Location • Aberfoyle/Stronachlachar
Species • brown trout, pike and perch
Permit • Altskeith Hotel, Kinlochard by Aberfoyle, Perthshire, Tel: 01877 387 266 (Bank fishing £5 per rod per day, boats £15 per day. Fishing is free to hotel guests).
• Inversnaid Hotel, Inversnaid by Aberfoyle, Perthshire, Tel: 01877 382 223 (Prices as above).
• Inverard Hotel, Lochard Road, Aberfoyle, Perthshire, Tel: 01877 382 229 (Prices as above).

LOCH ARKLET

Location • Stronachlachar/Inversnaid
Species • wild brown trout
Permit • W M Meikle, 41 Buchany, Doune, Perthshire, Tel: 01786 841 692 (Boat fishing only, £20 per day, electric motors £7 per day. Concessions for OAPs and unemployed.

LOCH CHON

Location • Aberfoyle/Callander
Species • pike perch and brown trout
Permit • Forest Enterprise, Aberfoyle Tel: 01877 382 383 (Adults £3. Juniors £1.50. Bank fishing only).
• David Marshall Lodge, QEFP Visitor Centre, Aberfoyle Tel: 01877 382 258 (Prices as above).
• James Bayne, 76 Main St., Callander Tel: 01877 330 218 (Prices as above).

LOCH COULTER

Location • Denny/Fintry
Species • brown trout
Permit • Alistair Steel, Topps Farm, Fintry, Carronbridge, Denny, Tel: 01324 822 471 (Costs in the region of £24 per day).

LOCH DRUNKIE

Location • Aberfoyle
Species • brown trout
Permit • Forest Enterprise, Aberfoyle Tel: 01877 382 383 (Adults £3. Juniors £1.50. Bank fishing only. Access via Forest Drive 10:00-18:00).
• David Marshall Lodge, QEFP Visitor Centre, Aberfoyle Tel: 01877 382 258 (Prices as above).
• James Bayne, 76 Main St., Callander Tel: 01877 330218 (Prices as above).

DIRECTORY

LOCH FITTY
Location • Dunfermline/Kelty
Species • brown trout and rainbow trout
Season opens Saturday 22 February, 2002
Permit • Game Fisheries Ltd., The Fishing Lodge, Loch Fitty, Kingseat, Dunfermline, Fife, Tel: 01383 620 666 Specimen Bay £24 – 4hrs, 2 trout, no catch and release.
Main loch: 10.00am - Dusk
Bank £17 day session, £ 14 evening session
Boat fishing £19 per rod day session, £16 per rod evening session
East Bay (Bait) £ 13 for any 5 hours
Concessions for retired or out-of-work anglers, Tuesdays and Thursdays.

LOCH KATRINE
Location • Stronachlachar
Species • brown trout
Permit • W M Meikle, 41 Buchany, Doune, Perthshire, Tel: 01786 841 692 (Boat fishing only, £20 per day, electric motors £7 per day. Concessions for OAPs and unemployed).
• Estate Office, Stronachlachar Tel: 01877 386 256 (Prices on request. Fly fishing only. Boat fishing only. 3 persons per boat. 2 rods per boat).

LOCH LOMOND
Location • Dunbarton/Crianlarich
Species • salmon, sea trout and brown trout
Permit • Tulliechewan Caravan Park, Balloch, Tel: 01389 759 475 (Adult day permit £15, £40 per week. Juniors £2.50 per day. Boat hire around £35 per day.
• Balloch Hotel, Balloch, Loch Lomond, Tel: 01389 752 579 (Prices as above).
• Gibson's Fishing Tackle, 225 Bank Street, Alexandria Tel: 01389 752 037 (Prices as above).
• McFarlane and Son, The Boatyard, Balmaha Tel: 01360 870 214 (Prices as above).
• A Wallace, Flat-a-float, Ardlui, Loch Lomond, Tel: 01301 704 244 (Prices as above).
• Rowardennan Hotel, Rowardennan, Loch Lomond, Tel: 01360 870 273 (Prices as above).
• Country Lines, 29 Main Street, The Village, East Kilbride, Tel: 01355 228 952 (Prices as above).
• Glasgow Angling Centre, 8 Claythorne Street, Glasgow, Tel: 0141 552 4737 (Prices as above).
• Cafaro Bros, 140 Renfield Street, Glasgow, Tel: 0141 332 6224 (Prices as above).
• W M Robertson, 61 Miller Street, Glasgow, Tel: 0141 221 6687 (Prices as above).

LOCH LOMOND & RIVER LEVEN
Location • Alexandria
Species • salmon, sea trout and brown trout
Permit • Gibson's Fishing Tackle, 225 Bank Street, Alexandria Tel: 01389 752 037 (Adult day permit £15, £40 per week. Juniors £2.50 per day.

LOCH LOMOND & RIVER LEVEN
Location • Balloch to Ardlui
Species • salmon and trout
Permit • Loch Lomond Angling Association Tel: 0141 781 1545 (Adult day permit £15, £40 per week. Juniors £2.50 per day.

LOCH LOMOND & RIVER LEVEN
Location • Balmaha
Species • salmon, sea trout, brown trout, pike, roach, perch
Permit • McFarlane & Son, The Boatyard, Balmaha Tel: 01360 870 214 (Adult day permit £15, £40 per week. Juniors £2.50 per day.

LOCH LOMOND & RIVER LEVEN
Location • Rowardennan by Drymen
Species • salmon, sea trout and pike
Permit • Rowardennan Hotel, Rowardennan, Loch Lomond, Tel: 01360 870 273 (Adult day permit £15, £40 per week. Juniors £2.50 per day).

LOCH LOMOND & RIVER LEVEN
Location • Luss
Species • salmon, sea trout and brown trout
Permit • Loch Lomond Park Centre, Luss Tel: 01436 860 601 (Adult day permit £15, £40 per week. Juniors £2.50 per day.

LOCH LOMOND & RIVER LEVEN
Location • Inveruglas
Species • salmon and trout
Permit • Loch Lomond Holiday Park, Inveruglas by Tarbet Tel: 01301 704 224 (Adult day permit £15, £40 per week. Juniors £2.50 per day).

LOCH LUBNAIG
Location • Callander/Lochearnhead
Species • salmon, trout and perch
Permit • James Bayne, 76 Main St., Callander Tel: 01877 330 218 (Brown trout and sea trout £4 per day. Salmon £5.50 per day. No Sunday fishing for salmon or sea trout. To launch boat and fish, £60 per season, £30 per week, £6 per day.
• Forest Enterprise, Aberfoyle Tel: 01877 382 383 (prices as above).

- QEFP Visitor Centre, Aberfoyle
  Tel: 01877 382 258 (prices as above).
- Immervoulin Caravan & Camping Park,
  Strathyre Tel: 01877 384 285 (prices as
  above).
- I P R Winter, Laggan Farm, Strathyre,
  Tel: 01877 384 614 (prices as above).
- Kings House Hotel, Balquhidder, Perthshire
  FK19 8NY Tel: 01877 384 646 (prices as
  above).
- Munro Hotel, Strathyre, by Callander,
  Perthshire, Tel: 01877 384 263 (prices as
  above).
- Trossachs Fishings, Mr. M. Meikle
  Tel: 0850 558 869 (day) 01786 841 692
  (evening) (prices as above).

LOCH ORE
Location • Lochgelly/Scotlandwell
Species • brown trout and rainbow trout
Permit • Park Centre, Lochore Meadows Country Park,
Crosshill, nr Lochgelly, Fife,
Tel: 01592 414 312 (From £7 – £8 for bank
fishing (8 hours, 5 fish). 3 man boat £42, full
day, includes engine).

LOCH VENACHAR
Location • Callander/Trossachs
Species • brown trout, sea trout, salmon, pike
and perch
Permit • W M Meikle, 41 Buchany, Doune, Perthshire,
Tel: 01786 841 692 (£8 per rod per day, boat
with outboard and fuel £30 approx. Season
tickets available. Sunday fishing allowed).
- James Bayne, 76 Main St., Callander
  Tel: 01877 330 218 (Adults £8 per day, £40
  per season. Juniors £4 per day, £20 per
  season. Boats for hire. Sunday fishing
  allowed).
- Trossachs Fishings, Mr. M. Meikle
  Tel: 0850 558 869 (day) 01786 841 692
  (evening) (prices as above).

LOCH VOIL & DOINE
Location • Balquhidder
Species • salmon, sea trout, brown trout and char
Permit • Mrs Catriona Oldham Muirlaggan,
Balquhidder, Lochearnhead, Perthshire,
Tel: 01877 384 219 (£3 per day. South shore
only on Loch Voil. Boats £27 per day).
- James Bayne, 76 Main St., Callander
  Tel: 01877 330 218 (Prices as above).
- Kings House Hotel, Balquhidder, Perthshire
  FK19 8NY Tel: 01877 384 646 (Prices as
  above).

- Munro Hotel, Strathyre, by Callander,
  Perthshire, Tel: 01877 384 263 (Prices as
  above).
- Stronvar Country House Hotel, Balquhidder,
  Lochearnhead, Perthshire,
  Tel: 01877 384 688. (Prices as above).
- C Marshall, Craigruie Farm, Balquhidder,
  Lochearnhead, Perthshire,
  Tel: 01877 384 262. (Prices as above).

LOGANLEA TROUT FISHERY
Location • Edinburgh
Species • brown trout
Permit • East of Scotland Water, Comiston Springs,
55 Buckstone Terrace, Edinburgh,
Tel: 0131 445 6462 (call for details).

MARKLE FISHERIES
Location • Markle, East Lothian
Species • rainbow trout, blue trout, brown trout
Permit • The Lodge, Markle Fisheries,
Tel: 01620 861213.
Excellent big-water fishery, run by Jonathan
Swift. Disabled anglers access. Bank fishing
only. Three lochans including mixed coarse
and rainbow fishery. Corporate days. Tackle
shop and snacks available.

MILLHALL FISHERY
Location • Briar Brae
Species • brown trout and rainbow trout
Permit • call: 01324 714 190 (Call for details).

MORTON FISHERY
Location • Livingston/West Calder
Species • brown trout, rainbow trout and American
brook trout
Permit • Ms Julie Hewitt, Morton Fishery, Morton, Mid
Calder, West Lothian, Tel: 01506 882 293/
01506 880 087 (Bank fishing £16.50 (6 fish
limit). Boat £4. Evening or half day ticket £11
(3 fish limit). You may bring your own
outboard).

NORTH THIRD RESERVOIR
Location • Carron Bridge, Stirling
Species • wild brown trout and rainbow trout
Permit • George Holdsworth, Greathill House, Stirling,
Tel: 01786 471 967/Fax: 01786 447 388
(Bank fishing £15 (10am – 5pm, 10 fish),
1 man boat £18, 2 man boat £31. Evening
session (6pm – 11pm) is slightly cheaper).

DIRECTORY

RAITH LAKE
Location • Kirkcaldy/Auchertoul
Species • rainbow trout and brown trout
Permit • Robert Duffy, Raith Lake Fisheries, Kirkcaldy, Fife, Tel: 01592 646 466 (lake)/ 01592 643 830 (home) (Monday – Friday £10 per rod (3 fish). 2 man boat £16 (Tuesday and Thursday, 10am – 4pm), weekends £15 per rod. 2 for £28, 3 for £36. 4 fish per rod, thereafter C&R).

RATHEN REEL AFFAIR
Location • Fraserburgh
Species • rainbow trout
Permit • Fishery manager, Tel: 01346 513329

RESCOBIE LOCH DEVELOPMENT ASSOCIATION
Location • Forfar
Species • rainbow trout
Permit • Fishery manager 01307 830367

SELMMUIR FISHERY
Location • Edinburgh/West Calder
Species • brown trout, rainbow trout and brook trout
Permit • G Gowland, Selmmuir Fishery, nr Mid Calder, West Lothian, Tel: 01506 884 550 (4 hours – 2 fish £12, 8 hours – 4 fish £14.50. Barbless C&R thereafter).

SWANSWATER FISHERY
Location • Chartershall
Species • rainbow, brown trout, steelheads, goldies
Permit • Alastair Lohoar, Swanswater Fisheries, Cultenhove, nr Chartershall, Stirling, Tel: 01786 814 805 (£9 for 2 hours/2 fish. £20 for 8 hours/5 fish. Bank fishing on Mill and Meadow ponds from £7.50 – £17. Fly only. Boats available from £3 – £6).

TEITH
Location • Callander
Species • salmon, sea trout, brown and rainbow trout
Permit • Angling Centre, Stirling, Tel: 01786 430400
• Hooked on Scotland Ltd, 74 Port Street, Stirling, Tel: 01786 446 564 (call for details)
• Country Pursuits, 46 Henderson St., Bridge of Allan Tel: 01786 834 495/Fax: 210 (Prices on request. No Sunday fishing. Bank fishing only. Advance booking advisable. 10 rods max. Fly fishing only).
• James Bayne, 76 Main St., Callander Tel: 01877 330 218 (Prices on request).
• Stirling District Council, Beechwood House, St Ninnian's Road, Stirling, Tel: 01786 432 348 (Prices on request).

• Ross Muirhead, Unit 1, Kildean Market, Stirling, Tel: 01786 461 597 (Prices as above).
• D Crockart & Son, 47 King Street, Stirling, Tel: 01786 465 517 (Prices on request).
• Mitchell's Tackle Shop, 13 Bannockburn Road, Stirling, Tel: 01786 445 587 (Prices on request).
• Lanrick Castle Estate, Broich Farm, Doune, Tel: 01786 841 866 (Prices on request)..
• Strutt & Parker, 13 Hill Street, Berkley Square, London, Tel: 0171 629 7282 (Prices on request).
• Finlyson Hughes, 29 Barossa Place, Perth, Tel: 01738 451 111 (Prices on request).
• Visitor Centre, David Marshall Lodge, Queen Elizabeth Forest Park, Aberfoyle, Tel: 01877 382 258
• Keir & Cawder Estates, Craigarnhall, Doune, Perthshire, Tel: 01786 833 858 (Prices on request).

THREIPMUIR RESERVOIR
Location • Currie and Balerno, Midlothian
Species • brown trout & rainbow trout
Permit • A Fleming, 42 Main Street, Balerno, Edinburgh, Tel: 0131 449 3833 (Day tickets from 7am onwards, buy on the day you intend to fish. £8 for adults, £6 for juniors and OAPs. Bank fishing only. Wading is unsafe).

TYNE
Location • Gifford/Haddington/East Linton
Species • brown trout, occasional salmon and sea trout
Permit • Mikes Tackle Shop, 46 Portobello High Street, Edinburgh EH51 1QA, Tel: 0131 657 3258. J S Main, 87 High Street, Haddington, East Lothian, Tel: 01620 882 148 (£5 per rod per day).

WATER OF LEITH
Location • Edinburgh
Species • brown trout, some wild fish
Permit • City of Edinburgh Council, 17 Waterloo Place, Tel: 0131 229 9292 (No spinning. Regulations on permit).
• Balerno Post Office, Tel: 0131 529 7913 (Condtions as above).
• Currie Post Office, Tel: 0131 449 6224 (Condtions as above).
• Colinton Post Office, Tel: 0131 441 1003 (Condtions as above).
• Juniper Green Post Office, Tel: 0131 453 3103 (Condtions as above).
• Water of Leith Conservation Trust, Tel: 0131 455 7367 (Condtions as above).

ALTSKEITH HOTEL
Kinlochard, By Aberfoyle, Perthshire.
Tel: (01877) 387266

Good base for **Loch Ard**, a scenic fishery at the head of the River Forth, 2 miles long and up to half a mile wide. Fly fishing for brown trout. Pike and perch also present. Charges £5 per rod for bank fishing. Boats £15 per day.

BUNRANNOCH HOTEL
Kinloch Rannoch, Perthshire.
Tel: (01882) 632367

Excellent location for Loch Rannoch and surrounding lochans. Rannoch produces large ferox every season and excellent shoreline sport with more modest brown trout. The fishings are managed by the Rannoch Conservation Association. Bank fishing £4.00 per day and boat with outboard around £30.00 per day for up to 3 anglers.

CLACHAN COTTAGE HOTEL
Lochearnhead, Perthshire.
Tel:(01567) 830247

Well positioned for **Loch Earn**, a busy fishery which is covered by a Protection Order. Angling is controlled by Loch Earn Fishings who stock the loch each season with 7,500 brown trout, between 10oz and 2.5lbs. Fish grow on quickly and the loch can produce beautiful brown trout up to 7lbs and larger.

All legal methods are allowed, although fly fishing using traditional loch-style techniques still produce some of the best baskets. Day tickets cost only £5 for adults and under 16s fish for £1. Boat charges range from £15 for short 4 hour hires, to £29 for a full day, inclusive of outboard motor and fuel.

DRUMMOND ARMS HOTEL
St Fillans, Perthshire.
Tel: (01764) 685212

Excellent area for hill walking, good brown trout fishing and a number of rivers. Good base for **Loch Earn** and other Trossachs lochs. Loch Earn is stocked annually with 7500 brown trout and offers excellent fishing from shore and boats. Limit of 6 fish per rod. Day tickets for brown trout £5. Boats 4 hours £15, 6 hours £22, 8 hour hire £29 inclusive of outboard and full tank of fuel.

DRUMTOCHTY ARMS HOTEL
The Square, Auchenblae, Kincardineshire
Tel: (01561) 320210

Loch Saugh is one of the notable lochs in the area, with brown trout averaging 1.25lbs, stocked and managed by the Brechin AC.

Excellent salmon and sea trout fishing by arrangement on **North** and **South Esk**, with the latter producing some exceptional sea trout sport in the summer of 2000.

Improving spring runs on the North Esk, with the Balmakewan beat producing 4 springers on opening day

of the 2001 season. West Water available through Brechin AC costs £10-£17 per day depending on season. Lets on North and South Esk from £35 per day, but expect to pay much more for prime time fishing.

FEUGHSIDE INN
Strachan, By Banchory, Kincardineshire
Tel: (01330) 850225

Fishing on the **River Feugh**, a major spawning tributary of the lower River Dee. Inexpensive sea trout and salmon fishing. Late summer, many of the fish are coloured and should be returned carefully to the water. Charges on application.

GOBLIN HA' HOTEL
Main Street, Gifford.   **SEE FEATURE ON PAGE 58**
Tel: (01620) 810244,
Fax: (01620) 810 718
www.goblin-ha-hotel.com

A short drive from Edinburgh on the edge of the Lammermuirs, the hotel has an excellent bistro and bar. Good loch fishing and stillwater rainbow fisheries nearby. Gifford has its own Golf Course and many famous links courses within easy driving distance. (See Pastime Publications' Scotland Home of Golf)

The Lothian **River Tyne** is a small stream at Gifford with good light tackle fly fishing for browns. The lower reaches from Haddington to the sea can produce big sea trout. The sea trout runs are less prolific than 20 years ago, but surprisingly occasional salmon are also caught nowadays. Poaching is a problem below East Linton when sea trout are running.

Hopes Reservoir in the Lammermuirs is a 35 acre fishery well stocked with brown trout, averaging 8-12oz with fish better than a pound regularly taken. Boat fishing only. Charges £22.00 for 2 rods per boat. The River Tyne costs £5 per rod per day and tickets are available from Mike's Tackle Shop, High Street Portobello, Edinburgh (0131) 657 3258.

INVERARD HOTEL
Lochard Road, Aberfoyle, Perthshire
Tel: (01877) 382229

Good base for **Loch Ard** with free fishing for hotel guests. Boat and bank fishing for brown trout. Traditional loch-style drifting works best from boats. Castle Bay is a noted drift.

Bank fishing around £5 per rod per day. Boat charges £15 per day.

INVERSNAID HOTEL
Inversnaid, by Aberfoyle, Perthshire
Tel: (01877) 382223

Ideally located for **Loch Ard** and the Trossachs. Plentiful brown trout fishing and salmon and sea trout on the

River Forth and **River Teith**. Large pike and perch are present in many of the lochs and offer good sport to spinning enthusiasts. Trout fishing £5 per day and boat charges £15 per day. See also Inverard Hotel, Aberfoyle and Altskeith Hotel, Kinlochard.

KINGS HOUSE HOTEL
Balquidder, Lochearnhead, Perthshire
Tel: (01877 384646

Well placed for trout fishing in the **Trossachs**, and particularly the top end of **Loch Earn**, stocked annually with brown trout and offering good sport from boats and bank.

Loch Voil at the head of the River Teith, **Loch Lubnaig** and the **River Balvag** offer excellent budget sport in wonderful scenery. Salmon, sea trout, brown trout, ferox, char and specimen pike. The hotel also has fishing also on **Loch Doine**. Bank fishing for brown trout from £3 per day and boats £27 including outboard motor.

LOCH ACHRAY HOTEL
The Trossachs, By Callander.
Tel: (01887) 376229

Excellent centre for touring and loch fishing for brown trout. Some lochs also produce big pike and perch: and spinning is allowed.

Main base for **Loch Venacher**, a large loch extending to 3.5 miles and some half a mile wide and **Loch Achray**. Pike and perch are present as well as brown trout and the chance of salmon and sea trout. Some large ferox trout which feed on the char, are taken every year, mainly trolling from boats. Bait fishing allowed, but fly fishing can produce nice baskets of trout. £7 per rod per day for bank fishing and £27 for boat and outboard.

MUNRO HOTEL
Strathyre, By Callander, Perthshire
Tel: (01877) 384263

Access to fishing on the **River Teith** for salmon and sea trout, as well as some good loch fishing. Pike and perch fishing in many of the Trossachs lochs. Trout fishing from £5 per day per rod. Other prices on application.

ROWARDENNAN HOTEL
Rowardennan, Loch Lomond
Tel: (01360) 870273

Whether you fish the 'Big Loch' for salmon and sea troutor its record-breaking pike, Rowardennan Hotel is well placed and can also arrange boats and visitor permits.

Excellent boat fishing for salmon and sea trout, as well as coarse fishing for specimen perch, roach and double

figure pike. Scenically stunning, **Loch Lomond** is famous for its 'Bonny banks.' The River Leven drains from the loch, and offers good budget fishing for salmon and sea trout, although numbers of farm escapees continue to plague this fishery.

Boating stations on the loch include Macfarlane & Sons at Balmaha (01360) 870273, ideal for the Endrick bank and good salmon drifts. Boats with outboards £35 per day. The Loch Lomond Angling Improvement issues day tickets at £15 per week River Leven and £35 per week for Loch Lomond and River Leven.

STRONVAR COUNTRY HOUSE HOTEL
Balquidder, Lochearnhead, Perthshire
Tel: (01877) 384688

Good base for the Trossachs, with inexpensive loch fishing for brown trout, ferox, char, perch and pike.

Loch Voil offers salmon and sea trout fishing on a budget. Good fishing available on **Loch Doine** and interconnecting rivers fish well particularly after a spate. Boat fishing offers the best chance of success on this large fishery. Charges £3 bank fishing. Boats £27 including outboard motor.

THE INN
Muckhart
Tel: (01259) 781324

In recent years, the **River Devon** has received improving runs of migratory fish, with a recent fish pass at the Cambus cauld. Salmon and sea trout run from June, peaking in the autumn.

Spinning and bait fishing allowed. The Devon AC stocks the river with around 4,000 brown trout each year. The river receives compensation water from **Castlehill** reservoir, which also offers boat and bank fishing for brown trout. Charges £9 per rod per day.

ROMAN CAMP COUNTRY HOUSE HOTEL
Callander FK17 8BG
Tel: (01877) 330003/ (01877) 331533
www.roman-camp-hotel.co.uk

17th century country mansion adjacent to the **River Teith** in the Trossachs. Excellent touring centre and free salmon and trout fishing on the hotel's own private beat.

Early spring salmon can be caught from opening day on the River Teith but fishing peaks in late summer and autumn. Given water, the summer months can be just as productive with grilse and sea trout. Trout fishing from £5 per day per rod: Salmon and trout fishing from around £20 per day per rod.

Great Glen & Skye

BROGAIG
Location • North Skye/Staffin Bay
Species • trout, salmon, sea trout
Permit • Jansports, Wentworth Street, Portree, Isle of Skye, Tel: 01478 612 559
• Neil Cameron, Secretary, Portree Angling Association, Hillcroft, 2 Teraslane, by Portree, Skye, Tel: 01470 582 304

FARRAF
Location • Struy
Species • salmon, grilse, brown trout
Permit • Juliet and Frank Spencer-Nairn, Culligran Cottages, Struy, nr Beauly, Inverness-shire, Tel: 01463 761 285 (From £15 – £45 per rod per day for salmon. Brown trout fishing £10 per rod per day).
• Glen Affric Hotel, Cannich, Inverness-shire, Tel: 01456 415 214 (Prices as above).

GARRY
Location • Fort Augustus/Fort William
Species • salmon, brown trout, pike and char
Permit • Invergarry Hotel, Invergarry, Inverness-shire PH35 4HG, Tel: 01809 501 206/ fax: 01809 501 236 (Lower River Garry and Loch Oich, weekly lets preferred, from £400 – £1,800. Day lets cost £18 per rod per day, when available).
• Tomdoun Hotel, by Invergarry, Inverness-shire, Tel: 01809 511 218/244 /fax: 511 216 (Upper River Garry and surrounding lochs. Boats £12 approx per day, outboards £12 per day (2 rods). Fishing free to hotel guests).

GLASS
Location • Struy
Species • salmon, grilse, brown trout
Permit • Ardochy Lodge, by Invergarry, Inverness-shire, Tel: 01809 511 232 (£18 per boat per day, outboards £12 approx).
• River Glass Syndicate, Tel: 01463 761 252 (From £15 - £45 per rod per day. Trout fishing £10 per rod per day).
• Juliet & Frank Spencer-Nairn, Culligran Cottages, Struy, nr Beauly, Inverness-shire, Tel: 01463 761 285 (Prices as above).

KILMALUAG
Location • Port Gobhlaig
Species • grilse and sea trout
Permit • Glen Affric Hotel, Cannich, Inverness-shire, Tel: 01456 415 214 (From £15 - £45 per rod per day. Trout fishing £10 per rod per day.
• Neil Cameron, Secretary, Portree Angling Association, Hillcroft, 2 Teraslane, by Portree, Skye, Tel: 01470 582 304 (Salmon fishing £10 per session, dawn till 1pm or 2pm till dusk).

LEALT
Location • Portree/Staffin
Species • salmon & sea trout
Permit • Neil Cameron, Secretary, Portree Angling Association, Hillcroft, 2 Teraslane, by Portree, Skye, Tel: 01470 582 304 (Bank fishing £10 per day).

LOCH ARKAIG
Location • Fort Augustus
Species • wild brown trout, ferox, char, occasional salmon, sea trout and pike (Loch Arkaig is joined to Loch Lochy by the short River Arkaig. Salmon and sea trout enter the system via the River Lochy and Loch Lochy).
Permit • West Highland Estates, Estate Office, 33 High Street, Fort William, Inverness-shire, Tel: 01397 702 433 (£3 per rod per day, boat launch charge £10 per day with 2 anglers fishing).
• Mrs Yates, 2 Clunes, Achnacarry, by Fort William, Tel: 01397 712 719 (Prices as above).

LOCH BRAN
Location • Inverness/Fort Augustus
Species • brown trout
Permit • Rod & Gun Shop, 18 High Street, Fort William, Tel: 01397 702 656 (£3 per rod per day, boat launch charge £10 per day with 2 anglers fishing).

LOCH DOCHFOUR
Location • Inverness
Species • brown trout
Permit • The Shop, Dochgarroch Locks, Inverness, Tel: 01463 861 265 (£4 per rod per day).

LOCH DOILET
Location • Corran/Acharacle
Species • salmon, sea trout and brown trout
Permit • Strontian Angling Club, c/o Harry Whitney, Biggans End, Monument Park, Strontian PH36 48Z, Tel: 01967 402 480 (Boat with 2 anglers costs £10 per day).

LOCH GARRY
Location • Invergarry/Tomdoun
Species • salmon, brown trout, pike and char
Permit • Tomdoun Hotel, by Invergarry, Inverness-shire, Tel: 01809 511 218, fax: 01809 511 216 (Upper River Garry and surrounding lochs. Boats £12 approx per day, outboards £12 per day (2 rods). Fishing free to hotel guests).

LOCH INCHLAGGAN & UPPER LOCH GARRY
Location • Tomdoun
Species • salmon, brown trout, pike and char
Excellent wild brown trout and occasional char in the Lochs. Upper River Garry offers superb fly fishing for brown trout, which can run up to 4lbs. The char in Loch Garry are of record size, and are often to be found feeding near the smolt-rearing cages. Specimen ferox trout are regularly caught in both Loch Garry and Loch Quoich.
Permit • Tomdoun Hotel, by Invergarry, Inverness-shire. Tel: 01809 522 218 (outboards £12 approx).
• Garry Gualach Adventure Centre, Tel: 01809 511 230

LOCH INSH
Location • Aviemore, Inverness-shire
Species • salmon, sea trout, brown trout, char and pike
Loch Insh forms part of the River Spey system, is readily accessible and a major watersports centre, so anglers have to share this popular loch with other users. Best spots are around the islands at the northern end or working the south shore.
Permit • Dalraddy Holiday Park, by Aviemore, Inverness-shire, Tel: 01479 810 330
• Alvie Estate office, Kincraig. Tel: (01540) 651 255.
• Loch Insh Watersports, The Boat House, Kincraig, tel. (01540) 651 272 (Boat with outboard, 2 rods fishing, £40. Bank fishing £10 per day).

LOCH KILLIN
Location • Gorthleck, Inverness-shire
Species • brown trout, ferox and arctic char
Loch Killin lies in a narrow valley to the south-east of Whitebridge. Bank fishing only and trout average around 8 oz. The loch is glacial and lies around 1,000 feet above sea level and fishes best from June onwards.
Permit • Neil Cameron, Secretary, Portree Angling Association, Hillcroft, 2 Teraslane, by Portree, Skye, Tel: 01470 582 304 (Bank fishing £8 per day).

LOCH KNOCKIE
Location • Knockcarrach
Species • trout and char
Permit • Ewan MacDonald, 4 St Cumin's House, Morar, by Mallaig, Tel: 01687 462 520 (Boat with outboard and fuel £35 per day, £20 per evening, 2 rods. Bank fishing £4.50).
• The Morar Hotel, Morar, by Mallaig, Tel: 01687 462 346 (Boat with outboard and fuel £35 per day, £20 per evening, 2 rods. Bank fishing £4.50).
• Knockie Lodge Hotel, Whitebridge, Stratherrick, Tel: 01456 486 27 / fax: 01456 486 389 (Hotel guests have priority. Otherwise £25 per day for the boat)
• Whitebridge Hotel, Stratherrick, Gorthleck, Inverness IV1 2UN. Tel: (01456) 486226/ 486272

LOCH LAGGAN & LOCH MOY
Location • Kingussie – Spean Bridge Road (A86)
Species • brown trout, ferox, pike
Permit • The In at Roy Bridge, Roy Bridge, Inverness-shire PH31 4AG. Tel: (01397) 712 253
• James Coutts, Fishing Scotland, Tel/ fax: 01397 712 812

LOCH MEALT
Location • Portree/Flodigarry
Species • brown trout and char
Permit • Morar Motors, Tel: 01687 462 118 (Boat with outboard and fuel £35 per day, £20 per evening, 2 rods. Bank fishing £4.50).
• Jack Meredith, Highland Sports Fishing Ltd., Clunebeg House, Drumnadrochit, Inverness-shire, Tel: 01456 450 387/854 (Costs from £4 – £6 per hour for boat with ghillie).

LOCH MORAR (& HILL LOCHS)

Location • Morar
Species • salmon, sea trout, brown trout, ferox trout, char
Permit • Glenmoriston Lodge Estate, Invermoriston, Inverness-shire, Tel: 01320 351 300 (Boat with outboard and ghillie – 2 rods – at £70 per day).
• J Graham & Co, 37 Castle Street, Inverness, Tel: 01463 233 178/fax: 01463 710 287 (Boat hire and ghillie can be arranged).
• A C Humphrey, Balvoulin, Flichty, Inverness, Tel: 01808 521 283 (Boat fishing only, no outboards. £15 per boat per day, 2 rods).

LOCH NESS

Location • Inverness/Fort Augustus
Species • salmon, sea trout, brown trout, ferox trout, char
Permit • J Graham & Co, 37 Castle Street, Inverness, Tel: 01463 233 178/fax: 01463 710 287 (Boat fishing only, no outboards. £15 per boat per day, 2 rods).
• Whitebridge Hotel, Stratherrick, Inverness, Tel: 01456 486 272/01456 486 226, Fax: 413 (Boat fishing only, no outboards. £15 per boat per day, 2 rods).
• D MacAukay, Dalilea Farm, Acherachle, Tel: 01967 431 253 (Boat and outboard £35 approx, per day).

LOCHS RAVAG, CONNON & DUAGRICH

Location • Struan, Isle of Skye
Species • brown trout
Connan trout average around 12 ounces, but can run up to 2 lbs., with baskets of a dozen or more fish when conditions are right. Loch Duagrich produces larger quantities of smaller trout averaging 8 oz. Ravag is a weedy loch with good stock of free-rising wild trout.
Permit • Ullinish Lodge Hotel, Struan, Isle of Skye, Tel: 01470 572 214 (£10 per rod per day, hotel guests have priority. Other fishing available).

LOCH RUTHVEN

Location • Elrig
Species • brown trout
Permit • Glenfinnan House Hotel, Glenfinnan, Tel: (01397) 722 235 (Boat and outboard £35 approx, per day).
• Prince's House, Glenfinnan, Tel: (01397) 722 246 (subject to availability) (Prices as above).

• Mrs N D Stewart, Kinlochmoidart House, Lochailort, Inverness-shire, Tel: 01967 431 609

Location • Flichtry, Inverness-shire
Species • brown trout
Boat fishing only, with excellent quality browns, regularly stocked by the estate, average weight 1lb. but plenty of larger fish up to 4 lbs.
Permit • A C Humphrey, Balvoulin, Flichty, Tel. (01808) 521283
• John Graham and Co., Inverness, Tel. (01463) 233178

LOCH SHIEL

Location • Glenfinnan/Acharacle
Species • brown trout
Permit • Mrs Lees-Millais, Glenmoidart House, Lochailort, Inverness-shire, Tel: 01967 431 254 (Fishing on Estate waters is let with the Glenmoidart Estate cottage).
• Glenmoriston Lodge Estate, Invermoriston, Inverness-shire, Tel: 01320 351 300 (Salmon fishing £15 – £35 per rod per day. Boat hire £20 approx. trout £5 per rod per day).
• Grant Harris, Balintombuie, Dalchreichart, Glenmoriston, Tel: 01320 340 225 (Salmon £12 per rod, brown trout £6 per rod, per day).

MOIDART

Location • Glen Moidart
Species • salmon, sea trout and wild brown trout
Permit • P Fraser, TV & Radio, 41 High Street, Nairn, Nairnshire, Tel: 01667 453 038 (Lower beat. £13.50 per day, £41 per week. Juniors half price).
• Calva Holiday Homes, Culloden Moor, Inverness-shire, Tel: 01463 790 228/405/ fax: 01463 790 228 (Offers accommodation including salmon fishing. Day lets £6 per rod per day).

MORISTON

Location • Invermoriston/Kyle of Lochalsh
Species • salmon and brown trout
The river flows from Loch Cluanie and runs parallel to the A887 Invermoriston-Kyle of Lachalsh road, joining the north shore of Loch Ness at Invermoriston. The river is affected by hydro and river heights can fluctuate suddenly. Best of the sport occurs in the afternoon as the river drops after the

Moriston cont'd

'artificial spates'. The river can produce large spring salmon. There are some good hill lochs nearby for wild brown trout.

Permit • The Rod & Gun Shop, 18 High Street, Fort William, Tel/Fax: 01397 702 656 (£5 per rod per day, first come first served, from 9am).
• Glenmoriston Lodge Estate, Tel. (01320) 351 300

NAIRN

Location • Perth/Inverness
Species • salmon and sea trout
Permit • Jansports, Wentworth Street, Portree, Isle of Skye, Tel: 01478 612 559 (Salmon and sea trout cost £7.50 – £12. Trout £5 per rod per day).
• Skeabost House Hotel, Skeabost Bridge, Isle of Skye, Tel: 01470 532 202 (£15 per rod per day. Free for hotel guests staying 3 or more days).

NEVIS

Location • Fort William
Species • salmon, sea trout and brown trout
Permit • The Rod & Gun Shop, 18 High Street, Fort William, Tel/Fax: 01397 702 656

POLLOCH

Location • Corran/Acharacle
Species • salmon, sea trout & brown trout
Permit • The Rod & Gun Shop, 18 High Street, Fort William, tel/fax: 01397 702 656 (£12 per rod per day).

PORTREE ANGLING ASSOCIATION

Location • Isle of Skye
Species • brown trout, salmon and sea trout
Permit • For all Portree AA waters, visitors can obtain permits from Jansports, Wentworth Street, Portree, Isle of Skye, Tel: 01478 612 559
• The Secretary, Portree Angling Association, Tel: 01478 612 559.

SLIGACHAN

Location • South Skye
Species • salmon, sea trout and brown trout
Permit • Jansports, Wentworth Street, Portree, Isle of Skye, Tel: 01478 612 559 (Fly only. Boat hire day £15, evening £10 (2 rods). Bank fishing £8. No Sunday fishing).
• Slighan Hotel, Tel. (01478) 650 204

SNIZORT

Location • North Skye
Species • salmon, sea trout and brown trout
Permit • The Secretary, Portree Angling Association, Hillcroft, 2 Teraslane, by Portree, Skye, Tel: 01470 582 304 (Fly only. Boat hire day £15, evening £10 (2 rods). Bank fishing £8. No Sunday fishing).
• Skeabost House Hotel, Skeabost Bridge, Isle of Skye, Tel: 01470 532 202 (£15 per rod per day. Free for hotel guests staying 3 or more days).
• Ullinish Lodge Hotel, Struan, Isle of Skye, Tel: 01470 572 214 (£10 per rod per day, hotel guests have priority. Other fishing available).

SPEAN & ROY

Location • Kingussie/Fort William
Species • salmon and sea trout in River Spean, salmon and brown trout in River Roy. Both spate rivers.
Permit • The Inn at roy bridge HotelL Roy Bridge, Inverness-shire PH31 4AG. Tel: (01397) 712 253
• The Rod & Gun Shop, 18 High Street, Forth William, Tel: 01397 702 656
• James Coutts, Fishing Scotland, Tel/fax: 01397 712 812

STORR LOCHS & HILL LOCHS

Location • Portree/Staffin. Three interlinked lochs form the Storr Lochs, lying to the north of Portree.
Species • brown trout
Permit • Jansports, Wentworth Street, Portree, Isle of Skye, Tel: 01478 612 559
• The Secretary, Portree Angling Association, Tel: 01478 612 559., or the Secretary, Portree Angling Association, Hillcroft, 2 Teraslane, by Portree, Skye, Tel: 01470 582 304 (Fly only. Boat hire day £15, evening £10 (2 rods). Bank fishing £8. No Sunday fishing).

STRONTIAN

Location • Strontian/Polloch
Species • salmon and sea trout
Permit • Bill Brailsford, Head Keeper, Garrogie Estate Office, Gorthleck, Inverness-shire, Tel: 01456 486 254 (Bank fishing only. Prices under review).

EILEAN IARMAIN HOTEL

Eilean Iarmain, An t'Eilean Sgitheanach IV43 8QR.
Tel: (01471) 833266 Fax: (01471) 833260

A number of excellent brown trout lochs and lochans including **Loch Lonachan**, lying north of Beinn nan Carn. Comfortable safe wading and traditional flies do the business. Brown trout average around the half pound mark, but with plenty of larger fish to keep you concentrated.

Fish a Soldier Palmer, Black Pennel or Blue Zulu on the top dropper, particularly effective in a good wave. Attractors such as Peter Ross and Silver or Bloody Butcher also work well. Charges £7.50 per day and only £25 per rod for a week's excellent sport.

FERRY INN

Uig, Isle of Skye
Tel: (01470) 542242

Plenty of choice for hill lochs and wild brown trout. The little **River Rha** can provide exciting sport and a chance of summer salmon and sea trout after rain. Timing is critical and your best chance is on a dropping river after a spate.

Spinning and bait fishing are allowed and the lower reaches produce most of the fish. Fly fishing can be just as productive and a single handed rod and floating line or sink tip line with small hairwing flies is all you need. Silver Stoat, Willie Gunn or trout flies such as Peter Ross and Black Pennel will all take grilse as well as sea trout.

For trout fishing, also contact the Uig Angling Association at Glenhinnisdale. Salmon fishing £15 per rod per day and £40 per week.

GLEN AFFRIC HOTEL

Cannich, Inverness-shire
Tel: (01456) 415214

Excellent choice of trout fishing: particularly **Loch Monar** and **Loch Mullardoch**, including a number of remote hill lochs. Of these **Loch Mor** and **Loch Beag** are reasonably accessible and well worth the effort. Fine trout fishing on the **River Cannich**. As well as trout, Loch Monar holds perch and pike as well as ferox which can run to double figures. Access can be restricted to hill lochs during the stalking season.

Charges around £25-£30 for a day boat for two anglers. Bank fishing from £5.

INVERGARRY HOTEL

Invergarry, Inverness-shire PH35 4HG
Tel: (01809) 511216

Situated on the lower **River Garry**, with salmon fishing available on the river and Loch Oich. Some good pike fishing also on **Lochs Oich**, **Quoich** and **Garry**. Excellent fly fishing for wild brown trout on Loch Garry, Inchlaggan (top end of Loch Garry) and the upper River

Garry, with ferox present in Lochs Garry and Quoich. Char have grown to record proportions in Loch Garry due to over-feed from smolt cages, and often run in excess of 5 lbs.

Trout fishing from £5 per day and free to guests on Loch Oich. Salmon fishing sometimes available from £18 a day when not previously let, otherwise the beats cost from £400 to £1800 per week. See also Tomdoun Hotel for Loch Garry and upper River Garry.

KNOCKIE LODGE HOTEL

Whitebridge, Stratherrick
Tel: (01456) 486276 fax: (01456) 486389

A comfortable lodge hotel offering excellent food and well-stocked bar. Excellent area for ornithology. Fishing on **Loch Knockie** which offers excellent brown trout fishing from the shoreline on its many bays or drift fishing from a boat. Trout average 10-12oz but with plenty of larger trout present.

Loch na Lann and several other hill lochs and lochans offer good trouting and some of the waters also contain pike to double figures. Deeper waters also contain char and the chance of ferox.

Flies to try include Soldier Palmer or Black Pennel on the bob (top dropper), Dunkeld, Kingfisher Butcher and Invicta.

Prices from £12 per rod per day and boat fishing £25 per day, with priority given to hotel guests.

LOCHCARRON HOTEL

Main Street, Lochcarron, Wester Ross
Tel: (01520) 722226
Fax: (01520) 722612   **SEE AD ON PAGE 49**

Anglers are well catered for – an ideal base from which to sample the excellent wild brown trout fishing of Ross-shire's hil lochs. Fishing can be arranged through the hotel, as well as stalking and rough shooting.

LOCH ERICHT HOTEL

Dalwhinne, Inverness-shire
Tel: (01528) 522257

Loch Ericht is some 15 miles long can be bleak and intimidating and boat fishing demands care and proper safety equipment, as the weather can quickly turn stormy. Bank anglers should also fish with extreme caution as the margins can be soft and unstable. Having said that, the loch offers excellent sport with trout averaging around 8-10oz and always the chance of much bigger fish close inshore.

The Ben Alder Estate allows access to a number of hills lochs which offer excellent sport with the fly rod, with restrictions imposed during the stalking season. Check with the estate factor (01540) 672000 before setting out for your enjoyable day in wonderful scenery. Fishing £5 per day per rod.

SKEABOST HOUSE HOTEL
Skeabost Bridge, Isle of Skye
Tel: (01470) 532202

Well known angling centre, with its own resident angling instructor. The hotel has access to the **River Snizort** which can be very productive following rain and running off after a coloured spate is the best time to be on the river. Salmon run around 6-7lbs and fishing is best in the autumn, where discretion should be used in returning any hen fish or ripe cock salmon. Small flies and a single handed rod, fish early and late and stalk your fish in lower water conditions. Spinning and bait fishing are allowed, but fly fishing on its day offers great sport.

Excellent loch fishing, including the famous **Lochs of Stoer** a short drive away. Also good sea angling from rocks and beaches as well as boat fishing.

Salmon fishing on the River Snizort is free to guests staying for 3 days or more, otherwise £15 per day. See Ullinish Lodge Hotel for upper river and loch fishing.

SLIGHAN HOTEL
Isle of Skye
Tel. (01478) 650 204

The Slighan Hotel is situated in the south-east of Skye and can offer fishing on the River Slighan. As with all rivers on the island, sport is dependent on rain and the river fishes best after a spate for salmon and sea trout.

THE INN AT ROY BRIDGE
Roy Bridge, Inverness-shire PH31 4AG
Tel: (01397) 712 253   **SEE AD ON PAGE 67**

(Formerly The Stronlossit Hotel). Comfortable and homely accommodation, where anglers are particularly welcome. Excellent fishing for wild brown trout and salmon in the area, with the added bonus of double-figure ferox trout and specimen pike in nearby Loch Laggan. Rods for salmon fishing can be arranged through the hotel on the local rivers Spean and Roy, which offer excellent summer sport with grilse and late-run salmon, particularly on a falling spate.

TOMDOUN LODGE
By Invergarry, Inverness-shire   **SEE AD ON PAGE 68**
Tel: (01809)511 218/ 244 fax: (01809) 511216

Excellent base for wild brown trout fishing, overlooking the Upper **River Garry**, **Inchlaggan** and **Loch Garry**. Superb wild brown trout which are free rising in the loch and upper river. Occasional salmon. Char also frequent Inchlaggan and Loch Garry, where they grown to abnormal sizes due to feeding from the smolt cages in the main loch. There are also double figure ferox and large pike present in the system and Loch Quoich further up the valley.

Trout fishing around £25 per boat per day including outboard for two anglers. Upper river and bank fishing on the loch is free to hotel guests.

ULLINISH LODGE HOTEL
Struan, Isle of Skye
Tel: (01470) 572214

Excellent lodge hotel with fishing on the upper **River Snizort** for salmon and several excellent lochs for wild brown trout. Prices on application.

WHITEBRIDGE HOTEL
Stratherrick, Gorthleck, Inverness IV1 2UN
Tel: (01456) 486226/ 486272 fax: (01456) 486413

Good fly fishing for wild brown trout sport on **Loch Ruthven**, fish average 12-14oz with plenty of larger specimens.

Loch a'Choire above Loch Ruthven is a deep, glacial loch containing both trout and char and ferox could also be present. Other lochans offer good sport with trout averaging 6-8oz. Boat charges £15 for two rods. Bank fishing from £5 per day.

Skye offers an excellent choice of angling, including many hill lochs, of which the Stoer Lochs are perhaps the most famous. Good sea angling too from the shoreline and boats.

North-East & Speyside

AVIELOCHAN
Location • Nethybridge/Inverdruie
Species • rainbow trout and brown trout
Permit • Mrs Margaret MacDonald, Avielochan, by
Aviemore, Inverness-shire,
Tel: 01479 810 847 (£20 per day for boat
with 2 rods).

AVON
Location • Avon/Glenlivet
Species • salmon, sea trout and brown trout
Permit • The Factor, Ballindalloch Estate Office,
Banffshire, Tel: 01807 500 205/Fax: 210
(From £8 per day on the upper river to £400
per rod per week on the lower river).
• Delnashaugh Hotel, Ballindalloch, Banffshire,
Tel: 01807 500 255/Fax: 389
(Prices as above).
• The Factor, Eastridge Estate Office, Ramsbury,
Malborough, Wiltshire, Tel: 01672 520 042
(Prices as above).
• Highland Sporting Estates, Kylnadrochit
Lodge, Tomintoul, Banffshire,
Tel: 01807 580 230/Fax: 01309 690 454
(Prices as above).
• Gordon Arms Hotel, The Square, Tomintoul,
Banffshire, Tel: 01807 580 206/Fax: 488
(Prices as above).
• Tomintoul Post Office, The Square, Tomintoul,
Banffshire, Tel: 01807 580 201
(3 permits per day for Tomintoul residents,
£8 per rod).

COWIE
Location • Stonehaven/Crathes
Species • salmon and sea trout
Permit • David's Sports Shop, 31 Market Square,
Stonehaven, Kincardineshire,
Tel: 01569 762 239 (£7 per rod per day).

CRIMONMOGATE LOCH
Location • St Coombs
Species • brown trout, rainbow trout, brook trout
Permit • Crimonmogate Trout Fishery, Crimonmogate,
by Fraserburgh, Tel: 01346 532 203
(Day ticket £20, half day £12. Evenings £10).

DEE
Location • Balmoral
• Cairntown/Aberdeen
Species • salmon and sea trout
Permit • Balmoral: J Somers, 13/15 Bon Accord
Terrace, Aberdeen Tel: 01224 210 008
(Prices on application).
• Countrywear, 15 Bridge Street, Ballater,
Aberdeenshire, Tel: 01339 755 453
(Prices on application).
• The Factor, North Lodge Estate, Kingcausie,
by Banchory, Aberdeenshire,
Tel: 01224 732 266 (Prices on application).
• G S Dawson, Red Brae, The Croft, Nether
Blainslie, Galashiels, Selkirkshire,
Tel: 01896 860 307 (Prices on application).
• Messrs Savills, 12 Clerk Street, Brechin,
Angus, Tel: 01356 622 187
(Prices on application).
• The Factor, Kincardine Estates, Kincardine
O'Neil, Aboyne, Aberdeenshire,
Tel: 01339 884 225 (Prices on application).
• The Factor, Auchnagathle House, Keig,
Alford, Aberdeenshire, Tel: 01975 562 525
(Prices on application).
• Messrs Smith Milligan, Chrtd Surveyors,
14 Golden Square, Aberdeen,
Tel: 01224 638 237 (Prices on application).
• The Factor, Glen Tannar Estate, Brooks House,
Glen Tannar, Aboyne, Aberdeenshire,
Tel: 01339 886 451 (Prices on application).
• Deeline Information service,
Tel: 0891 881 941 (Prices on application).
• Cairntown/Aberdeen: Banchory Lodge Hotel,
Banchory, Aberdeenshire,
Tel: 01330 282 2625
(£25 – £150 per rod per day).
• Bell-Ingram, 3 Rubislaw Terrace, Aberdeen,
Tel: 01224 644 272 (Prices as above).
• Ian Black, Meadowhead Farm, Newmachar,
Aberdeen, Tel: 01224 724 286 (Prices as
above).
• Ardoe House Hotel, Blairs, South Deeside
Road, Aberdeen, Tel: 01224 867 353
(Prices as above).
• Julie Nickols, Linc Holdings, Amber Hill,
Boston Lincs, Tel: 01205 290 444/Fax: 237
(Prices as above).

Dee cont'd

- Campbells', Altries, Maryculter, Aberdeen, Tel: 01224 733 258 (Prices as above).
- Carter Jonas, 20 Owen Street, Hereford, Tel: 01432 277 174 (Prices as above).
- Tilbouries Fishing, 15 Kelsey Gate, Court Down Road, Beckenham, Kent, Tel: 0181 658 1754 (Prices as above).
- Gordon Arms Hotel, Kincardine O'Neil, Aberdeenshire, Tel: 01339 884 236 (Prices as above).
- Dawn Ritchie, Marcliffe at Pitfodeles, North Deeside Road, Aberdeen, Tel: 01224 869 190 (Prices as above).
- Howie Irvine, Sporting Factors, 62 Bon Accord Street, Aberdeen, Tel: 01224 580 913 (Prices as above).
- Turner Hall, Cambus O'May, Ballater, Aberdeenshire, Tel: 01339 755 034 (Prices as above).

DEVERON

Location • Glenbuchat/Banff
Species • salmon, sea trout and brown trout
Permit • Grampian Fishing Line Service, Tel: 01891 881 941 (£5 – £50 depending upon location and dates).
- Banffshire Fishselling Company, 20 Shore Street, Macduff, Tel: 01261 832 891 (Prices as above).
- Insports, 1 Carmelite Street, Banff, Tel: 01261 818 348 (Prices as above).
- J Christie Murdoch McMath & Mitchell, 27 Duke Street, Huntly, Tel: 01466 792 291 (Prices as above).
- Ian Masson Fishing Tackle, 6 Castle Street, Turriff, Tel: 01888 562 428 (Prices as above).
- Huntly Castle Hotel, Huntly, Tel: 01466 792 696 (Prices as above).
- Forbes Arms Hotel, Rothiemay, Tel: 01466 711 248 (Prices as above).
- The Factor, Mayen Estate Office, Rothiemay, Tel: 01466 711 369 (Prices as above).
- R K Mann, Blencowe Hall, Blencowe, Penrith, Cumberland, Tel: 01768 483 628 (Prices as above).
- E MacKenzie, Marnoch Lodge Fishings, Huntly, Tel: 01466 780 872 (Prices as above).
- Mrs Joanne McRae, Estate Office, Forgue, Huntly, Tel: 01464 871 331 (Prices as above).
- Messrs Savills, 12 Clerk Street, Brechin, Angus, Tel: 01356 622 187 (Prices as above).

- Bell-Ingram Rural, 42 Queens Road, Aberdeen, Tel: 01224 324 282 (Prices as above).
- H Eggington, Laureston Lodge, Newton Abbot, Devon, Tel: 01626 630 81 (Prices as above).
- Ian Forbes Fishing Tackle, Gordon Street, Huntly, 01466 794 251 (Prices as above).
- Guy Bentinck, Messrs Perkins, 100 Union Street, Aberdeen, Tel: 01244 626 300 (Prices as above).

DON

Location • Alford/Cockbridge
- Tillyfoure/Bridge of Don
Species • salmon, sea trout and brown trout
Permit • Alford/Cockbridge: Colquhonnie Hotel, Strathdon, Aberdeenshire, Tel: 01975 651 210 (From £6 – £80 depending on dates and location).
- Kildrummy Fishings, Gateside, Milton of Kildrummy, Alford, Aberdeenshire, Tel: 01975 571 208 (Prices as above).
- Kildrummy Castle Hotel, Kildrummy, by Alford, Aberdeenshire, Tel: 01975 571 288 (Prices as above).
- Forbes Arms Hotel, Bridge of Alford, Aberdeenshire, Tel: 01975 562 108 (Prices as above).
- Tillyfoure/Bridge of Don: J Somers, 13 - 15 Bon Accord Terrace, Aberdeen Tel: 01224 210 008 (Parkhill & Fintray Beats) (From £6 – £80 depending on dates and location).
- Balgownie Sports, 23 Scotstown Road, Bridge of Don, Aberdeen, Tel: 01224 826 232 (Criche Beat) (Prices as above).
- J J Watson, 44/48 Market Place, Inverurie, Aberdeenshire, Tel: 01467 620 321 (Town Water and others).
- Rod & Mary Sloan, DIY Supplies, 129 High Street, Inverurie, Aberdeenshire, Tel: 01467 625 181 (Town Water and others) (Prices as above).
- D Wardhaugh & Son, 38 - 40 East High Street, Forfar, Angus, Tel: 01307 463 657 (Grandhome Fishings) (Prices as above).
- FJ & SL Milton, Kenmay, Aberdeenshire, Tel: 01467 642 220 (Kenmay Beats) (Prices as above).
- Richard Fyffe, Corsindae, Sauchen, by Inverurie, Aberdeenshire, Tel: 01330 833 295 (Fetternear Beat) (Prices as above).
- W & R Murray, Main Street, Alford,

Aberdeenshire, Tel: 01975 562 366
(Alford Fishings) (Prices as above).
- The Warden, Haughton House, Alford,
Aberdeenshire, tel; 01975 562 453 (Alford
Fishings) (Prices as above).
- Colin Hart, Grant Arms Hotel, Monymusk,
Aberdeenshire, Tel: 01467 651 226
(Prices as above).
- Castle Forbes Water, The Estate Office,
Whitehouse, by Alford, Aberdeenshire,
Tel: 01975 562 524 (Prices as above).
- Messrs Strutt & Parker, 68 Station Road,
Banochry, Aberdeenshire, Tel: 01330 824 888
(Towie Beat) (Prices as above).
- J Uren, Priory Farmhouse, Appledore Road,
Teddington, Middx, Tel: 01833 331 071
(Tilliefoure Fishings) (Prices as above).
- Don Line Information Service,
Tel: 01891 881 941 (Prices as above).

DULNAIN
Location • Elgin
Species • salmon, sea trout and brown trout
Permit • Grant Mortimer, 3 High Street, Grantown-on-
Spey, Moray, Tel: 01479 872 684/Fax: 211
(Call for details).

FINDHORN
Location • Elgin/Inverness
- Findhorn Bay
- Estate Waters
- Drynachan Beats
- Tomatin Beats
Species • salmon, sea trout and brown trout
Permit • Elgin/Inverness: Iain Grant, The Tackle Shop,
97D High Street, Forres, Morayshire,
Tel: 01309 672 936
(£10 – £50 per rod per day).
Permit • Findhorn Bay: Moray Water Sports, The Old
Fishery, Findhorn, Morayshire,
Tel: 01309 690 239 (£3.50 per week).
Permit • Estate Waters: Lethen Estate, Lethen, Nairn,
Tel: 01667 452 247/Fax: 456 449
(£400 – £1,500 depending upon dates).
- Glenferness Fishings, Earl of Leven,
Glenferness House, Nairn,
Tel: 01309 651 202 (Prices as above).
- Drynachan Beats: Cawdor Estates, Estate
Office, Cawdor, Nairn,
Tel: 01667 404 666/Fax: 787
(£400 – £1,500 depending upon dates).
- Tomatin Beats: Glenan Lodge, Tomatin,
Inverness-shire, Tel: 01808 511 217
(£20 – £35 per rod per day. Guests have
priority).

GAIRN
Location • Trustach/Balmoral
Species • salmon
Permit • see River Dee entry, Trustach – Balmoral
(Prices on application).

GLEN OF ROTHES TROUT FISHERY
Location • Rothes, Aberlour, Morayshire AB38 7AG
Species • rainbow trout, brown trout, brook trout, blue
rainbows and steelheads
Permit • Mike Payne, Tel: 01340 831994
2002 prices on application

GLEN TANAR LOCH
Location • Glen Tanar Estate
Species • rainbow trout
Permit • Glen Tanar Estate, Tel: 01339 886451
The Warden, Millbuies Country Park,
Longmorn, Elgin, Moray, Tel: 01343 860 234
(Boat fishing, £15 per day per rod).

GLENLATTERACH RESERVOIR
Location • Elgin/Craigelachie
Species • Brown trout, average 8-12 oz.
Boat and bank fishing.
Permit • Moray District Council, Department of
Recreation, High Street, Elgin,
Tel: 01343 545 121
- The Warden, Millbuies Loch, Longmorn,
Tel: 01343 860 234
- Grampian Regional Council, Water Services
Department, Grampian Road, Elgin,
Morayshire. Charges under review for 2002.

ISLA
Location • Glen Isla
Species • salmon, sea trout, brown trout and grayling
Permit • Jas Crockart and Son, 28 Allan Street,
Blairgowrie, Tel: 01250 872 056
(£20 per rod per day for salmon).
- Mr Snip, Hairdressers, Couper Angus,
Tel: 01828 627 148 (Prices as above).
- The Atholl Arms Public House,
Tel: 01828 627 205 (trout fishing permits £5
per rod per day).
- Alvie Estate Office, Kincraig, Kingussie,
Inverness-shire, Tel: 01540 651 255/249
(Boat with 2 rods £35, bank £10, per day).

LOCH ALVIE
Location • Kincraig
Species • brown trout and pike
Permit • Grant Mortimers, 3 High Street, Grantown,
Moray, Tel: 01479 872 684/Fax: 211
(£20 per day for boat with 2 rods).

DIRECTORY

LOCH DALLAS
Location • Nethybridge/Inverdruie
Species • rainbow trout and brown trout
Permit • Loch Ericht Hotel, Dalwhinne, Inverness-shire, Tel: 01528 522 257 (£5 per rod per day, also, check with the estate before fishing the hill lochs).

LOCH EINICH
Location • Aviemore/Coylumbridge
Species • brown trout and char
Permit • Mr Williams, Tollhouse Shop, Dalwhinne, Inverness-shire, Tel: 01528 522 274 (£5 per rod per day, also, check with the estate before fishing the hill lochs).

LOCH ERICHT
Location • Dalwhinne
Species • wild brown trout and ferox
Permit • Ian Crichton, Ben Alder Estate, Dalwhinne, Inverness-shire, Tel: 01540 672 000 (£5 per rod per day, also, check with the estate before fishing the hill lochs).
• Grant Mortimers, 3 High Street, Grantown-on-Spey, Moray, Tel: 01479 872 684/Fax: 211 (£20 per day for boat with 2 rods).
• Alvie Estate Office, Kincraig, Kingussie, Inverness-shire, Tel: 01540 651 255/249/Fax: 380 (Boat with 2 rods £40, bank £10, per day).

LOCH GARTEN
Location • Nethybridge/Inverdruie
Species • rainbow trout and brown trout
Permit • Laggan Stores, Laggan Bridge, by Newtonmore, Inverness-shire, Tel: 01528 544 257 (Bank fishing £6 per rod per day).

LOCH INSCH FISHERY
Location • Colpy
Species • rainbow trout
Permit • Grant Mortimers, 3 High Street, Grantown, Moray, Tel: 01479 872 684/Fax: 211 (£20 per day for boat with 2 rods).

LOCH INSH
Location • Kincraig
Species • salmon, sea trout, brown trout, char and pike
Permit • D Kinloch, Keeper's Cottage, Loch na Bo, Lhanbryde, Elgin, Moray, Tel: 01343 842 214 (Bank fishing £8.50 per session. 2 rod boat, £12 per session).

LOCH LAGGAN
Location • Kingussie/Fort William
Species • brown trout, ferox and pike
Bank fishing only from north shore. Boats are available for hire.
Permit • Mr Vallely, The Inn at Roy Bridge, Roy Bridge, Inverness-shire PH31 4AG, Tel. 01397 712 253
• Badenloch AA, Kingussie
• Loch Laggan Estates, Estate Office, Dalwhinnie
• Iain Grant, The Tackle Shop, 97D High Street, Forres, Morayshire, Tel: 01309 672 936 (Boat fishing only. Single angler £15 per day. 2 anglers sharing a boat – price on application).

LOCH MOR
Location • Nethybridge/Inverdruie
Species • rainbow trout and brown trout
Permit • Drumtochty Arms Hotel, The Square, Auchenblae, Kincardineshire, Tel: 01561 320 210 (£10 per rod per day, bag limit of 4 fish).

LOCH NA BO
Location • Elgin/Fochabers
Species • brown trout
Permit • Keeper's Cottage, Lhanbryde, Tel: 01343 842 214

LOCH OF BLAIRS
Location • Forres/Grantown
Species • rainbow trout
Permit • G Caroll, Tackle Shop, 15 Church Street, Brechin, Angus, Tel: 01356 625 700 (£10 per rod per day, bag limit of 4 fish).

LOCH SAUGH
Location • Fettercarin/Strachan
Species • brown trout
Permit • Grant Mortimers, 3 High Street, Grantown, Moray, Tel: 01479 872 684/Fax: 211 (£20 per day for boat with 2 rods).
• Martin Holroyd, Ballater Angling Association, 59 Golf Road, Ballater, Aberdeenshire, Tel: 01339 755 454 (£7.50 per rod per day).
• Countrywear, 15 & 35 High Street, Ballater, Aberdeenshire, Tel: 01339 755 453 (Prices as above).

LOCH VAA

Location • Nethybridge/Inverdruie
Species • rainbow trout and brown trout
Permit • Iain Grant, The Tackle Shop, 97D High Street, Forres, Morayshire, Tel: 01309 672 936 (Boat with 2 rods, £10 for 1 session, £16 for 2 sessions, £22 for three sessions).

LOCH VROTICHAN

Location • Rattray/Braemar
Species • brown trout
Permit • Angus Stuart, Fishing Tackle, 60 High Street, Grantown-on-Spey, Tel: 01479 872 612 (Boat with 2 rods, £10 for 1 session, £16 for 2 sessions, £22 for three sessions).
• Caretaker's Cottage, Lochindorb, Glenferness, Tel. 01309 651 270 (Prices as above).
• Invercauld Estate Office, Braemar, Tel: 01339 741 224 (Prices as above).

LOCHINDORB

Location • Lochindorb Lodge
Species • brown trout
Permit • Iain Grant, The Tackle Shop, 97D High Street, Forres, Morayshire, Tel: 01309 672 936 (£6 per rod per day).
• Pitfour Fishery, Pitfour Estate, Mintlaw, Aberdeenshire, Tel: 01771 624 448 (£6 per session – £18 per day, depending upon bag limits and times).
• Grant Mortimers, 3 High Street, Grantown, Moray, Tel: 01479 872 684/Fax: 211(£30 – £250 depending upon location and dates).

MILLBUIES LOCH

Location • Elgin/Craigellachie
Species • rainbow trout and brown trout. Two lochs in woodland, 4 miles south of Elgin on A941. Boat fishing only.
Permit • The Warden, Millbuies Lochs, Elgin, Morayshire, tel. 0134 386 234.
• Department of Recreation, Moray District Council, 30/32 High Street, Elgin, Tel. 01343 454121. Prices on application

MUCKLE BURN

Location • Forres/Inverness
Species • salmon and sea trout
Permit • Aberlour Hotel, Tel: 01340 871 287 (Prices on application).

PITFOUR LOCH

Location • New Pitsligo/Mintlaw
Species • rainbow trout and brown trout
Permit • Craigard Hotel, Tel: 01479 831 206 (Prices on application).

ROTHIEMURCHUS ESTATE

Location • Aviemore/Coylumbridge
Species • brown trout
Permit • Rothiemurchus Fish Farm, Inverdruie, Tel: 01479 810703 Orton Management Company Ltd (Prices on application)

ROTHIEMURCHUS TROUT FISHERY

Location • Aviemore, Inverness-shire
Species • rainbow trout
Permit • Orton Management Company Ltd., Estate Office, Orton, Fochabers, Tel: 01343 880 240 (Prices on application).

SPEY

Location • Elgin
Species • salmon, grilse, sea trout and brown trout
Permit • W Roy, Wollburn, Speyview, Aberlour, Tel: 01340 871 217 (£30 – £250 depending upon location and dates).
• Messrs Bidwells, Etive House, Beechwood Park, Inverness, Tel: 01463 715 585/ Fax: 01340 831 687 (Prices as above).
• Finlyson Hughes, 29 Barossa Place, Perth, Tel: 01738 451 111 (Prices as above).
• Messrs Savills, 12 Clerk Street, Brechin, Angus, Tel: 01356 622 187 (Prices as above).
• The Factor, Strathspey Estates Office, Heathfield, Grantown-on-Spey, Moray, Tel: 01479 872 529 (Prices as above).
• Tulchan Sporting Estates Ltd, Estate Office, Tulchan, Grantown-on-Spey, Moray, Tel: 01807 510 200/Fax: 234 (Prices as above).
• Messrs Allen's, Deshar Road, Boat of Garten, Inverness-shire, Tel: 01479 831 372 (Prices as above).
• The Factor, Rothimurchus Estate, Inverdruie, by Aviemore, Inverness-shire, Tel: 01479 810 647 (Prices as above).
• W Grant, Mountain Lodges, Beechgrove, Mains of Garten Farm, Boat of Garten, Inverness-shire, Tel: 01479 831 551 (Prices as above).
• Colin Sutton, Speyside Sports, 64 Grampian Road, Aviemore, Inverness-shire, Tel: 01479 810 656 (Prices as above).

Spey cont'd

- Robertson's Sports, 1 - 3 Kirk Street, Peterhead, Tel: 01779 472 584 (Day tickets £15 per rod).
- Mrs Audrey Forbes, 3 Lea Cottages, Newburgh, Ellon, Aberdeenshire, Tel: 01358 789 297 (Day tickets £20 when available, private beats £440 – £605 per week, accommodation may be available).
- Buchan Hotel, Ellon, Aberdeenshire, Tel: 01358 720 208 (£15 per day in September, otherwise £7.50 per day).
- S French & Sons, Grocers, Methlick, Aberdeenshire, Tel: 01651 806 213 (£6 – £15 per day depending upon dates).
- J Mackie & Co., Lewes, Fyvie, Aberdeenshire, Tel: 01651 891 209 (£10 per rod per day).

UGIE
Location • Longside
Species • salmon, grilse and sea trout
Permit • Rothiemurchus Estate Office, by Aviemore, Inverness-shire, Tel: 01479 810 858/ Fax: 811 778 (Prices on application).

WAULKMILL
Location • New Deer
Species • rainbow trout
Permit • George Davidson, Waulkmill, New Deer, Tel: 01771 644 357. Limit 4 trout (day ticket) and 2 trout (half day ticket). Prices on application.

YTHAN
Location • Newburgh/Peterhead
Species • salmon and sea trout
Permit • Rathen Reel Affair, Fraserburgh Tel: 01346 513 329
- Estuary fishings are controlled by Ythan Fisheries, 3 Lea Cottages, Newburgh, AB41 0BN, Tel: 01358 789297
- Haddo House water: Estate Office, Mains of Haddo, Tel: 01651 851664
- Buchanan House Hotel, Ellon, Tel: 01358 720208

Setting out for the hill lochs: don't forget the sun block – it can be warm and sunny in the Scottish Highlands. And don't forget the anti-midge cream either!

ABERLOUR HOTEL
Banffshire
Tel: (01340) 871287

A Speyside hotel ideally located for the Spey valley: fishing on the **River Spey** and **River Dulnain**, a major tributary, with excellent salmon and sea trout angling on a budget. The Spey produces some 8000 fish annually, although spring salmon fishing has declined. Excellent fly fishing for summer sea trout and grilse, with salmon runs peaking in autumn. Association water charges £ 135 per week and 3 day ticket £ 80. Rods are also available on private beats through the hoTel: prices vary according to season.

ARDOE HOUSE HOTEL
Blairs, South Deeside Road, Aberdeen
Tel: (01224) 867353

Excellent up market base for the **Lower Dee**. Fishing lets sometimes available on **Ardoe** timeshare fishings. Spring salmon fishing has in recent years been delayed on a voluntary basis to help improve runs of spring fish.

Salmon beats may be accessible by arrangement, but are generally let on a year to year basis. Good trout fishing on lochs and rivers, including Dee tributaries and excellent golf courses nearby.

BANCHORY LODGE HOTEL
Banchory, Aberdeenshire
Tel: (013302) 822625

Excellent base for fishing middle and upper reaches of **River Dee**. Good trout fishing on hill lochs. Salmon rods from £25 – £150 per day depending on beats and time of year.

BUCHANAN HOTEL
Ellon, Aberdeenshire
Tel: (01358) 720208

The hotel has access to the Ellon fishings on the **River Ythan**, which still produces excellent numbers of sea trout from both the river and particularly from the Newburgh Fishings in the estuary. The Ythan itself is a spate river and can be heavily fished when the salmon and sea trout are running.

A trout rod of 9-11ft is adequate and most anglers fish typical sea trout patterns such as Teal, Blue & Silver, Peter Ross, Black Pennel and streamers. Spinning is the most popular method in saltwater. See also The Udny Arms Hotel and Gight House Hotel. Charges for Ellon fishings £7.50 per day and £15 in September.

COLQUHONNIE HOTEL
Strathdon, Aberdeenshire AB36 8UN
Tel: (019756) 51210

200 year old refurbished country house offering 8 miles of excellent brown trout fishing on the **River Don**, with occasional salmon and sea trout. Excellent dry fly water.

Good food and home cooking and cosy bar with log fires.

Trout fishing from £10 per rod per day. Salmon fishing by arrangement, from around £20 per day upwards, depending on beats and time of year.

CRAIGARD HOTEL
Speyside
Tel: (01479) 831206

Fishing on **River Spey** and **River Dulnain** for sea trout and salmon. Also excellent fly fishing for wild brown trout. Rods available on private beats by arrangement. Charges vary with beats and season.

The association water can get busy during the summer months and it pays to fish early and late: not only is the river quieter then, but both times are prime taking times for grilse and sea trout. Association water at Grantown on Spey offers visitor tickets from £ 80 for 3 days to £ 150 for a week's excellent sport with salmon and splendid sea trout.

DALLAS HOTEL
Aerial View, Dallas, Moray
Tel: (01343) 890323

Fishing for salmon, sea trout and brown trout on the **River Lossie**. Good saltwater sport spinning for sea trout in the estuary and up to 400 taken each season. Around 100 salmon are taken on the Lossie.

Day tickets available from the Elgin Angling Association cost £5 per day and £20 per week. The Dallas AC have fishing on the upper river also at £5 per rod per day, available from the hotel.

DELNASHAUGH INN
Ballindalloch, Banffshire AB3 9AS
Tel: (01807)500255 Fax: (01807) 500389

The **River Avon** is a major tributary of the River Spey and receives good runs of salmon and sea trout and is ideally suited to single-handed rods or light 12ft salmon rod. floating or sink tip lines and small hairwing flies for salmon.

Sea trout flies will also take grilse: recommended flies include Silver Stoat, Ally's shrimp, Blue Charm, Munro, Hairy Mary and Willie Gunn for salmon. And Peter Ross, Black Pennel, Alexandra, Silver Butcher for sea trout. The Avon and its own tributaries also offer good brown trout fishing. Charges from £8 per day up to £400 per week for prime time fishing on the lower river.

FORBES ARMS HOTEL
Bridge of Alford, Aberdeenshire
Tel: (019755) 62108 Fax: (019755) 62490

Small family run hotel on the banks of the **River Don** with over 3 miles of salmon, sea and brown trout fishing.

Special all-inclusive rates for fishing guests. See also Loch Rannoch Hotel.

FORBES ARMS HOTEL
Rothiemay AB5 5LT. Tel: (01466) 711248

Salmon and sea trout fishing available through the hotel on the beautiful and productive **River Deveron**. This deceptively long river is fed by several tributaries and provides spectacular rocky pools and falls in its upper reaches and gentler deeper reaches below Huntly.

Sea trout fishing is still good on the river and around 1500 fish are taken each season, and around 1000 salmon. Some of the sea trout can run well into double figures. Best sport is obtained following heavy rain and a dropping river can produce spectacular results. This is a popular river and can be booked well in advance. Fishing charges range from around £5 to £50 per day. Grampian Fishing Line (01891) 881941 can advise on cancellations and help with late bookings. See also Huntly Castle Hotel.

GARVE HOTEL
Garve, Ross-shire. Tel: (01997) 414205

Good base for wild brown trout fishing with large number of hill lochs and easy access. Taditional wet flies will all take trout, but try something bushy on the top dropper such as Soldier Palmer, or Black Pennel. Fishing from £5 per day.

GIGHT HOUSE HOTEL
Methlick. Tel: (01651) 806389

Good base for fishing on the upper **River Ythan**, which still produces excellent numbers of sea trout from both the river and particularly from the Newburgh Fishings in the estuary. The Ythan itself is a spate river and can be heavily fished when the salmon and sea trout are running. A trout rod of 9-11ft is adequate and most anglers fish typical sea trout patterns such as Teal, Blue & Silver, Peter Ross, Black Pennel and streamers. Spinning is the most popular method in saltwater. Prices for upper reaches on application to the hotel.

GORDON ARMS HOTEL
The Square, Tomintoul, Banffshire, AB37 9ET. Tel: (01807) 580206 Fax: (01807) 580488

The **River Avon** is a major tributary of the **River Spey** and receives good runs of salmon and sea trout and is ideally suited to single-handed rods or light 12ft salmon rod. floating or sink tip lines and small hairwing flies for salmon. Sea trout flies will also take grilse: recommended flies include Silver Stoat, Ally's shrimp, Blue Charm, Munro, Hairy Mary and Willie Gunn for salmon. And Peter Ross, Black Pennel, Alexandra, Silver Butcher for sea trout.

The Avon and its own tributaries also offer good brown trout fishing. Charges from £8 per day up to £400 per week for prime time fishing on the lower river. See also Delnashaugh Hotel for River Avon.

GORDON ARMS HOTEL
Kincardine O'Neil, Aberdeenshire. Tel: (013398) 84236

Centrally located on Royal Deeside with access to the **River Dee** by arrangement on a number of beats. Spring salmon has been in decline but conservation efforts, spawning habitat improvement and voluntary catch and release of salmon has helped turn the tide. Late spring and summer can produce splendid runs of salmon and good sport with sea trout. Some large salmon run Dee in September, fresh in from the sea, right to the end of the season. Good brown trout fishing in tributaries and lochs, some of which also contain pike.

Trout fishing from £5 per day. Salmon fishing varies depending on beat and time of year. See also Banchory Lodge Hotel (middle and upper reaches) and Ardoe House Hotel (lower river)

GRANT ARMS HOTEL
Monymusk, Aberdeenshire. Tel: (01467) 651226 Fax: (01467) 651494

18th century traditional coaching inn, lying at the foot of **Bennachie**. Exclusive fishing on 15 miles of the River Don, excellent fly fishing for wild brown trout and salmon sport on 11 beats and 29 named pools.

Ghillie by arrangement. £6.00 - £10.00 per day for brown trout £15- £18 for salmon rods.

HUNTLY CASTLE HOTEL
Huntly. Tel: (01466) 792696

Salmon and sea trout fishing is available through the hotel on the beautiful and productive **River Deveron**. This deceptively long river is fed by several tributaries and provides spectacular rocky pools and falls in its upper reaches and gentler deeper reaches below Huntly.

Around 1500 sea trout, some of them well into double figures, are taken each season and about 1000 salmon. Best sport occurs following heavy rain and a dropping river can produce spectacular results. This is a popular river and should be booked well in advance. Fishing charges range from around £5 to £50 per day. Grampian Fishing Line (01891) 881941 can also help with late bookings. See also Forbes Arms Hotel.

KILDRUMMY CASTLE HOTEL
Kildrummy, By Alford Aberdeenshire. Tel: (019755) 71288

Ideal base for **River Don**, set amidst beautiful scenery. Castle Forbes and Kildrummy beats are amongst the most productive beats on the river. Spring salmon fishing is fair, but most of the salmon are taken late summer and autumn. Excellent brown trout sport. Rods from around £ 10 per day.

MINMORE HOUSE HOTEL
Glenlivet , AB37 9DB. Tel: (01807) 590378

Quality food and accommodation in this country house hotel. Good double bank fishing for salmon and sea trout on **River Avon**, major tributary of the Spey, restricted to two rods on 1.5 miles of water. Weekly lets. Prices for Avon on application to hotel. Free fishing on **River Livet**.

PARK HOUSE
Deeside. Tel: (01334) 839218, www.park-leisure.co.uk

For anglers who want their own house party, Park House offers fully staffed inclusive packages, with private fishing on excellent fly water on the Park Beat of the **River Dee**. Ghillies available: good wading. Freezing and drying room facilities. Prices on application from Park House.

RAEMORE HOUSE HOTEL
Royal Deeside. Tel: (01330) 824884 Fax: (01330) 822171, Email: raemoirhse@aol.com

Georgian mansion set in 3500 acres of parkland and forests. Excellent and elegant dining. Fishing can be arranged on the **River Dee** for salmon and sea trout and local lochs for wild brown trout. Excellent golf courses a short drive away.

Special Spring breaks from £100 DBB per night for two people. Fishing charges on application.

RAMSAY ARMS HOTEL
Laurencekirk. Tel: (01561) 340334

Loch Saugh is one of the notable lochs in the area, with brown trout averaging 1.25lbs, stocked and managed by the Brechin AC. Excellent salmon and sea trout fishing by arrangement on North and South **Esk**, with the latter producing some exceptional sea trout sport in the summer of 2000.

Improving spring runs on the North Esk: Balmakewan beat produced 4 springers on opening day of the 2001 season, with Morphie Dyke, no longer a physical or temperature barrier for early-run salmon.

The South Esk is particularly noted for its splendid sea trout fishing. Several beats are available on both rivers. West Water is available through Brechin AC costs £10-£17 per day depending on season. Lets on North and South Esk from £35 per day, but expect to pay much more for prime time fishing. Both rivers are heavily pre-booked and many beats are let on a syndicate basis by the week, sometimes with on-river lodge accommodation, as at Balmakewan on the North Esk.

SEAFIELD LODGE HOTEL
Woodside Avenue, Grantown on Spey PH26 3JN. Tel: (01479) 872152

Fine food and hospitality combined with 7 miles of association water and access to private **Spey** beats such as Castle grant and Tulchan. The late Hugh Falkus and Arthur Oglesby ran hugely successful Spey Casting courses from here for many years. Special angling packages are available from the hotel (see Gems of Scotland)

UDNY ARMS HOTEL
By Newburgh, Aberdeenshire. Tel: (01358) 789444

Good base for the lower **River Ythan** and estuary. Sands of Forvie to the north of the Ythan is an important nature reserve and excellent centre for birders. The Ythan offers fly fishing and spinning for sea trout and around 80 salmon per season. The River Ythan, which still produces excellent numbers of sea trout (around 1000-2500 each year) from both the river and particularly from the Newburgh Fishings in the estuary. The Ythan itself is a spate river and can be heavily fished when the salmon and sea trout are running. A trout rod of 9-11ft is adequate and most anglers fish typical sea trout patterns such as Teal, Blue & Silver, Peter Ross, Black Pennel and streamers. Spinning is the most popular method in saltwater. Contact the hotel for rod charges and availability.

Orkney & Shetland

ORKNEY

LOCH BOARDHOUSE
Location • Twatt/Birsay, Mainland
Species • brown trout. Shallow weedy loch which gives excellent sport from boat and bank. Boats available from Barony Hotel.
Permit • Orkney Trout Fishing Association season ticket £15.
• Barony Hotel, Birsay, Orkney KW17 2LS, Tel: 01856 721327 Fax: 01856 721302
• WS Sinclair, Tackle Shop, 27 John Street, Stromness, Tel: 01856 850 469.

LOCH HARRAY
Location • Merkister, Mainland
Species • brown trout and occasional sea trout. Probably the most popular loch on Orkney. Six miles long and up to 1.5 miles wide.
Permit • Orkney Trout Fishing Association season ticket £15.
• Merkister Hotel, Harray, Orkney, Tel: 01856 773 66.
• W S Sinclair, Tackle Shop, 27 John Street, Stromness, Tel: 01856 850 469.

LOCH OF HUNDLAND
Location • Twatt/Hillside, Mainland
Species • brown trout. Lying between Swannay to the east and Boardhouse to the west.
Permit • Orkney Trout Fishing Association season ticket £15.
• W S Sinclair, Tackle Shop, 27 John Street, Stromness, Tel: 01856 850 469
• Boats available from Merkister Hotel, Tel: 01856 773 66, or Muckle Quoy Farm

LOCH OF HUXTER
Location • Symbister, Isle of Whalsay
Species • brown trout. Huxter is just one of several excellent lochs on the Isle of Whalsay, managed by the Whalsay Angling Association. A regular ferry service links Whalsey with Mainland Orkney.
Permit • Brian Polson, Whalsay Angling Association, Sheardaal, Huxter, Whalsay, Tel: 01806 566 472 (Visitor ticket £10).

ISBISTER LOCH
Location • Knowe of Holland, Isle of Whalsay
Species • brown trout
Permit • Brian Polson, Whalsay Angling Association, Sheardaal, Huxter, Whalsay, Tel: 01806 566 472 (Visitor ticket £10).

LOCH OF KIRBISTER
Location • Stromness/Kirkwall, Mainland (A964)
Species • brown trout & sea trout. Bank fishing only with good wading. Trout average 8-12 ounces and occasional bigger fish. Sea trout do enter this loch.
Permit • Orkney Trout Fishing Association season ticket £15.
• W S Sinclair, Tackle Shop, 27 John Street, Stromness, Tel: 01856 850 469.

MEIKLE WATER
Location • Isle of Stronsay, Orkney
Species • brown trout
Permit • Orkney Trout Fishing Association season ticket £15.
• Stronsay Hotel, Stronsay, Orkney Islands, Tel: 018576 616 213.

STENNESS
Location • Orkney, Stromness
Species • brown trout, sea trout, mullet, saithe (coalfish), herring, flounders and codling
Permit • Orkney Trout Fishing Association season ticket £15.
• Standing Stones Hotel, Stenness, Orkney, Tel: 01856 850 449.
• W S Sinclair, Tackle Shop, 27 John Street, Stromness, Tel: 01856 850 469.

LOCH SWANNAY
Location • Twatt/Chrismo, Orkney
Species • brown trout
Permit • Orkney Trout Fishing Association season ticket £15.
• W S Sinclair, Tackle Shop, 27 John Street, Stromness, Tel: 01856 850 469

SHETLAND

LOCH AITHSNESS
Location • Vassa, Shetland
Species • brown trout and sea trout
Permit • Shetland Tourist Information Centre, Market Cross, Lerwick, Tel: 01595 693 434 (Season ticket £20, day ticket £5, use of boats £20).

LOCH ASTA
Location • Tingwall Valley, Shetland
Species • brown trout and sea trout
Permit • Shetland Tourist Information Centre, Market Cross, Lerwick, Tel: 01595 693 434 (Season ticket £20, day ticket £5, use of boats £20).

LOCH BENSTON
Location • Vassa, Shetland
Species • brown trout and sea trout
Permit • Shetland Tourist Information Centre, Market Cross, Lerwick, Tel: 01595 693 434 (Season ticket £20, day ticket £5, use of boats £20).

LOCH GIRLSTA
Location • Lerwick/Hillside, Shetland
Species • brown trout, sea trout and char
Permit • Shetland Tourist Information Centre, Market Cross, Lerwick, Tel: 01595 693 434 (Season ticket £20, day ticket £5, use of boats £20).

LOCH SPIGGIE
Location • Littleness, Shetland
Species • brown trout and sea trout. The Shetland Anglers Association controls fishing on numerous excellent brown trout waters, some of them also containing sea trout.
Permit • Shetland Tourist Information Centre, Market Cross, Lerwick, Tel: 01595 693 434 (Check with Asta Farm if you want to launch a boat).

SHETLAND LOCHS – GENERAL
Location • Yell Island, Shetland
Brown trout & sea trout.
Permit • The Shetland Anglers Association controls fishing on numerous excellent brown trout waters, some of them also containing sea trout.Shetland Anglers Association, David Nisbet, Tel: 01957 702 037 (Season ticket £20, day ticket £5, use of boats £20).

Mainland Orkney's two main towns, Kirkwall and Stromness have a number of good hotels. Details of these and many others can be found on the official Orkney Tourist Association website at **visitorkney.com**

AYRE HOTEL
Ayre Road, Kirkwall, Orkney KW15 1QX
Tel: 01856 873001
F: 01856 876289
e-mail: ayre.hotel@orkney.com
www.ayrehotel.co.uk

Family owned hotel on harbour front, some rooms with sea views. Close to historic town centre and all amenities.

BALFOUR CASTLE
Isle of Shapinsay, Orkney
Tel: 01856 711282
Fax: 01856 711283
e-mail: balfourcastle@btinternet.com.
www.balfourcastle.co.uk

Rooms, some with 4-posters £70, DB&B £100. "This is listed as a 'guest house' but check out their website! Wonderful hosts and wonderful accommodation and food" (The Editor) Listed Victorian baronial mansion, designed by David Bryce and built in 1848. 70 acres of wooded grounds, including original walled garden. Still a family home, now open to guests. Informal hospitality, traditional elegant surroundings. Highly recommended. Sea trout fishing from the shoreline and sea angling, bird watching trips can be arranged. Specimen common skate, porbeagle shark and elusive halibut swim in these waters. Excellent ling, pollack and cod fishing.

BARONY HOTEL
Birsay, Orkney KW17 2LS
Tel: 01856 721327
Fax: 01856 721302

Orkney's oldest fishing hotel with panoramic views of Boardhouse Loch and Brough of Birsay. Central to the main bird life sanctuaries and archaeological sites. Fine cuisine, local surf & turf. Vegetarian. Closed October to April.

CREEL RESTAURANT & ROOMS
Front Road, St Margaret's Hope, South Ronaldsay, Orkney KW17 2SL
Tel: 01856 831311
e-mail: alan@thecreel.freeserve.co.uk .
www.thecreel.co.uk

Owned since 1985 by chef Alan and his wife Joyce. Food is prepared with originality, flair and imagination. Modern cooking with a hint of Orcadian influence. Bedrooms have sea view – ideal to enjoy your food and stay awhile.

MERKISTER HOTEL
Harray, Orkney KW17 2LF
Tel: 01856 771366/289,
Fax: 01856 771515
e-mail: merkister-hotel@ecosse.net

Excellent fishing hotel, located right on the banks of Loch Harray, with boats available from the hotels own boathouse. Egon Ronay featured restaurant. 15 minutes drive from both Kirkwall and Stromness.

SMITHFIELD HOTEL
Dounbie, Orkney KW17 2HT
Tel: 01856 771215, fax: 01856 771494

A small family run hotel specialising in the personal touch. Friendly comfortable atmosphere, only six bedrooms. Good food. Closed November to April.

STANDING STONES HOTEL
Stenness, Orkney KW16 3JX
Tel: 01856 850449
Fax: 01856 851262
e-mail: standingstones@sol.co.uk

Overlooking the Loch of Stenness, this comfortable hotel sits at the gateway to the heart of neolithic Orkney. A warm welcome to anglers, good food and a unique location close to Orkney's World Heritage sites.

THE MURRAY ARMS HOTEL
Back Road,
St Margaret's Hope, Orkney KW17 2SP
Tel: 01856 831205
e-mail: murrayarms@freeuk.com
www.murrayarmshotel.com

Typically traditional small stonebuilt hotel with 5 en-suite rooms and licensed restaurant. Close to all the local village amenities and the car ferry service to mainland Scotland (Wick).

WOODWICK HOUSE
Woodwick Bay, Evie, Orkney KW17 2PQ
tel: 01856 751330 fax: 01856 751383
e-mail: woodwickhouse@appleonline.net

Warm welcoming country house. Idyllic surroundings. 12 acres of grounds, burn, secluded bay and bluebell woodland. Candlelit meals – 'Taste of Scotland'. Open fires. Cultural events. Open all year.

For information on accommodation in Shetland, check out the official website at **www.visitshetland.com** or contact Shetland Isles Tourism Market Cross, Lerwick, Shetland ZE1 OLU. Central reservation number for bookings and enquiries: Tel 01595 69 34 34, Fax: 01595 69 58 07

BUSTA HOUSE HOTEL
Busta, Brae ZE2 9QN
Tel: 01806522506
Fax: 01806522588

Busta is situated 23 miles North of Lerwick and is reputed to be the oldest continuously inhabited house in Shetland with parts dating from the 16th and 18th Century. A charming mansion overlooking its own harbour and Busta Voe, Busta House offers high standards of comfort and cuisine.

SHETLAND HOTEL
Homsgarth Road, Lerwick ZE1 OPW
Tel: 01595 695 515
Fax: 01595 695 828

The Shetland Hotel is part of Shetland's premier hotel group. The hotel is situated on a prime site in Lerwick, Shetland's main town. Special hotel packages are available with either flights from UK airports or overnight ferry from Aberdeen included, and packages can include car hire arrangements.

SUMBURGH HOTEL,
Sumburgh Crescent, Virkie, Sumburgh
Tel: 01950460201

Great base for the south end of Shetland. Excellent sea angling.

THE WESTINGS HOTEL
Whiteness
Tel: 01595840242

The Westings, situated very close to the summit of Wormadale Hill, is surrounded by the natural moors of the Whiteness Valley. The views overlooking the whole of the south west of Shetland are stunning. Fingers of land reach out into the Atlantic. Islands break the seas. Lighthouses signal in the distance.

North of Scotland

A'GHARBH-BHAID BEAG, LOCH

Location • Rhiconich

Species • salmon and sea trout

Permit • The Novar Estates Office, Evanton, Ross-shire, Tel: 01349 830 208 (£10 – £35 per rod per day, depending upon dates).
• The Alness Angling Club, c/o George Ross, 127 Kirkside, Alness, Ross-shire, Tel: 01349 883 726 (Prices as above).

ALNESS

Location • Cromarty Firth

Species • salmon and sea trout, fishing on 20 miles of river from: Loch Morie to Alness. Fishes best after a spate, 1.5/2 feet above summer level.

Permit • The Novar Estates Office, Evanton, Ross-shire, Tel: 01349 830 208 (£15 – £40 per rod per day. Prices under review).
• The Alness Angling Club have 3 beats on 5 miles of river, including the stretch from Alness golf course to the sea. Contact Alness Angling Club, George Ross, 127 Kirkside, Alness, Ross-shire. Tel: 01349 883 726 (Prices as above).
• Day tickets from J Patterson, Ironmongers, High Street, Alness, Tel: 01349 830 208

BEAULY

Location • Lovat Bridge/Cannich

Species • salmon and sea trout
The river was purchased in 1990 for a record price by the River Beauly Fishings Co. who undertook extensive improvements and a timeshare scheme. The Lower River includes the Falls, Home and Downie beats, Middle River, the Dam and Ferry beats and Upper River, Eskdale and Aigas beats.

Permit • The River beauly Fishing Co., Broomy Bank, Hampton Heath, Malpas, Chesire, SY14 8LT, Tel: 01948 820 393/Fax: 01948 820 264 (Weekly lets from £500 – £3,500. 3-5 rods. Priority to those who book a complete beat and/or accommodation).
• R Morison, Ironmongers, West End, Beauly, Inverness-shire, Tel: 01463 782 213 (From £20 per rod per day on the Lovat Bridge/Wester Lovat beat. Thursdays and Saturdays reserved).

• Timeshare and lease: Knight, Frank & Rutley, Edinburgh, Tel: 0131 225 8171

BLACK LOCH

Location • Near Achiltibuie

Species • brown trout

Permit • Peter MacGregor, The Borgie Lodge Hotel, Skerray, by Sutherland, Tel: 01641 521 332 (Bank fishing only).
• Polly Estates Ltd., Inverpolly, Ullapool IV26 2YB, Tel: 01854 622452

BORGIE & SKERRAY HILL LOCHS

Location • Bettyhill/Tongue

Species • salmon in the River Borgie, brown trout in the hill lochs

Permit • The Factor, Sutherland Estates Office, Duke Street, Golspie, Sutherland, Tel: 01408 633 268/Fax: 01408 633 800 (Prices on application).
• Finlyson Hughes, 29 Barossa Place, Perth, Tel: 01738 451111/630926 (Weekly salmon lets on the River Borgie with accommodation from £2,000 – 7,000 per week, 4 rods plus guests).
• Peter MacGregor, The Borgie Lodge Hotel, Tongue, Sutherland, Tel/Fax: 01641 521 332.

BROOM

Location • Ullapool/Braemore

Species • salmon and sea trout

Permit • Most of the fishing is let through agents:
• Finlyson Hughes, 29 Barossa Place, Perth, Tel: 01738 451111/630926
• Strutt and Parker, London, Tel: 0171 629 7282

BRORA (UPPER AND LOWER)

Location • Brora, Sutherland

Species • salmon and sea trout

Permit • Sutherand Estates (Upper and Lower beats), Estate Office, Duke Street, Golspie, Sutherland KW10 6RP, Tel: 01408 633 268.
• Finlyson Hughes (Lower Beat North Bank), 29 Barossa Place, Perth, Tel: 01738 451111/630926
• Scriberscross Lodge (Upper Brora by arrangement), Strath Brora, Rogart, Tel: 01408 641246. (Also boats on several hill lochs for brown trout).

CARRON
Location • Achnasheen/Strathcarron
Species • salmon, sea trout and brown trout
Permit • The Factor, Benmore Estates office,
Balnagowan, Ross-shire, Tel: 01862 843 601
(Duchally Fishing. Early booking essential.
£100 – £600 per rod per week).
• Finlyson Hughes (Lower beat North Bank),
29 Barossa Place, Perth,
Tel: 01738 451111/630926.

CASSLEY
Location • Rosehall, Sutherland
Species • salmon and sea trout
Permit • Bell Ingram, Estate office, Bonar Bridge,
Sutherland IV24 3EA, Tel: 01863 766 683,
Fax: 01863 766 736 (Upper Cassley. Early
booking essential. £100 – £600 per rod per
week, charges under review).
• Glenrossal Estate, Rosehall, by Lairg,
Sutherland IV27 4BG, Tel: 01549 441 203/
Fax: 01549 441 323 (Glenrossal Fishings,
charges as above).
• Achness Hotel, Rosehall by Lairg, Sutherland
IV27 4BD, Tel: 01549 441 239 (Rosehall
Fishings, charges as above).

CONON
Location • Contin-Conon Bridge, Dingwall
Species • salmon and sea trout
Boats are provded on most beats with ghillie.
Spinning is allowed in certain water heights.
Permit • Fairburn Estates Office, Urray, Muir of Ord,
Ross-shire IV6 7UT, Tel: 01997 433273,
Fax: 01997 433274.
• Coul House Hotel, Contin, by Strathpeffer,
Ross-shire IV14 9EY, Tel: 01997 421487/
Fax: 01997 421945.
• Loch Achonachie AC, The Post Office, Contin,
Ross-shire IV7 8ER, Tel: 01997 421351.
• East Lodge Hotel, Strathconon, by Muir of
Ord, Ross-shire IV6 7QQ, Tel: 01997 477222,
Fax: 01997 477243,
e-mail: elh@btinternet.com

DUBH-NAN-GEODH
Location • Loch More
Species • trout
Permit • Scourie Hotel, Scourie by Lairg, Sutherland,
Tel: 01971 502 396 (£5 per rod per day).

DUNNET HEAD LOCHS
Location • Dunnet Head, Caithness
Species • brown trout
Permit • Northern Sands Hotel, Dunnet, Caithness,
Tel: 01847 851 270 (Day ticket £5, evenings
£5. No Sunday fishing).
• Harper's Fly Fishing Services, 57 High Street,
Thurso, Caithness, Tel: 01847 893 170
(Prices as above).
• Hugo Ross, 56 High Street, Wick, Caithness,
Tel: 01955 604 200 (Prices as above).

EILEANACH LOCH
Location • Altnabreac, Caithness
Species • brown trout. Also Lochan Dubh Nan Geodh
and Loch Gaineimh.
Permit • The Ulbster Arms Hotel, Bridge Street,
Halkirk, Caithness, Tel: 01847 831 206
(£10 per rod. £15 for boat).

EILEANACH LOCH
Location • Altnaharra/Tongue
Species • brown trout. Hot spots around the islands
from bank or boat.
Permit • Jack Paterson, The Halladale Inn, Melvich,
Sutherland, Tel: 01641 531 282
(£5 per rod per day).

EILEANACH LOCH
Location • Scourie, Sutherland
Species • brown trout. Fish up to 3lbs can be
taken here.
Permit • Scourie Hotel, Scourie, Sutherland IV27 4SX,
Tel: 01971 502396. Fishing from £6 per day
and angling packages from £260 including
full board and fishing. Other loch fishing
available.
• Forsinard Hotel, Strath Halladale, Sutherland,
Tel: 01641 571 221 (£9 per rod per day).

EUN LOCH
Location • Altnabreac, Caithness
Species • brown trout
Permit • The Ulbster Arms Hotel, Bridge Street,
Halkirk, Caithness, tel: 01847 831 206
(£10 per rod. £15 for boat: Charges
under review).

GAINEIMH LOCH
Location • Thurso/Bettyhill
Species • trout
Permit • Glen Affric Hotel, Cannich, Inverness-shire,
Tel: 01456 415 214 (£15 – £45 per rod per
day depending upon dates).

GAINEIMH LOCH
Location • Lairg/Altnaharra
Shieldaig, Badachro, Gairloch
Species • brown trout
Permit • Lairg/Altnaharra: Crask Inn, Lairg,
Tel: 01749 81241
Shieldaig, Badachro, Gairloch: Shieldaig
Lodge Hotel, Badachro, tel: 01445 741 250.
The loch also has fishing on other lochs
including Loch Maree.

GLASS
Location • Lovat Bridge/Cannich
Species • salmon, brown trout and grilse
Permit • Brian Lyall, Badanloch, by Kinbrace,
Sutherland, Tel: 01431 831 232 (£15 per rod
per day).
• Angus Ross, Head Keeper, Achentoul Estate,
Kinbrace, Sutherland, Tel: 01431 831 227
(£15 per rod per day).

HALLADALE
Location • Forsinard
Species • salmon and some sea trout
Permit • Ms Audrey Imlach, Bunahoun, Forsinard,
Strath Halladale, Sutherland KW13 6YU,
Tel: 01641 571 271 (£200 – £1000 for a
3 rod beat, prices under review).

HELMSDALE
Location • Helmsdale, Sutherland
Species • Fly only for salmon & sea trout on
association water. Excellent wild brown trout
in the hill lochs.
Permit • The Bridge Hotel & Tackle Shop, Dunrobin
Street, Helmsdale, Sutherland. Hotel,
Tel: 01431 821100, Fax: 01431 821101;
Tackle Shop, Tel: 01431 821102, F
ax: 01431 821103. (Day tickets for River
Helmsdale Town Water from £17.62 – £21.15
per day and £82.25 – £105.75 per week.
Trout and occasional salmon fishing available
on hill lochs and tributaries on Badenloch and
Auchentoul Estates.
• Brian Lyall, Badanloch Estate, by Kinbrace,
Sutherland, Tel: 01431 831 232 (£15 per rod
per day. Various hill lochs and occasional
salmon from Upper River Helmsdale below
Badanloch.)
• Angus Ross, Head Keeper, Achentoul Estate,
Kinbrace, Sutherland, Tel: 01431 831 227
(£15 per rod per day. Fishing for brown trout
on the Banock Burn and occasional salmon
from a tributary of the Helmsdale.)

KIRKAIG
Location • Lochinver
Species • salmon
Permit • Inver Lodge Hotel, Lochinver, by Lairg,
Sutherland, Tel: 01571 844 496
(From £30 per rod per day).

KYLE OF TONGUE & LOCAL LOCHS
Location • Kyle of Tongue
Species • sea trout
Permit • Scriberscross Lodge, Strath Brora, Rogart,
Sutherland, Tel: 01408 641 246/Fax: 465
• The Mountainman, West Argyle Street,
Ullapool, Ross-shire, Tel: 01854 613 383
(Bank fishing £6 per day).

LOCH AILSH
Location • Benmore, Sutherland
Species • brown trout, sea trout and occasional
salmon. This lovely loch offers excellent
brown trout fishing. Lying below Benmore
Assynt at the head of the Upper Oykel, the
loch can also produce migratory fish. Best
drifts are on the north shore, around the
island and adjacent to the outflow.
Species • Inver Lodge Hotel, Lochinver, by Lairg,
Sutherland, Tel: 01571 844 496 (boat fishing
only, guests have priority. Prices under review.
The hotel can also arrange fishing on the
River Inver, Kirkaig and Upper Oykel and
other lochs.)

LOCH A'CHROISG
Location • Achnasheen/Gairloch
Species • pike, perch, brown trout and ferox
Permit • Ledgowan Lodge Hotel, Achnasheen,
Tel: 01445 720252. (Fishing free to residents)

LOCH AN RUTHAIR
Location • Helmsdale/Melvich
Species • brown trout
Permit • Tony Henderson, Garvault Hotel,
Kinbrace, Sutherland, Tel: 01431 831 224
(Boats £15, outboards £15, bank £5).
Garvault Hotel has a choice of excellent hill
lochs with wild brown trout. Fly only.

LOCH ASCAIG
Location • Borrobol Estate, Helmsdale
Species • wild brown trout
Permit • Sir Michael Wigan, Borrobol Estate,
Kinbrace, Helmsdale, Sutherland,
Tel: 01431 831 264 (£226 – £339 per week,
with cottage. Spate river free to tenants,
offering occasional salmon and sea trout)

Loch Ascaig cont'd

Permit • The Sutherland Sporting Company, New Buildings, Lairg, Sutherland, Tel: 01549 402 239 (£15 per boat with 2 rods fishing. No outboards).

LOCH ARICHLINIE
Location • Badanloch, Helmsdale
Species • wild brown trout, occasional salmon
Permit • Brian Lyall, Badanloch Estate, by Kinbrace, Sutherland, Tel: 01431 831 232 (£15 per rod per day. Various hill lochs and occasional salmon from Upper River Helmsdale below Badanloch.)
• Angus Ross, Head Keeper, Achentoul Estate, Kinbrace, Sutherland, tel: 01431 831 227
• The Bridge Hotel & Tackle Shop, Dunrobin Street, Helmsdale, Sutherland, Tel: 01431 821102, Fax: 01431 821103.

LOCH BAD NA H'ERBA
Location • Sciberscross
Species • wild brown trout
Permit • Sciberscross Lodge, Strath Brora, Rogart, Tel: 01408 641246. (Fishing on several hill lochs from £10 per rod per day)

LOCH BAD NA H-ACHLAISE (GREEN LOCH)
Location • Achiltibuie /Ullapool
Species • brown trout and char, occasional sea trout. Fly fishing only.
Permit • Polly Estates Ltd., Inverpolly, Ullapool IV26 2YB, tel: 01854 622452.

LOCH BADANLOCH (& OTHER HILL LOCHS)
Location • Kinbrace/Syre
Species • brown trout, ferox, char, occasional salmon
Permit • Brian Lyall, Badanloch Estate, by Kinbrace, Sutherland, Tel: 01431 831 232 (£15 per rod per day. Various hill lochs and occasional salmon from Upper River Helmsdale below Badanloch.)
• Angus Ross, Head Keeper, Achentoul Estate, Kinbrace, Sutherland, Tel: 01431 831 227
• The Bridge Hotel & Tackle Shop, Dunrobin Street, Helmsdale, Sutherland, Tel: 01431 821102, Fax: 01431 821103.

LOCH BEANNACH
Location • Inchnadamph/Lochinver
• Lairg/Altnaharra
Species • brown trout
Permit • Inchnadamph/Lochinver: The Sheiling Guest House, Garve Road, Ullapool, Wester-Ross, Tel: 01854 612 947 (Fishing is free to guests).

• Lairg/Altnaharra: David Walker, Park House, Lairg, Sutherland, Tel: 01549 402 208, Fax: 01549 402693
(Other lochs, including Loch Shin and Loch Craggie. Salmon fishing on the Shin and shooting can be arranged. Prices under review for 2002.)

LOCH BORRALAN
Location • Oykel/Ledmore
Species • brown trout and char. Boats are moored across the road from the motel. A lovely loch with free-rising brown trout and beautifully coloured char.
Permit • The Alt Bar, Altnacealagach Motel, Elphin, by Lairg, Sutherland, Tel: 01854 666 220/ 260 (Prices for 2002 under review).

LOCH BORRALIE
Location • Cape Wrath, Sutherland
Species • brown trout and char. One of a series of superb limestone lochs, offering some of the best brown trout fishing in the north of Scotland.
Permit • Jack Watson, Cape Wrath Hotel, Keodale, Durness, Sutherland, Tel: 01971 511212, Fax: 01971 511313 (A weeks board & fishing from £450 per person. Daily lets £15).

LOCH BRORA
Location • Brora
Species • salmon, sea trout, brown trout and char
Permit • Guns & Tackle, Rosslyn Street, Brora, Sutherland, Tel: 01408 621 373 (boat with 2 rods, £30 per day)
• Sciberscross, Strath Brora, Rogart, Tel: 01408 641246. (Also boats on several hill lochs for brown trout)
• Sutherland Estates, Estate Office, Duke Street, Golspie, Sutherland KW10 6RP, Tel: 01408 633 268

LOCH CALADAIL
Location • Durness, Sutherland
Species • brown trout. One of several limestone lochs which produce magnificent fish up to 6 lbs. and more. Small flies and fish fine. Boat and bank fishing available through the hotel.
Permit • Jack Watson, Cape Wrath Hotel, Keodale, Durness, Sutherland, Tel: 01971 511 212, Fax: 01971 511 313 (A weeks board & fishing from £450 per person. Daily lets £15).

LOCH CALDER
Location • Glengolly/Halkirk
Species • brown trout, ferox and char. Bank anglers should proceed with caution, with soft banks and sudden drop-off. Boat fishing most productive.
Permit • Harper's Fly Fishing Services, 57 High Street, Thurso, Caithness, Tel: 01847 893 170
• Hugo Ross, 56 High Street, Wick, Caithness, Tel: 01955 604 200

LOCH CAM
Location • Ledmore/Ullapool
Species • brown trout, ferox. A big loch set in magnificent surroundings. Fish round the islands and skerries which often produce a surprise larger trout. Look for good fishing around the burn mouths running off Suilven and Canisp. This can be a wild and windy loch, but shelter around the main, wooded island, will still give fine sport.
Permit • David Walker, Park House, Lairg, Sutherland, Tel: 01549 402 208 (£20 per boat, no outboards, no bank fishing).
• Oykel Bridge Hotel, Oykel Bridge, by Lairg, Ross-shire, Tel: 01549 441 218 (Boat with 2 rods £20 per day).
• The Alt Bar, Altnacealagach, Elphin, by Lairg, Sutherland, Tel: 01854 666220 (boat with 2 rods, £20 per day)
• Inver Lodge Hotel, Lochinver, by Lairg, Sutherland, Tel: 01571 844 496 (Boat £18 per day, bank £5 per day).
• Birchbank Holiday Lodge, Knockan, Elphin, by Lairg, Sutherland, Tel: 01854 666 203, Fax: 01854 666 215

LOCH CRAGGIE
Location • Lairg/Saval
Species • brown trout
Permit • David Walker, Park House, Lairg, Sutherland, Tel: 01549 402 208 (£20 per boat, no outboards, no bank fishing).

LOCH CRAGGIE
Location • Bonar/Ledmore
Species • brown trout
Permit • The Alt Bar, Altnacealagach, Elphin, by Lairg, Sutherland, Tel: 01854 666220, (Boat £15 per day, prices under review).
• The Inchnadamph Hotel, Assynt, by Lairg, Sutherland, Tel: 01571 822 (Salmon fishing available, brown trout lochs free to guests).

LOCH CRAGGIE
Location • Tongue/Altnaharra
Species • brown trout
Permit • Altnaharra Hotel, Altnaharra, by Lairg, Sutherland, Tel: 01549 411 222 (Bank £5, boat £10, outboard £5, per day.)
• Tongue Hotel, Tongue, tel. 01847 611 206. (Prices on application)

LOCH CROISPOL
Location • Balnakeil, Cape Wrath
Species • brown trout
Permit • Jack Watson, The Cape Wrath Hotel, Keodale, Durness, by Lairg, Sutherland, Tel: 01971 511 212, Fax: 01971 511 313 (A weeks board & fishing from £450 per person. Daily lets £15).

LOCH CULAG
Location • Lochinver/Inverkirkaig
Species • brown trout, salmon and sea trout
Permit • Culag Hotel, Lochinver, Tel. 01571 844 270, Fax: 01571 844 483 (boat fishing only, guests have priority. Prices under review. The hotel can also arrange fishing on the River Inver and River Kirkaig and local lochs.)

LOCH GLASS
Location • Evanton
Species • brown trout
Permit • Hugo Ross, 56 High Street, Wick, Caithness, Tel: 01955 604 200 (£5 per rod per day).

LOCH HEILAN
Location • Greenland Mains Farm, Caithness
Species • brown trout. Excellent fly fishing, good wading and boat fishing. Trout can run better than 3 lbs. Excellent fly hatches including mayfly, so have your dry fly box handy as well as traditional wets.
Permit • Mr Ian MacDonald (Loch Keeper), Tel/Fax: 01847 601 272 (Prices on application).
• Harper's Fly Fishing Services, 57 High Street, Thurso, Caithness, Tel: 01847 893 170
• Forss House Hotel, by Thurso, Caithness, Tel: 01847 861 201. The hotel also has fishing on other lochs and occasional lets on the River Forss for salmon.
• Hugo Ross, 56 High Street, Wick, Caithness, Tel: 01955 604 200

LOCH HEMPRIGGS

Location • Wick
Species • brown trout. Bank fishing only on this exposed loch and wade with care. Look for trout around the larger rocks just sub-surface. Great sport with always the chance of bigger fish.
Permit • Thrumster Garage, Thrumster, by Wick, Caithness, Tel: 01955 651 252 (£5 per rod per day.)

LOCH HOPE

Location • Altnaharra/Tongue
Species • sea trout and salmon
Permit • Altnaharra Hotel, Altnaharra, by Lairg, Sutherland, Tel: 01549 411 222 (£35 per day, outboard included, 2 rods).
• Peter MacGregor, The Borgie Lodge Hotel, Skerray, Sutherland, Tel: 01641 521 332 (Prices as above).
• Loch Maree Hotel, Loch Maree, Wester Ross, Tel: 01445 760 288 (£35 per day, Ghillie £35).

LOCH LOYAL

Location • Altnaharra/Tongue
Species • brown trout, ferox and occasional salmon
Permit • Altnaharra Hotel, Altnaharra, by Lairg, Sutherland, Tel: 01549 411 222 (£35 per day, outboard included, 2 rods).
• Ben Loyal hotel, Tongue, Sutherland, Tel: 01847 611 216
• Tongue Hotel, Tongue, Tel: 01847 611206

LOCH MAREE

Location • Kinlochewe/Achnasheen
Species • sea trout, brown trout & occasional salmon
Permit • Kinlochewe Hotel, Kinlochewe, Wester Ross, Tel: 01445 760 253 (£35 per day, Ghillie/boatman available. Prices under review).
• Loch Maree Hotel, by Achnasheen, Ross-shire IV22 2HL, tel: 01445 760288 (Boats available with ghillies, prices under review)

LOCH MEADIE

Location • Altnaharra
Species • brown trout
Permit • Estate Office, Inverpolly Estate, Ullapool, Wester Ross, Tel: 01854 622 452 (Bank fishing £6 per rod per day).

LOCH MEADIE

Location • Westerdale, Halkirk
Species • brown trout. One of 12 excellent lochs, fished out from Halkirk, with plenty of free-rising trout. Traditional loch-style drift fishing.
Permit • The Ulbster Arms Hotel, Bridge Street, Halkirk, Caithness, tel: 01847 831 206 (£10 per day, subject to availability. Guests have priority.)

LOCH MERKLAND

Location • Lairg/Scourie
Species • brown trout and ferox. A deep loch, which produces browns around 8-12 ounces. Traditional flies.
Permit • Overscaig Hotel, by Lairg, Sutherland, Tel: 01549 431203. The hotel has fishing on several hill lochs, Loch Shin and the River Tirry. Salmon fishing can be arranged on the River Shin).

LOCH MIGDALE

Location • Bonar Bridge, Sutherland
Species • brown trout
Permit • Dunroamin Hotel, Lairg Road, Bonar Bridge, Sutherland, Tel: 01863 766236 (The hotel can arrange fishing on the Kyle of Sutherland for salmon and sea trout and nearby brown trout lochs. Dedicated 2-bedroom flat with wheelchair access).

LOCH MORE

Location • Westerdale
Species • salmon & brown trout
Lying at the head of the Thurso River, this large, shallow loch offers good brown trout fishing and salmon are also taken, mainly above the sluices at the head of the river.
Permit • The Ulbster Arms Hotel, Bridge Street, Halkirk, Caithness, Tel: 01847 831 206 (Prices on application)

LOCH NA DAIL (POLLY LOCH)

Location • Badnagyle/Achiltibuie/Lochinver, Sutherland
Species • brown trout
Permit • Polly Estates Ltd., Inverpolly, Ullapool IV26 2YB, Tel: 01854 622452 (Fly fishing only, boat available. The estate also has fishing on the River Polly and River Oscaig, with boat and bank fishing on Lochs Soinascaig and Badagyle and Lurgainn.)

LOCH NAN CLAR
Location • Badanloch, Kinbrace, Sutherland
Species • brown trout
Fly fishing only, boats available. Occasional salmon can be taken in the narrows above Loch Rimsdale.
Permit • Brian Lyall, Badanloch Estate, by Kinbrace, Sutherland, Tel: 01431 831 232
• The Bridge Hotel & Tackle Shop, Dunrobin Street, Helmsdale, Sutherland, Tel: 01431 821102, fax: 01431 821103.
• Tony Henderson, Garvault Hotel, Garvault, Kinbrace, Sutherland, Tel: 01997 414 205 (Prices under review.)

LOCH NAVER
Location • Altnaharra, Sutherland
Species • salmon, sea trout and brown trout. Dapping is popular as well as traditional loch-style. Trolling allowed for salmon on some beats on Loch Naver.
Permit • Altnaharra Hotel, Altnaharra, by Lairg, Sutherland, Tel: 01549 411 222 (Boat fishing, 2 rods, from £20, outboards available. No bank fishing on Loch Naver. The hotel has some excellent hill lochs and also sea trout fishing on Loch Hope, as well as summer salmon on the River Mudale above Loch Naver and River Borgie by arrangement).

LOCH PALM
Location • Kinbrace/Syre
Species • brown trout
Permit • Tony Henderson, Garvault Hotel, Garvault, Kinbrace, Sutherland, Tel: 01997 414 205 (From £5 per rod per day).

LOCH RHIFAIL
Location • Kinbrace/Syre
Species • brown trout
Permit• Tony Henderson, Garvault Hotel, Garvault, Kinbrace, Sutherland, Tel: 01997 414 205 (From £5 per rod per day).

LOCH RIMSDALE
Location • Kinbrace/Syre
Species • brown trout, char and occasional salmon
Permit • The Bridge Hotel & Tackle Shop, Dunrobin Street, Helmsdale, Sutherland, Tel: 01431 821102, Fax: 01431 821103.
• Tony Henderson, Garvault Hotel, Garvault, Kinbrace, Sutherland, tel: 01997 414 205

LOCH ROSAIL
Location • Kinbrace/Syre
Species • brown trout
Permit • Tony Henderson, Garvault Hotel, Garvault, Kinbrace, Sutherland, Tel: 01997 414 205 (From £5 per rod per day.)

LOCH SHIN
Location • Lairg/Altnaharra
Species • brown trout, ferox
Permit • Peter MacGregor, The Borgie Lodge Hotel, Skerray, by Thurso, Sutherland, Tel: 01641 521 332
• Altnaharra Hotel, Altnaharra, by Lairg, Sutherland, Tel: 01549 411
• Sutherland Sporting Company, Main Street, Lairg, Sutherland IV27 4AR, Tel: 01549 402229 (Fishing tackle, advice and permits for other local lochs).
• The Lairg Angling Club, St Murie, Lairg, Sutherland, Tel: 01549 402 010 (Bank fishing £5 per day, £15 per week. Boats £30 approx)
• B Macleay, Achnairn, Shinness by Lairg, Sutherland IV27 4DN, Tel: 01459 402 131 /402 420, Fax: 01549 402519 (Boat Hire including half cabin cruising boats and tackle hire, guides.)

LOCH SIONASCAIG
Location • Inverpolly National Nature Reserve, Lochinver
Species • brown trout & ferox. A magnificent loch set in spectacular grandeur, dotted with islands and numerous bays.
Permit • Polly Estate Office, Inverpolly, Ullapool IV26 2YB, Wester Ross, Tel: 01854 622 452 (Boat and 2 rods £15 per day, outboard £10. The estate has fishing on 9 other trout lochs)

LOCH SKERRAY
Location • Bettyhill/Tongue
Species • brown trout. This loch together with Loch A'Chaoruinn is controlled by the Tongue & District AC. Best drifts are around the island.
Permit • Borgie Lodge Hotel, Skerray, Tongue, Sutherland, Tel/Fax: 01641 521 332
• Ben Loyal Hotel, Tongue, Sutherland.

LOCH SLAIM
Location • Tongue, Sutherland
Species • brown trout, salmon, sea trout & char
Permit • Borgie Lodge Hotel, Skerray, Tongue, Sutherland, Tel/Fax: 01641 521 332 (Boat fishing only, £20 a day. Charges under review.)

LOCH ST. JOHN'S
Location • Thurso/Dunnet
Species • brown trout. St John's Loch Improvement Association work hard to keep this beautiful loch producing magnificent, pink -fleshed, silvery trout. A wheely boat for handicapped anglers is available, booked through Harper's.
Permit • Hugo Ross, 56 High Street, Wick, Caithness, Tel/Fax: 01955 604 200 (Boat £15).
• Harper's Fly Fishing Services, 57 High Street, Thurso, Caithness, Tel: 01847 893 179
• St Clair Arms Hotel, Castletown, Tel: 01847 821 656/ 821 214
• Forss House Hotel, Forss, by Thurso, Tel: 01847 861 201

LOCH STACK
Location • Lairg/Scourie
Species • sea trout, salmon, brown trout
Permit • Scourie Hotel, Scourie IV27 4SX, Tel: 01971 502396 (Boat fishing only with ghillie/boatman and is mainly for salmon and sea trout, although the loch does contain good brown trout. Prices on application)

LOCH STAINK
Location • Altnaharra/Tongue
Species • brown rout
Permit • Altnaharra Hotel, Altnaharra, by Lairg, Sutherland, Tel: 01549 411 222 (Boat with 2 rods. £20 per day. Good boat and bank fishing for free-rising trout. Black Zulu or Black Pennel on the bob and you'll have enough for breakfast within an hour. As with all of the Altnaharra lochs, the scenery and birdlife is splendid).

LOCH STEMSTER
Location • Achavanich/Lybster
Species • brown trout
Permit • Dunbeath Hotel, Dunbeath, Caithness KW6 6EG, tel: 01593 731 208, Fax: 01593 731 242 (Fly fishing only, boats available. Prices on application)

LOCH TOFTINGALL
Location • Watten/Mybster, Caithness
Species • brown trout. 130 acres and shallow, so wind can sometimes cause problems.
Permit • The Loch Watten Hotel, Watten, Caithness, Tel: 01955 621 232
• Hugo Ross, 56 High Street, Wick, Caithness, Tel: 01955 604 200
• John Swanson, Aspen Bank, Banks Road, Watten, Caithness, Tel: 01955 621 326

LOCH UIDH TARRAIGEAN (UPPER POLLY LOCHS)
Location • Badnagyle / Achiltibuie, by Lochinver
Species • brown trout
Permit • Polly Estates Ltd., Inverpolly, Ullapool IV26 2YB, Tel: 01854 622452

LOCH URIGILL
Location • Ledmore/Ullapool
Species • brown trout & ferox. Lying to the south of Borrolan this large, weedy loch has a good mayfly hatch in June and July. Boat fishing and good results bank fishing and safe wading.
Permit • Inchnadamph Hotel, Assynt, Lochinver, Sutherland, Tel: 01571 822202, Fax: 01571 822203
• Culag Hotel, Lochinver, Sutherland, Tel: 01571 844270, Fax: 01571 844483

LOCH VEYATIE
Location • Ledmore/Ullapool
Species • brown trout and ferox. This is a big loch, 4 miles long and outboards are recommended, as it can be windy. Good mayfly hatches through June and July. Loch a'Mhadail, separated by a rocky skerry from Veyatie is also well worth a cast. Wild and wonderful scenery, as with all the Ledmore lochs.
Permit • Inchnadamph Hotel, Assynt, Lochinver, Sutherland, Tel: 01571 822202, Fax: 01571 822203
• Culag Hotel, Lochinver, Sutherland, Tel: 01571 844270, Fax: 01571 844483
• The Alt Bar, Altnacealagach, Elphin, by Lairg, Sutherland, Tel: 01854 666220

LOCH WATENAN
Location • Ulbster
Species • brown trout
Permit • D Gunn, Watten Lodge, Watten, Caithness, Tel: 01955 621 217/01955 823 90 (Boat with 2 rods, £15 per day, outboards £15, bank fishing £5 per rod per day).

LOCH WATTEN
Location • Watten Village
Species • brown trout. One of the region's finest lochs, with beautiful, silvery brown trout around 10-12 ounces and better. Don't expect huge baskets, but do expect wonderful sport.
Permit • Hugo Ross, 56 High Street, Wick, Caithness, Tel: 01955 604 200 (£15 for use of boat, per rod per day. Bank fishing £10).

- Loch Watten Hotel, Watten, Caithness, Tel: 01955 621232 (Boat charges under review for 2002)
- Harper's Fly Fishing Services, 57 High Street, Thurso, Caithness, tel: 01847 893 179 have priority).

LOCH WESTER
Location • Bridge of Wester/Lyth
Species • salmon, sea trout and brown trout. Loch Wester is a shallow loch, which fishes well wading, as well as from a boat.
Permit • Mrs. G Dunnet, Auckhorn, Lyth, by Wick KW1 4UD, Tel: 01955 604200
- Hugo Ross, 56 High Street, Wick, Caithness, Tel: 01955 604 200
- Harper's fly Fishing Services, 57 High Street, Thurso, Caithness, Tel: 01847 893 179

LOCHS AIRIGH LEATHAID
Location • Westerdale
Species • brown trout. Three lochans on Loch Dubh Estate. Well worth the walk.
Permit • The Ulbster Arms Hotel, Bridge Street, Halkirk, Caithness, Tel: 01847 831 206

OYKEL
Location • Oykel Bridge
Species • salmon and sea trout. There is excellent salmon and sea trout fishing on the Kyle, especially from the mouth of the River Carron to Bonar Bridge. Being tidal, this fishes best on an ebbing tide. Fly only and restrictions apply. Private beats below Oykel Falls are rarely available, but Oykel Bridge Hotel and Inver Lodge Hotel have fishing available on the upper beats and Loch Ailsh. Early booking is essential for the river.
Permit • Oykel Bridge Hotel, Oykel Bridge, by Lairg, Sutherland, Tel: 01549 441 218 (Private beats below Oykel Falls are let on an annual basis and rarely become available. The hotel has beats on the Upper Oykel: advance booking only, prices on application).
- Inver Lodge Hotel, By Lairg, Lochinver, Sutherland, IV27 4LU, Tel: 01571 844496 (Upper beats below Loch Ailsh and Loch Ailsh)
- M Brown, Kyle of Sutherland Angling Club, Balleigh Wood, Edderton, Ross-shire, Tel: 01862 821 230 (£20 per day approx).
- Dunroamin Hotel, Lairg Road, Bonar Bridge, Sutherland, Tel: 01863 766236 (Fishing on nearby trout lochs. Dedicated 2-bedroom flat with wheelchair access.)

RHICONICH
Location • Rhiconich
Species • salmon, sea trout and brown trout. The river offers fly fishing along with boat fishing on Loch Garbet Beag for salmon and sea trout. The hotel also has boats on 8 trout lochs and fishing on more than a dozen excellent hill lochs. No Sunday fishing.
Permit • The Rhiconich Hotel, Richonich, by Lairg, Sutherland, Tel: 01971 521 224 (Prices under review for 2002).

SARCLET LOCH
Location • Gearty Head, Thrumster Village
Species • brown trout.
Permit • Thrumster Garage, Thrumster, by Wick, Caithness, Tel: 01955 651 252 (Boat £16 per day, £8 per half day, (2 rods), plus permit at £4 per rod).

STONEYFIELDS LOCHS
Location • Invergordon
Species • rainbow trout and brown trout. Bank fishing on three stocked lochans, two miles north of Invergordon.
Permit • Stoneyfield House, Invergordon, Ross-shire, Tel: 01349 852 632 (Fly fishing on two lochs of 3 and 5 acres and one bait loch. Trout average 2 lbs. up to double figures. Prices on application).

TARVIE LOCHS TROUT FISHERY
Location • Contin, Strathpeffer, Ross-shire
Species • rainbow trout and brown trout Stocked fishery with rainbows to 15lbs and brown trout to 6 lbs. member of the Association of Stillwater Fisheries, tackle hire and flies for sale, R.E.F.F.I.S & S.T.A.N.I.C. approved instructor by appointment. Troutmaster Water.
Permit • Bookings and rates for 2002, contact Tarvie Lochs Trout Fishery, Tarvie, Contin, by Strathpeffer, Ross-shire IV14 9EJ, Tel: 01997 421 250 (Boat fishing and fly fishing only on main loch, limit 4 fish per rod, thereafter C&R. Separate bait loch. Open all year round – rainbows only – weather permitting.)

THURSO

Location • Westerdale/Halkirk/ Westerdale, Caithness

Species • salmon. Excellent fly fishing on a rotating beat system, which covers the whole river. Fishes well throughout the year with a prolific grilse run and some sea trout. First class brown trout lochs available through the hotel.

Permit • The Ulbster Arms Hotel, Bridge Street, (2002 charges on application.)

• Thurso Fisheries, Estate Office, Thurso East, Caithness, Tel: 01847 893 134

WESTER

Location • Wick/John O'Groats

Species • salmon and sea trout. This short river is fished in conjunction with the loch and can provide good sport, particularly in the late season.

Permit • Mrs. G Dunnet, Auckhorn, Lyth, by Wick KW1 4UD, Tel: 01955 604200

• Hugo Ross, 56 High Street, Wick, Caithness, Tel: 01955 604 200

• Harper's fly Fishing Services, 57 High Street, Thurso, Caithness, Tel: 01847 893 179

WICK

Location • Wick/Thurso

Species • salmon and sea trout. Some 9 miles of excellent club water for salmon and sea trout, offering fly and bait fishing on a budget for visitors. Managed by the Wick Angling Association, this superb spate stream is fast flowing, with some excellent pools and can be easily covered from the banks. Catch and release is practiced voluntarily in the autumn.

Permit • Hugo Ross, 56 High Street, Wick, Caithness, Tel: 01955 604 200 (2002 prices on application)

YARROWS LOCH

Location • Thrumster Village

Species • brown trout. A deep loch, unsuitable for bank fishing. Trout are plentiful but small; an excellent loch for beginners to fly fishing.

Permit • Hugo Ross, 56 High Street, Wick, Caithness, Tel: 01955 604 200

ACHNESS HOTEL

Rosehall by Lairg, Sutherland IV27 4BD
Tel: (01549) 441239 Fax: (01549) 441324

Quiet, comfortable fishing hotel by **River Cassley**. Salmon fishing on Cassley and by arrangement on other Sutherland rivers. Good loch fishing for brown trout. Easy access to local golf courses including Royal Dornoch. Trout fishing from £5 per day. Salmon and sea trout fishing from around £30 per day.

AULTBEA HOTEL & RESTAURANT

Aultbea, Ross-shire IV22 2HX. Tel. (01445) 731 201

Situated on the shores of Loch Ewe with views to the Torridon Mountains. Ideal centre for trout hill lochs and sea angling. Salmon fishing can be arranged.

ACKERGILL TOWER

Ackergill, By Wick, Caithness.
Tel: (01955) 603556 Fax: (01955) 602140

If accommodation in the grand manner is your choice, then it doesn't come any better than Ackergill Tower, dramatically situated above the craggy shoreline of Sinclair's Bay, overlooking the broody waters of the **Pentland Firth**. In days gone by, you could arrive by boat to the stone pier below the battlements or horse-drawn carriages, but nowadays, it's more likely to be by limousine or helicopter.

Ackergill comes not only complete with house staff, but its own wardrobe of Barbour jackets and wellies for all sizes of guest. There is a private lochan, the only one in Caithness stocked with rainbow trout averaging close to two pounds. They make an obliging change if the salmon and sea trout or wild brown trout are rather more fickle. Ackergill can make arrangements for all your sporting and corporate requirements.

ALTNAHARRA HOTEL

Altnaharra, By Lairg, Sutherland IV27 4UE.
Tel: (01549) 411222 Fax: (01549) 411222

Great fishing hotel, set in majestic scenery close to the head of **Loch Naver**. Good salmon, sea trout and brown trout on Loch Naver and on tributaries of the famed **River Naver**, the **River Mallart** and **River Mudale**, with occasional lets also on the main river. Several other trout lochs and sea trout on nearby Loch Hope. Loch Naver: Salmon sea trout and brown trout. Boats available with outboard. 50-70 salmon per season with good spring fishing. Trolling allowed but restricted to fly at west end of loch.

River Mallart: Principal tributary of River Naver. Good spate river for salmon, including famous Washing Pool. Around 50 fish per season. Loch Meadie: occasional salmon, excellent brown trout, good baskets of fish average 6-8 oz but up to 4 lbs. Boat fishing best with outboard to cover all the water.

Loch Loyal: a deep loch which offers good bank fishing and boat sport. Occasional salmon and ferox are also taken trolling. Trout fishing from £5 per day and boats from £20 per day for two rods. outboards £15 per day. Ghillies £35 + gratuities.

BELGRAVE ARMS HOTEL
Helmsdale, Sutherlan
Tel: 01431 821463

Friendly Georgian Inn, pub grub adjacent to the A9. Close to harbour. Sea angling and salmon and trout on town water. See also the Bridge Hotel and Tackle Shop. Salmon and sea trout from £17.62 per day per rod.

BLADNOCH INN
Bladnoch, Wigtown
Tel: (01988) 402200

Fishing on **River Bladnoch** for salmon and fine brown trout. Some sea trout. Good centre for sea angling and coarse angling for bream, roach, perch and specimen pike. Trout fishing from £5 per day: salmon fishing from £15-£25 per day per rod.

BORGIE LODGE HOTEL
Skerray, Tongue, Sutherland
Tel: (01641) 521332
Email: info@borgielodgehotel.co.uk,
www.borgielodgehotel.co.uk

Delightful traditional fishing lodge set in a peaceful secluded glen on the banks of the **River Borgie** in North Sutherland, with plenty of choice for trout fishers, offering both boat and bank sport on more than 20 lochs, including **Loch an Tigh-Choimhid** and **Lochan Arbhair**. Traditional flies do the business.

Salmon fishing available on the River Borgie and **Halladale**, with sea trout on **Loch Hope** and saltwater sport for sea trout from the **Kyle of Tongue**. Add inclusive sporting packages, including shooting and stalking in season, and you have the perfect escape from office life.

Trout angling: boats £15 per day and bank fishing £5. Salmon charges vary with season and choice of beats.

BRIDGE HOTEL & TACKLE SHOP
Dunrobin Street, Helmsdale, Sutherland.
Hotel: (01431) 821100 Fax: (01431) 821101
Tackle Shop: (01431) 821102 Fax: (01431) 821103
SEE AD ON PAGE 63

Opening for the 2002 season after extensive renovation, The Bridge Hotel and Tackle Shop is ideally situated for salmon and trout fishing, golf and sea angling. Stalking and shooting by arrangement through the hotel. The Tackle Shop is very much open for business and carries a full range of flies for salmon, sea trout and brown trout, as well as an extensive range of freshwater and saltwater rods, reels, tackle, waders, clothing and accessories.

Visitor's tickets are available for the **River Helmsdale** Town Water which can produce excellent sport with salmon, grilse, sea trout and finnock. Tickets run from 9am -9am the following day and fishing late and early offers the best chance of success. Fly only with strictly enforced rules on fly size and no trebles.

This prolific section of the river produces around 300 salmon every season. Salmon and trout fishing is also available on the upper river between **Badenloch** and **Loch Achnamoine**, as well as the extensive loch fishing on Badenloch Estate. A number of other rivers including the **Brora**, **Fleet**, and **Berriedale** (Caithness) are only a short drive away. Trout fishing from £15 per day on Badenloch and Auchentoul Estates, including hill lochs, the upper river and tributaries.

Helmsdale Town Water for salmon and sea trout: 8 visitor day tickets are available from the Bridge Hotel & Tackle Shop (01431) 821102. Visitor charges are £17.62 per day or £82.25 per week and from July through to the end of September £21.15 per day and £105.75 for the week.

CAPE WRATH HOTEL
Durness, Sutherland
Tel: (01971) 511212

One of the great Scottish fishing hotels, run by anglers for anglers. Some of the wonderful limestone lochs of Durness are only a short walk away from the hotel and all offer challenging fly fishing for superb, wild brown trout which can run better than 8 lbs. Don't expect large baskets, but do expect beautifully presented trout up to and in excess of 2 lbs. Hill lochs include **A'Gheodha Ruaidh**, **A'Phuill Bhuidhe** and **Bad An Fheur-Loch**.

Closer to the hotel, **Loch Borralie** is a beautiful limestone loch with excellent trout averaging around the pound, with much larger specimens.

Outboards are not allowed on **Lochs Caladail** and **Croispol** are other superb limestone lochs which produce challenging sport and splendid trout. Salmon fishing is available on the small spate stream, the **River Daill** and the excellent **River Dionard** which produced good numbers of salmon and sea trout each season. Heavily booked in advance. All inclusive packages for one week's full board and fishing at the Cape Wrath Hotel from £450. Daily lets from £15 per rod per day.

COUL HOUSE HOTEL
By Strathpeffer, Ross-shire. Tel: (01997) 421487 Fax: (01997) 421945

Access to excellent and inexpensive wild brown trout fishing on many hill lochs. Dingwall and District AC offer visitor access to their waters. The **River Conon** is a fine salmon stream and much of the fishing is either preserved or booked from year to year. Some lets may be available and rods can make enquiries through the hotel. Trout charges from £5 per day.

CRASK INN
By Altnaharra, Sutherland. Tel: (01549) 411241

Comfortable fishing inn in excellent location, with self-catering accommodation also available. Wild brown trout on **Loch Shin** and **River Tirry** and hill lochs. Traditional loch-style drifting on Loch Shin. Dry fly and small nymphs work well on the river. Downstream wet fly if the river is running off following rain can produce some surprisingly large browns. Tickets for bank fishing from £5 per day.

CULAG HOTEL & VALHALLA CHALETS
Lochinver, Sutherland
Tel: (01571) 844270 Fax: (01571) 844483

Excellent centre for trout and salmon fishing as well as sea angling. Assynt AC and Assynt Crofters Trust permits are available for numerous local brown trout lochs. Valhalla Chalets, Inverkirkaig, Sutherland offer self-catering accomodation, close to the River Kirkaig.

DUNROAMIN HOTEL
Lairg Road, Bonar Bridge, Sutherland
Tel: (01863) 766236

Excellent base for salmon and sea trout fly fishing on the Kyle of Sutherland, including the popular stretch from the mouth of the River Carron to Bonar Bridge. Trout fishing on local hill lochs. Self-contained 2 bedroom flat with wheelchair access and all hotel bedrooms en suite. Panoramic views over the Kyle and River Carron.

EDDRACHILLES HOTEL
Achiltibuie, Sutherland

Wonderful views across the bay of islands. Number of hill lochs available for brown trout fly fishing, ranging from typical, free-rising 3 or 4 to the pound up ro much larger specimens of 2lbs and more. Charges from £5 per day.

FORSINARD HOTEL
Forsinard, Sutherland, KW13 6YT. Tel: (01641) 571221

Excellent trout fishing including **Loch Buidhe Mor**, average 10/12 oz but much larger browns present. Bank fishing particularly good near stream mouths. **Loch Crocach** offers easy fishing for wild browns averaging around half a pound, an ideal beginners loch. Flies to try: Red hackled Invicta, Black Pennel and red tag, silver March Brown and Kingfisher Butcher. Bank fishing from £5 per day.

FORSS HOUSE HOTEL
by Thurso, Caithness. Tel: (01847) 861201

Situated on the **River Forss** which is timeshared on the main middle and lower reaches, above which it is private. An improving spring run and excellent sport with grilse and summer salmon when there is enough water. Occasional sea trout, but these can run between 5 and 10 lbs. Excellent base for Caithness lochs including nearby **Reay Lochs**, **Calder**, **Watten**, **St Johns** and **Heilan**. (see Gems of Scotland).

Bank fishing for trout from £ 5 per day. Boats from £ 15. Salmon fishing on the River Forss: lets are sometimes available on the lower river through the hotel. apply to Jamie MacGregor (01847) 86201 for availability and charges.

GARVAULT HOTEL
Badanloch, by Kinbrace, Sutherland. Tel: (01431) 831224

A true anglers' hotel, run by angler Tony Henderson for many years and offering an excellent selection of lochs holding hard-fighting wild brown trout. Both boat and bank fishing are available. Occasional lets for salmon and sea trout.

Loch Rimsdale: over 3 miles long and boat and outboard is essential for best results. Brown trout average 8/10oz and larger fish as well, best fish recently weighed 9lbs 8oz.

River Alt Lon A'Chuil: a substantial burn which flows into Loch Rimsdale and evidently benefits from the same fine fish which can run to 2lbs and more. Try a dry 'Daddy' or Claret Hopper: if that doesn't work, a Black Pennel should do the business. Boats from £15 per day with two anglers fishing. Bank fishing from £5 per day.

GLENMORANGIE HOUSE
Cadboll, Easter Ross. Tel: (01862) 871671

Glenmorangie House is situated in Cadboll in historic Easter Ross near the Glenmorangie Distillery in Tain and stands close to the picturesque ruins of Cadboll Castle. The earliest part of the house dates from the 1500's and most of the rest from the 1800's.The extensive grounds and walled gardens are only two hundred yards from the sea where rocky and sandy beach provides great walks.

Fishing is available as part of any visit to Glenmorangie House. Sea angling boats cater for groups up to a maximum of 20 and tackle can be provided. There are numerous trout lochs within an hour's drive. Salmon fishing is available on rivers **Shin**, **Carron**, **Cassley**, **Alness**, **Brora**, **Fleet** and others.

Experienced ghillies can be arranged, as well as tackle hire, transport and lunches. Bespoke packages are available, as is exclusive use of the House for parties of more than six people. Alternative activities for non-fishers include golfing and horse-riding.

HALLADALE INN
Melvich, Sutherland KW14 7YJ. Tel: (01641) 531282

A number of good lochs and lochans in wilderness country, including lochs an **Fheoir**, **Caol**, **Preas an Lochan**, **Lochan na Ceardach** and **Crasgach**.

Pony trekking and marvelous beaches nearby. And a

first class links course for golfers at Reay.

Salmon fishing can sometimes be arranged on the **River Halladale** which produces fish throughout the season. Traditional backing up in a good wind often produces results even during low-water conditions.

Easy and productive bank fishing for loch trout from £5 per day. The River Halladale is heavily pre-booked so advance enquiries are recommended. rates vary with season and beats. Prices on application.

THE HARBOUR LIGHTS HOTEL
Garve Road, Ullapool, Wester Ross IV26 2SX.
Tel: (01854) 612222 Fax: (01854) 612574

Good sea angling in Little Loch Broom and hill lochs for brown trout.

INCHBAE LODGE HOTEL
By Garve, Ross-shire IV23 2PH
Tel: (01997) 455269, Fax: (01997) 455207

A former hunting lodge set in 7 acres of grounds with free fishing for residents on hill lochs and the River Blackwater. Salmon fishing can be arrange on the River Conon.

INCHNADAMPH HOTEL
Assynt, By Lairg, Sutherland IV27 4HN
Tel: (01571) 822202 Fax: (01571) 822203

Overlooking the waters of **Loch Assynt** and the mountains of **Ben More Assynt** and **Quinnag**, **Inchnadamph** is a true fishing hotel, catering mainly for brown trout anglers. Cosy log fires and excellent malts compliment good Scottish fayre including local seafood and game. Trolling is allowed on Loch Assynt and produces occasional salmon and ferox. Excellent hill lochs and salmon fishing available on **River Inver** and **Upper Oykel** by arrangement.

Angling packages include free salmon and trout fishing for guests. True fishing hotel, catering mainly for brown trout anglers. Trolling allowed on **Loch Assynt** for occasional salmon and ferox. Excellent hill lochs and salmon fishing available on River Inver and Upper Oykel by arrangement.

INVERSHIN HOTEL
Invershin, by Lairg, Sutherland IV27 4ET.
Tel: (01549) 421202

The hotel has half a mile of its own fishings on the Kyle of Sutherland as well as trout fishing on nearby lochs. Salmon fishing can be arranged on the River Shin. En-suite rooms, packed lunches and freezer facilities.

INVER LODGE HOTEL
By Lairg,Lochinver, Sutherland IV27 4LU
Tel: (01571) 844496

Excellent base for superb wild brown trout sport on Sutherland lochs and salmon and sea trout fishing on Upper Oykel and **Loch Ailsh**, **River Kirkaig** and **River Inver**. Good sea angling out from Lochinver, including cod, ling, pollack (lythe), coalfish (saithe) and occasional halibut and porbeagle shark. Mackerel, pollack, coalfish, rock codling and wrasse can be taken from shore marks, while beaches will provide flatfish, particularly near burn mouths.

Excellent sport with salmon and sea trout can be had in summer and autumn, particularly following rain. Trout fishing from £5 per day. Salmon and sea trout fishing from around f25 per day upwards depending on season and river.

KINLOCHEWE HOTEL
Kinlochewe, Wester Ross.
Tel: (01445) 760253

This comfortable former coaching inn is situated at the top of **Loch Maree**, the hotel offers boats on the main loch and access to local lochs and the river above Loch Maree. Sea trout and salmon, with dapping most popular style of fishing on Maree. Good brown trout with char and ferox also present.

Boat charges £35 per day. Charge for ghillies/ boatmen £35 per day + gratuities.

KYLESKU HOTEL
Kylesku, by Scourie, Sutherland.
Tel: (01971) 502231

Excellent base for hill lochs and wild brown trout, mostly in the 6-10 oz range, but with bigger fish. Also reasonable sea trout fishing in saltwater bays on **Loch Beag** and **Loch Glendhu**, most productive where burns enter the sea, especially after rain. Sea trout fishing in recent years however has declined due to fish farm development and infestation of wild fish by sea lice. Charges £5 per day.

LEDGOWAN HOTEL
Achnasheen, Ross-shire.
Tel: (01445) 720252

Loch a'Chroisg, also known as **Loch Rosque**, sits below the A832 Gairloch/ Achnasheen road and is probably amongst the most northerly lochs to contain pike and perch. This deep, bleak loch also holds brown trout and some large ferox. Salmon enter the system although not recorded on rod and line. Dangerous to wade but own boats can be used.

Little Loch Rosque at the top of the system is great fun for pike and perch, which can be caught on the fly.

Shallower than the main loch and reedy, it also has very soft banks and wading in not recommended. Free fishing for hotel guests.

THE LINKS & ROYAL MARINE HOTELS
Golf Road, Brora, Sutherland KW9 6QS
Tel: (01408) 621 252 Fax: (01408) 621 181

Two more splendid hotels for the man who likes combining fishing & golf! James Braid's excellent 18 hole Brora Links course is a short 'drive' away. The River Brora and Loch Brora offer splendid salmon and sea trout fishing and there are numerous hill lochs in the area.

LOCH MAREE HOTEL
Loch Maree, Wester Ross. Tel: (01445) 760228

A great fishing hotel on the shores of **Loch Maree**, once famed for its dapping techniques and huge sea trout: stocks are again improving and most fishing is done on a catch and release basis by anglers keen to see this magnificent loch returned to its former glory.

Occasional salmon are also taken and the brown trout have increased in size significantly in recent years. Char and ferox are both present. Boat fishing on Loch Maree and fishing on nearby lochs and feeder rivers can be arranged.

Charges for boats £35 per day for two rods and ghillie/boatman £35 + gratuity. See also Shieldaig Lodge Hotel and Kinlochewe Hotel.

LOCH TORRIDON HOTEL
Torridon, Wester Ross. Tel: (01445)791242

Variety of hill lochs for brown trout. Bank fishing available on **Loch Damh** at the head of the **River Balgy**. Sea trout and salmon fishing may be arranged on the River Balgy and Loch Damh. Excellent sea fishing in **Loch Torridon** and out from Gairloch for pollack (lythe), cod, coalfish (Saithe), common skate and thornback ray. (see Gems of Scotland) Charges £6 per day for bank fishing for brown trout on Loch Damh. Fly fishing only.

LOCH WATTEN HOTEL
Watten, Caithness. Tel: (01955) 621232

Loch Watten is probably the most famous of Caithness lochs, and produces wonderfully-conditioned, silvery brown trout, averaging close to the pound. Don't expect huge baskets, but do expect excellent, challenging sport and a good brace or more for breakfast. Many anglers return most of their fish to the water. Normal loch-style techniques work best and the trout can be fickle. Boats are available through the hotel and Hugo Ross Fishing Tackle Shop, 56 High Street, Wick (01955) 604200. Charges £15 per day for two rods + £15 for outboard and fuel. Hugo Ross also has a comfortable fishing hut by the lochside for guests.

Hugo also has permits for **Loch Wester** and the **Wick River**, both excellent salmon and sea trout fisheries with day tickets on the Wick River at £20 per day and junior/OAPs a modest £5 per day.

MALLIN HOUSE HOTEL
Church Street, Dornoch, Sutherland IV25 3LP.
Tel: (01862) 810335 Fax: 01862 810810

Special three, five and seven day packages as well as weekend breaks. Excellent base for river and loch fishing, as well as sea angling. And for golfers, Royal Dornoch is just down the road.

NAVIDALE HOUSE HOTEL
Helmsdale, Sutherland KW8 6JS. Tel: (0143) 821258
Fax:(01431) 821531 Email:
sharon@navidalehouse.fsnet.co.uk

Comfortable, up market hotel, excellent food and acocmodation, well located for **River Helmsdale** and Sutherland lochs. Sea angling boats are available from Helmsdale harbour. For golfers, there's a short but challenging 9 hole golf course in Helmsdale, with Brora and Royal Dornoch a short drive away. Trout fishing from £15 per day on **Badenloch** and **Auchentoul** Estates, including hill lochs, the upper river and tributaries.

Helmsdale Town Water for salmon and sea trout: 8 visitor day tickets are available from the Bridge Hotel & Tackle Shop (01431) 821102. Visitor charges are £17.62 per day or £82.25 per week and from July through to the end of September £21.15 per day and £105.75 for the week. Remarkable value for money with an excellent chance of salmon and sea trout. See also Bridge Hotel, Helmsdale.

NORTHERN SANDS HOTEL
Dunnet, Caithness. Tel: (01847) 851270

Spectacular scenery on the edge of Dunnet Bay. **Dunnet Head** lochs offer good sport for wild brown trout, run and stocked by the Dunnet Head Angling Association, including **Black Loch**, **Long Loch** and **Sanders Loch**.

Nearby **Loch St Johns** offer boat only angling and prolific mayfly hatches in summer. Association water on the Wick River and Thurso Town Water on the **Thurso River** can produce good, inexpensive sport with salmon and occasional sea trout. Charges from £5 per day for trout and from £10-£25 per day for salmon.

OVERSCAIG LOCHSIDE HOTEL
By Lairg, Sutherland. Tel: (01549) 431203

Ideally situated for **Loch Shin**, upper **River Shin** and numerous lochs and hill burns. The **River Tirry** can give excellent sport with wild brownies following a spate. Loch Shin is one of the largest lochs in Scotland – some 17 miles by up to one mile wide. Brown trout from 8oz to 7lb specimens. Trout fishing from £5-£10 per day.

OYKEL BRIDGE HOTEL

Oykel Bridge, by Lairg, Ross-shire. Tel: (01549) 441218

Another fishing hotel catering almost exclusively for the rods on the **River Oykel**. The fishings on the lower river are let through the hotel as are the lower beats on the Upper Oykel above the falls. Sport is more modestly priced on the upper river and is more often available to visitors than the lower river. Voluntary catch and release has shown a marked improvement, particularly with the spring run in recent years.

River Oykel (lower) Approximately 5 miles of fishing .Exclusive Salmon fishing, normally booked from season to season with occasional vacancies. River Oykel (Upper) : Salmon fishing and improving sea trout rarely need to wade. Beats available through hotel. Good hill loch fishing for brown trout. Book early to avoid disappointment. For prices, please enquire at the hotel.

RHICONICH HOTEL

Rhiconich, By Lairg, Sutherland. Tel: (01971) 321224
Email: rhiconichhotel@cs.com, www.rhiconichhotel.co.uk

Excellent fishing hotel, well positioned for a bewildering choice of trout and salmon fishing. **Rivers Rhiconich** and Shinary and loch fishing for salmon, sea trout and wonderful brown trout fishing from boat and bank.

Lochs and lochans include Aisir Mor, An Eas Ghairbh, Crocach, Cul Na Creige, Dubha, Maithair A'Gharbh Uilt, Na Caise Luachraich, na Claise Carnaich, Na Laire Duibhe, Na Thule, Sandwood, Sgier A'Chadha and Tarbhaidh. Some deeper lochs such as **Na Thull** also support ferox trout to double figures.

Loch Shin offers excellent sport with wild brown trout and a good chance of sea trout and occasional salmon. The River Shin still produces fair numbers of salmon and offers exciting fly sport amidst dramatic scenery, deep runs and rocky banks.

Costs: Boat fishing £10-£25 per day, Bank fishing £5-£10 per day depending on lochs fished. Special courses run at Rhiconich from July 2 – 14 by STA fly fishing/ fly tying instructor Roger Beck. Contact Roger on www.beckfisher.ukf.net

SCOURIE HOTEL

Sutherland IV27 4SX. Tel: (01971) 502396 Fax: (01971) 502423, Email: patrick@scourie-hotel.co.uk
www.scourie-hotel.co.uk

Another superb, comfortable fishing hotel, catering specifically for keen fly fishers looking for wild brown trout fishing at its best.

Lochs include A'Bhagh Ghainmhich, A'Mhuirt, An Easan Uaine, An Fheidh, An Nighe Leathaid, An T-Seana Phuill, An Tigh Shelg and Bad An T-Seabhaig. From £5 per day for bank fishing. Boats available on some lochs. Special angling packages from £260 pp per week inclusive of full board and fishing.

SHIELDAIG LODGE HOTEL

Badachro, Gairloch, Wester Ross. Tel: (01445) 741250
Fax:01445 741305

Excellent base for wild brown trout fishing, with a wide range of lochs and lochans offering superb traditional loch fishing from bank and boat.

Fishing also available on **Loch Maree**, once famed for its dapping techniques and huge sea trout: stocks are again improving and most fishing is done on a catch and release basis by anglers keen to see this magnificent loch returned to its former glory.

Occasional salmon are also taken and the brown trout have increased in size significantly in recent years. Char and ferox are both present Boat fishing on Loch Maree: charges £35 per day for two rods and ghillie/ boatman £35 + gratuity. Hill lochs from £5 per rod per day. For Loch Maree, see also Loch Maree Hotel and Kinlochewe Hotel.

STRATHMORE LODGE

Westerdale, by Halkirk, Caithness KW12 6UP. Tel: (01847) 841227 Fax:(01847) 841264

At the top end of the **Thurso River** in flow country, now punctuated by forestry development. Some fine trout lochs, offering bank and boat fishing, with wild brown trout ranging from half a pound to two pounders and better. Prices on application.

STRATHMORE LODGE

Altnaharra, By Lairg, Sutherland

The lodge has a boat available for sea trout on Loch Hope (south end) and two rods on the lower **Strathmore** river, which receives runs of sea trout and salmon from Loch Hope which peak in July.

Sport is dependent on good water and rain. Booked well in advance and Strathmore Lodge has 5 weeks only. Fishing on **Loch Hope** (South end) £35 per rod per day. Ghillie £35 per day + gratuities.

SUMMER ISLES HOTEL

Achiltibuie, Ullapool, Wester Ross. Tel: (01854) 622282

Magnificent scenery: wild brown trout lochs and lochans, sate streams, with pollack (lythe), rock codling, coalfish (saithe) and flatfish from the saltwater shoreline.

Excellent hill climbing country, ornithology and wilderness treks, but remember to let someone know where you are going. And don't forget the anti-midge spray! Film producer and keen angler, Robert Irvine used to own the hotel and daughter Lucy Irvine ('Castaways') finished writing the book at the hotel. Trout fishing from £5 per rod.

THE BEN LOYAL HOTEL
Tongue, by Lairg, Sutherland IV27 4XE.
Tel: (01847) 611216, Email:
thebenloyalhotel@btinternet.com

Another good fishing hotel, four poster beds and a 'taste of Scotland', with local produce and their own well-stocked vegetable garden. And a choice of drams of course in the bar.

A number of good brown trout lochs including lochs **Cormaic** and **A'Mhuilinn** which produce good bags of trout averaging 8 oz to traditional wet flies.

Jewel in the crown is **Loch Hakel**, with hard fighting, well-presented, free-rising trout averaging 3 to the pound. Flies to try: Soldier Palmer or Red Tag on the bob, Black Pennel, Invicta and silver butcher.

Loch Nam Breac Buidge – the loch of the golden trout - can produce fish up to 2 lbs. Bank fishing only and good wading. Flies to try: Soldier Palmer, Woodcock and mixed, Invicta, Silver March Brown

Loch Craggie shared with Borgie Lodge Hotel and Altnaharra Hotel offers good trout fishing with a chance of occasional salmon which run in from the River Borgie. Bank fishing from £ 3-£5 and boats from £ 10 per day.

THE TONGUE HOTEL
Tongue. Tel: (01847) 611206

Traditional highland hospitality in this comfortable hotel. Ideally situated for the **River Borgie**, numerous lochs and sea trout fishing on the Kyle. Ghillies available, freezing and drying facilities. Trout fishing from £5 per day, salmon fishing from around £15 per rod per day.

Borgie Beach

TIGH AN EILEAN HOTEL
Shieldaig, Wester Ross. Tel: (01520) 755251

Wonderful location, scenery and walking in this remote part of Wester Ross. Good trout fishing on a number of lochs. The **River Balgy**'s short run from **Loch Damh** to the sea can produce good sport with salmon and sea trout. The sea trout run quickly through to the loch and can provide good sport there.

Nearby salmon farms have adversely affected both sea trout and salmon runs into this system, which still produces around 50-80 every year. As with the Loch Maree system, farm escapee also turn up. There is cautious optimism, that with increasing catch and release amongst anglers and better management and control of commercial fish farming on the west coast, that the tide has turned and the we can hope for gradually improving runs of both wild salmon and sea trout throughout the area.

Salmon rods can be booked through the hotel on the River Balgy: Tuesdays, Thursdays and Saturdays only: charges are £22.50 per day. Fly fishing for wild brown trout from £5 per rod per day.

TORWOOD HOUSE HOTEL
Glass, Glenluce, Newton Stewart, Wigtownshire.
Tel: (01581) 300469

Good base for Solway rivers and local lochs, including rivers **Cree**, **Urr** and **Water of Fleet**. Good shore fishing for bass and flatfish from the beaches and codling and mackerel from rocky marks.

The hotel has its own small 1.5 acre stillwater fishery, **Loch Torwood**, offering rainbows and browns averaging around the pound up to 6lbs. Small buzzers and nymphs on floating lines do best on this shallow lochan. Trout from £5 per day and salmon from £10-£15 per day per rod upwards.

ULBSTER ARMS HOTEL
Halkirk, Caithness, KW12 6XY. Tel: (01847) 831641

Situated adjacent to the **Thurso River** at Halkirk, the Ulbster Arms Hotel epitomises the Scottish angling hotel and is the main base for salmon anglers visiting the Thurso River for its splendid fly fishing. Beats are fished on a rotation basis which allows the whole river to be covered in a week. The Ulbster Arms is also an excellent base for trout fishing on 12 hill lochs in the area, 8 with boats, which are regularly stocked with native brown trout. Limestone outcrops ensure a number of the lochs produce wild trout in excess of 2-3 lbs every season.

The Thurso River carries an excellent stock of salmon, with the spring run peaking in April and May, quickly followed by the grilse and summer salmon. The main runs of larger fish occur in the autumn and the season closes on October 5.

For charges and inclusive angling packages, please contat the hotel.

Strathclyde

NORTH STRATHCLYDE

AROS
Location • Aros/Dervaig, Isle of Mull
Species • salmon and sea trout
Permit • Tackle & Books, 11 Main Street, Tobermory, Isle of Mull, Argyll, Tel: 01688 302 336, Fax: 140 (£4 – £14 per rod per day).
• Mrs Ursula Bradley, Old Byre, Dervaig, Isle of Mull, Tel: 01688 400 229 (May have accommodation).
• Mr & Mrs C Scott, Kilmore House, Kilmore, by Oban, Isle of Mull, Argyll, Tel: 01631 770 369(Cottages at Glenaros Farm, with fishing on the Aros River).

AROS LAKE
Location • Aros/Dervaig, Isle of Mull
Species • rainbow trout and brown trout
Permit • Tobermory Angling Association (Bank fishing only, average about a pound, occasional rainbows up to double figures. 2002 Prices on application)
• The Anglers Corner, 114 George Street, Oban, Argyll PA34 5NT, Tel/Fax: 01631 566 374
• Tackle & Books, 11 Main Street, Tobermory, Isle of Mull, Argyll, Tel: 01688 302 336 Fax: 01688 302 140
• Mrs Ursula Bradley, Old Byre, Dervaig, Isle of Mull, Tel: 01688 400 229 (May have accommodation).
• Mr & Mrs C Scott, Kilmore House, Kilmore, by Oban, Isle of Mull, Argyll, Tel: 01631 770 369(Cottages at Glenaros Farm, with fishing on the Aros River).

AWE
Location • Dalmally/Taynuilt
Species • salmon
Permit • Inerawe Fisheries, Taynuilt, Argyll, Tel: 01866 822 446 (£10 – £35 per rod per day, £110 – £140 per week, depending upon dates). Inverawe also has an excellent rainbow fishery.
• Mr Lorne Nelson, Kilmaronaig, Connel, Argyll, Tel: 01631 710 223 (£300 – £500 per beat per week, book well in advance).

• Sir Charles McGriggor, Upper Sonachan, Dalmally, Argyll, Tel: 01866 833 229 (£300 – £500 per beat per week, book well in advance).

BALLYGRANT LOCH
Location • Port Askaig/Bridgend, Isle of Islay
Species • brown trout
Permit • Port Askaig Shop, Port Askaig, Island of Islay, Argyll, Tel: 01496 840 245 (Boats from £10 – £15 per day, bank fishing £3).

BIG FEINN LOCH
Location • Kilmelford, Argyleshire (A816 Kilmelford – Loch Avich road)
Species • brown trout
Permit • The Village Store, Kilmelford, Tel: 01852 200 271 (Fishing is managed by Oban & Lorn AC. Excellent bank fishing in picturesque surroundings. Boat available. 2001 permit prices: Day £6, week-end £12, week £25, 2002 TBC. See also 'Wee Feinn' entry.).
• The Anglers Corner, 114 George Street, Oban, Argyll PA34 5NT, Tel/Fax: 01631 566 374
• David Graham, 9 – 15 Combie Street, Oban, Argyll, Tel: 01631 562 069
• The Anglers Corner, 114 George Street, Oban, Argyll PA34 5NT, Tel/Fax: 01631 566 374

BLACKMILL LOCH
Location • Furnace/Lochgilphead
Species • brown trout
Permit • Forest Enterprise, West Argyll Forest District, Whitegates, Lochgilphead, Argyll, Tel: 01546 602 518, Fax: 603 381(boat available, prices on application).
• A MacGilp, Fyne Tackle, 22 Argyll Street, Lochgilphead, Argyll, Tel: 01546 606 878

CUR
Location • Dunoon/Stachur
Species • salmon, sea trout and brown trout
Permit • Dunoon & District AC, Purdie's of Argyll,
112 Argyll Street, Dunoon,
Tel: 01369 703 232 (Excellent spate river ,
controlled by Dunoon and District AC, with
some deep holding pools above Loch Eck.
Salmon and specimen sea trout tend to run
late in the year from late August onwards.
Bait and fly fishing allowed. Day tickets also
available for River Massan. Prices on
application. The hotel also has boats
on Loch Eck.)
• Coylet Inn, Loch Eck, Dunoon.
Tel: (01369) 840322

DUNOON RESERVOIR
Location • Bishop's Glen, 1 mile from Dunoon
Species • rainbow trout
Permit • Dunoon & District AC, Purdie's of Argyll, 112
Argyll Street, Dunoon, Tel: 01369 703 232
(£7 per rod per day, bank fishing
only).

EDERLINE LOCHS
Location • Kilneuair Church
Species • brown trout
Permit • The Ederline Estate Office, Ford, Argyll,
Tel: 01546 810 215 (30 lochs to choose from,
some of which are stocked and boats are
available. £10 per rod per day for bank
fishing and boats on application.)
• The Ford Hotel, Ford, Argyll, Tel: 01546
810 273/ fax: 230. Permits available as above.

FINNART
Location • Larach Hill, 12 miles from Dunoon
Species • sea trout and salmon
Permit • Dunoon & District AC, Purdie's of Argyll,
112 Argyll Street, Dunoon,
Tel: 01369 703 232 (Occasional salmon, best
after a spate. All legal methods allowed.
2002 permit price on application).

GOIL
Location • Lochgoilhead
Species • salmon and sea trout
Permit • Purdie's of Argyll, 112 Argyll Street, Dunoon,
Tel: 01369 703 232 (Bank fishing, £7 – £10
per day).
• John Lamont, Shorehouse Inn, Lochgoilhead,
Tel: 01301 703 340 (£10 per day, £15 per
week).

IASG LOCH
Location • Glean Mor
Species • brown trout
Permit • The Anglers Corner, 114 George Street,
Oban, Argyll PA34 5NT,
Tel/Fax: 01631 566 374 (Day £6, week-end
£12, week £25. Other lochs include Loch Na
Sailm and Loch A'Cheigein).

INVERAWE FISHERY
Location • Dalmally/Taynuilt
Species • rainbow trout
Permit • Inverawe Fisheries, Taynuilt, Argyll,
Tel: 01866 822 446 (Several excellent stocked
lochs with rainbows up to double figures,
accomodation packages available. Prices on
application).

KINNABUS LOCHS
Location • Port Ellen/Lower Killeyan, Isle of Islay
Species • brown trout
Permit • Ian Laurie Newsagents, 19 Charlotte Street,
Port Ellen, Island of Islay, Argyll,
Tel: 01496 630 2264 (Bank fishing, £5 per
rod per day).

LAGGAN
Location • Bowmore, Isle of Islay
Species • salmon and sea trout
Permit • Mrs Eva Hay, Laggan Estate, Bridge House, by
Bowmore, Island of Islay, Argyll,
Tel: 01496 810 388 (£850 per beat – 2 to 4
rods – per week).
• Brian Wiles, Head Gamekeeper's House,
The Square, Bridgend, Tel: 01496 810 293
(Prices on application, fish run from July,
given good water conditions. Two other spate
streams, the Sorn and Grey as well as a large
number of hill lochs can be fished through
the estate).

LOCH A'BHARRAIN
Location • Kilmore, Isle of Islay
Species • brown trout
Permit • Ian Laurie Newsagents, 19 Charlotte Street,
Port Ellen, Island of Islay, Argyll,
Tel: 01496 630 2264 (Bank fishing, £5 per
rod per day).

LOCH A'CHAORAINN

Location • near Kilmeford

Species • wild brown trout

Permit • The Village Store, Kilmelford, Tel: 01852 200 271 (£10 per rod per day, approx).
- The Anglers Corner, 114 George Street, Oban, Argyll PA34 5NT, Tel/Fax: 01631 566 374 (Day £6, week-end £12, week £25).
- David Graham, 9–15 Combie Street, Oban, Argyll, Tel: 01631 562 069 (£10 per rod per day, approx).

LOCH A'CHEIGEIN

Location • near Kilmelford

Species • brown trout

Permit • The Village Store, Kilmelford, Tel: 01852 200 271 (Fishing is managed by Oban & Lorn AC. 2001 permit prices: Day £6, week-end £12, week £25, 2002 TBC).
- The Anglers Corner, 114 George Street, Oban, Argyll PA34 5NT, Tel/Fax: 01631 566 374 (Day £6, week-end £12, week £25).
- David Graham, 9–15 Combie Street, Oban, Argyll, Tel: 01631 562 069 (Fishing is managed by Oban & Lorn AC. 2001 permit prices: Day £6, week-end £12, week £25, 2002 TBC).

LOCH A'CHLACHAIN

Location • Kilmelford

Species • brown trout

Permit • The Village Store, Kilmelford, Tel: 01852 200 271 (Fishing is managed by Oban & Lorn AC. 2001 permit prices: Day £6, week-end £12, week £25, 2002 TBC).
- The Anglers Corner, 114 George Street, Oban, Argyll PA34 5NT, Tel/Fax: 01631 566 374
- David Graham, 9 – 15 Combie Street, Oban, Argyll, Tel: 01631 562 069

LOCH A'CHREACHAIN

Location • Glean Mor

Species • brown trout

Permit • David Graham, 9–15 Combie Street, Oban, Argyll, Tel: 01631 562 069.
- Oban Sports Centre, 4 Craigard Road, Oban, Argyll, Tel: 01631 563 845.
- The Anglers Corner, 114 George Street, Oban, Argyll PA34 5NT, Tel/Fax: 01631 566 374.

LOCH A'CRUAICHE

Location • Oban/Lochgilphead

Species • brown trout

Permit • David Graham, 9/15 Combie Street, Oban, Argyll, Tel: 01631 562 069 (Fishing is managed by Oban & Lorn AC. 2001 permit prices: Day £6, week-end £12, week £25, 2002 TBC).
- Oban Sports Centre, 4 Craigard Road, Oban, Argyll, Tel: 01631 563 845
- The Anglers Corner, 114 George Street, Oban, Argyll PA34 5NT, Tel/Fax: 01631 566 374

LOCH AIRIGH-SHAMRAIDH

Location • Musdale Farm

Species • trout

Permit • David Graham, 9/15 Combie Street, Oban, Argyll, Tel: 01631 562 069(Fishing is managed by Oban & Lorn AC. 2001 permit prices: Day £6, week-end £12, week £25, 2002 TBC).
- Oban Sports Centre, 4 Craigard Road, Oban, Argyll, Tel: 01631 563 845
- The Anglers Corner, 114 George Street, Oban, Argyll PA34 5NT, Tel/Fax: 01631 566 374

LOCH A'MHINN

Location • near Kilmeford

Species • rainbow trout and wild brown trout

Permit • David Graham, 9/15 Combie Street, Oban, Argyll, Tel: 01631 562 069 (Bank fishing only. Fishing is managed by Oban & Lorn AC. 2002 permit prices TBC).
- Oban Sports Centre, 4 Craigard Road, Oban, Argyll, Tel: 01631 563 845
- The Village Store, Kilmelford, Tel: 01852 200 271
- The Anglers Corner, 114 George Street, Oban, Argyll PA34 5NT, Tel/Fax: 01631 566 374

LOCH AN DAIMH

Location • near Kilmeford

Species • brown trout

Permit • David Graham, 9/15 Combie Street, Oban, Argyll, Tel: 01631 562 069 (Bank fishing only. Fishing is managed by Oban & Lorn AC. 2002 permit prices TBC).
- The Anglers Corner, 114 George Street, Oban, Argyll PA34 5NT, Tel/Fax: 01631 566 374

LOCH AN LOSGAINN BEAG

Location • Kilmelford
Species • brown trout
Permit • David Graham, 9–15 Combie Street, Oban,
Argyll, Tel: 01631 562 069 (Bank fishing only.
Fishing is managed by Oban & Lorn AC. 2002
permit prices TBC).
• The Anglers Corner, 114 George Street,
Oban, Argyll PA34 5NT,
Tel/Fax: 01631 566 374

LOCH AN LOSGAINN MOR

Location • Kilmelford
Species • brown trout
Permit • David Graham, 9/15 Combie Street, Oban,
Argyll, Tel: 01631 562 069 (Bank fishing only.
Fishing is managed by Oban & Lorn AC. 2002
permit prices TBC
• Oban Sports Centre, 4 Craigard Road, Oban,
Argyll, Tel: 01631 563 845 (Prices as above).
• Ford Hotel, Ford, Argyll, tel; 01546 810 273,
fax: 230 (Prices as above).

LOCH A'PHEARSAIN

Location • Oban/Lochgilphead
Species • brown trout and char
Permit • David Graham, 9/15 Combie Street, Oban,
Argyll, Tel. 01631 562 069 (Bank fishing only.
Fishing is managed by Oban & Lorn AC. 2002
permit prices TBC
• The Anglers Corner, 114 George Street,
Oban, Argyll PA34 5NT,
Tel/Fax: 01631 566 374

LOCH ARDNAVE

Location • Bridgend, Isle of Islay
Species • brown trout
Permit • Brian Wiles, Head gamekeeper's House,Islay
House Square, Bidgend, Islay,
Tel: 01496 681 293

LOCH ASCOG

Location • Argyll
Species • brown trout and rainbow trout
Permit • Kyles of Bute AC, Tighnabruiaich PA21 2BE,
Tel: 01700 811 486

LOCH ASSAPOL

Location • Bunessan, Isle of Mull
Species • salmon, sea trout and brown trout
Permit • Argyll Arms Hotel, Bunessan,
Tel: 01681 700 240

LOCH AVICH

Location • Taynuilt
Species • brown trout and rainbow trout
Permit • Norman Clark, 11 Dalavich, by Taynuilt
Argyll, Tel: 01866 844 209
(Bank fishing £3 per rod, boat with outboard
and fuel £30, boat only, £20).
• Croggan Crafts, Dalmally, Argyll,
Tel: 01838 200 201OCH

LOCH AWE

Location • Lochgilphead
Species • brown trout, ferox, char, escapee rainbow
trout, salmon, sea trout, pike & perch
Permit • T C Macnair Esq, Secretary, Loch Awe
Improvement Association, Boswell House,
Argyll Square, Oban, PA34 4BD
(Minimum donation of £5 for membership,
include name and address).
• Norman Clark, 11 Dalavich, by Taynuilt,
Argyll, Tel: 01866 844 209
(Bank fishing £3 per rod, boat with outboard
and fuel £30, boat only, £20).
• The Anglers Corner, 114 George Street,
Oban, Argyll PA34 5NT,
Tel/Fax: 01631 566 374 (Prices as above).

LOCH BEALACH GHEARRAN

Location • Furnace/Lochgilphead
Species • brown trout
Permit • David Graham, 9 –15 Combie Street, Oban,
Argyll, Tel: 01631 562 069
(Bank fishing £3 per rod, boat with outboard
and fuel £30, boat only, £20).
• Oban Sports Centre, 4 Craigard Road, Oban,
Argyll, Tel: 01631 563 845
(Prices as above).

LOCH CAM

Location • Loch Awe
Species • brown trout, ferox
Permit • T C Macnair Esq, Secretary, Loch Awe
Improvement Association, Boswell House,
Argyll Square, Oban, PA34 4BD
(Minimum donation of £5 for membership,
please include name and address).

LOCH DUBH-MOR

Location • Barcaldine/Inversragan
Species • brown trout
Permit • Ford Hotel, Ford, Argyll, Tel: 01546 810 273,
Fax: 230 (Bank fishing £3 per rod, boat with
outboard and fuel £30, boat only, £20).

LOCH ECK
Location • near Dunoon
Species • salmon, sea trout, brown trout and powan
Species • Coylet Inn, Loch Eck, Dunoon.
Tel: (01369) 840322
(Fly fishing for salmon, sea trout and brown trout. Powan are also present but rarely caught and are preserved. Trolling for migratory fish allowed. Boat hire available from hotel. Day tickets also available for the loch and for Rivers Massan and Cur from Dunoon and District AC. Prices on application.)
• Dunoon & District Angling Club, Ashgrove, 28 Royal Crescent, Dunoon, Argyll, Tel: 01369 705 732

LOCH FAD
Location • Rothesay/Isle of Bute, Straad
Species • brown trout and rainbow trout
Species • Isle of Bute Trout Company Ltd., Ardmaleish, Isle of Bute, Tel: 01700 504 871 (Prices on application).

LOCH FINLAGGAN
Location • Port Askaig/Bridgend, Isle of Islay
Species • wild brown trout
Permit • Islay Estate Office, Bowmore, Tel: 01496 810221 (Numerous small brown trout, £3 per day, £12 per week, f17 per season, £14 boat)

LOCH FRISA
Location • Isle of Mull
Species • salmon, sea trout and brown trout
Permit • Tackle & Books, 11 Main Street, Tobermory, Isle of Mull, Argyll, Tel: 01688 302 336, fax: 140 (£3 per rod per day. Mull's largest loch (5 miles long) containing excellent brown trout up to 5 lbs and more: occasional salmon and sea trout.).
• Archibald Brown & Son, 21 Main Street, Tobermory, Isle of Mull, Argyll, Tel: 01688 302 020(Prices as above).
• Forest Enterprise, Aros, Isle of Mull, Argyll, Tel: 01680 300 346(Prices as above).

LOCH GLASHAN
Location • Furnace/Lochgilphead
Species • brown trout and escapee salmon smolts
Permit • Forest Enterprise, West Argyll Forest District, Whitegates, Lochgilphead, Argyll, Tel: 01546 602 518 /fax: 603 381 (£3.50 per rod per day. Beware fluctating water levels).

• A MacGilp, Fyne Tackle, 22 Argyll Street, Lochgilphead, Argyll, Tel: 01546 606 878 (£3.50 per rod per day).

LOCH GLEANN A'BHEARRAIDH
Location • Kilbride and Leargs
Species • brown trout
Permit • The Barn Bar, Cologin, Leargs, by Oban, Argyll, Tel: 01631 564 501 (£6 per rod per day).

LOCH GULLY
Location • Lochgilphead
Species • brown trout
Permit • The Anglers Corner, 114 George Street, Oban, Argyll PA34 5NT, Tel/Fax: 01631 566 374 (Oban & Lorn Angling Club, prices on application).
• David Graham, 9/15 Combie Street, Oban, Argyll, Tel: 01631 562 069 (Prices on application).
• Oban Sports Centre, 4 Craigard Road, Oban, Argyll, Tel: 01631 563 845 (Prices on application).

LOCH NELL
Location • Barran, near Oban
Species • salmon, sea trout, brown trout and char
Permit • The Anglers Corner, 114 George Street, Oban, Argyll PA34 5NT, Tel/Fax: 01631 566 374 (Day £6, week-end £12, week £25).
• David Graham, 9/15 Combie Street, Oban, Argyll, Tel: 01631 562 069 (Prices on application).
• Oban Sports Centre, 4 Craigard Road, Oban, Argyll, Tel: 01631 563 845 (Prices on application).

LOCH RIGH MOR
Location • Craighouse/Ardlussa, Isle of Jura
Species • brown trout
Permit • John Connors, Craighouse, Isle of Jura, Argyll, Tel: 01496 820292 (Day tickets £5 through the estate)

LOCH SEIL
Location • Lochgilphead
Species • brown trout
Permit • Mrs E Mellor, Barndromin Farm, Kilninver, by Oban, Argyll, Tel: 01852 316 273 (Mainly small brown trout, formerly excellent sea trout loch, £5 per day.)

LOCH SOIR
Location • Oban/Kilmore
Species • brown trout
Permit • The Village Store, Kilmelford,
Tel: 01852 200271 (£10 per day, wade with
caution)
• The Anglers Corner, 114 George Street,
Oban, Argyll PA34 5NT,
Tel/Fax: 01631 566 374 (Charges as above).
• David Graham, 9/15 Combie Street, Oban,
Argyll, Tel: 01631 562 069
(Charges as above).
• Oban Sports Centre, 4 Craigard Road, Oban,
Argyll, Tel: 01631 563 845
(Charges as above).

LOCH TARSAN
Location • Glen Lean
Species • brown trout
Permit • Eleraig Highland Chalets, Kininver, by Oban,
Argyll, Tel/Fax: 01852 200 225
(£5 per rod per day (bank fishing). Free to
guests of Eleraig Chalets).

LOCH TRALAIG
Location • Oban/Kilmelford
Species • brown trout
Permit • Eleraig Highland Chalets, Kininver, by Oban,
Argyll, Tel/Fax: 01852 200 225
(Bank fishing £5 per rod per day. Free to
guests of Eleraig Chalets)
• Peter Menzies, Corylorn Farm, Kilninver, by
Oban, Argyll, Tel: 01852 200 221
(Bank fishing £5 per rod).

MACKAYS LOCH
Location • Oban
Species • rainbow trout and brown trout
Permit • The Anglers Corner, 114 George Street,
Oban, Argyll PA34 5NT,
Tel/Fax: 01631 566 374 (Put and take fishery,
trout average 1.5 lbs. £22 per rod per
day,£10 per boat, 2 rods

MASSAN
Location • Garrachra Glen/Eckford
Species • salmon and sea trout
Permit • Purdie's of Argyll, 112 Argyll Street, Dunoon,
Tel: 01369 703 232 (Bait fishing allowed and
the river fishes best after a spate. Fly rod access
difficult. £7 per rod per day).
• Dunoon & District Angling Club, Ashgrove,
28 Royal Crescent, Dunoon, Argyll,
Tel: 01369 705 732ORCHY

ORCHY
Location • Taynuilt/Tyndrum
Species • salmon and sea trout
Permit • L Campbell, Arichastilch, Glen Orchy,
Dalmally, Argyll, Tel: 01838 200 282
(£15 – £50 per rod per day).
• Croggan Crafts, Dalmally, Argyll,
Tel: 01838 200201 (£15 – £50 per rod
per day).

OUDE RESERVOIR
Location • Oban/Kilmelford
Species • brown trout
Permit • The Anglers Corner, 114 George Street,
Oban, Argyll PA34 5NT,
Tel/Fax: 01631 566 374
(Charges as above).
• David Graham, 9/15 Combie Street, Oban,
Argyll, Tel: 01631 562 069
(Charges as above).
• Oban Sports Centre, 4 Craigard Road, Oban,
Argyll, Tel: 01631 563 845
(Charges as above).

RUEL
Location • Colintravie/Strachur
Species • salmon and sea trout
Permit • Glendaruel Hotel, Clachan of Glendaruel,
Argyll, Tel: 01369 820 274 (£15 per rod
per day, fishes best after a spate).
• Purdie's of Argyll, 112 Argyll Street, Dunoon,
Tel: 01369 703 232 (£12 per rod per day).
• Dunoon & District Angling Club, Ashgrove,
28 Royal Crescent, Dunoon, Argyll,
Tel: 01369 705 732(£12 per rod per
day).

WEE FEINN LOCH
Location • Glean Mor
(A816 Kilmelford – Loch Avich road)
Species • brown trout
(Managed by Oban & Lorn AC, this loch lies
west of and close by Big Loch Feinn: see also
'Big Feinn' entry).
Permit • The Anglers Corner, 114 George Street,
Oban, Argyll PA34 5NT,
Tel/Fax: 01631 566 374
(Day £6, week-end, £12, week £25).
• David Graham, 9/15 Combie Street, Oban,
Argyll, Tel: 01631 562 069
(Charges as above).
• Oban Sports Centre, 4 Craigard Road, Oban,
Argyll, Tel: 01631 563 845
(Charges as above).

SOUTH STRATHCLYDE

ANNICK
Location • Kilmarnock
Species • salmon, sea trout and brown trout
Permit • T C McCabe, 8 East Park Crescent, Kilmaurs, Tel: 01563 538 652(Important tributary of the River Irvine. The River Irvine Angling Improvement Association has done excellent work on this system, to enhance runs of salmon and sea trout. £8 – £20 per rod per day depending upon dates).
• P & R Torbet, 15 Strand Street, Kilmarnock, Tel: 01563 541 734 (Prices as above).
• J Steven, 25 New Road, Galston, Tel: 01563 822 096 (Prices as above).

ARDGOWAN FISHERY
Location • Greenock/Largs
Species • brown trout and rainbow trout
Permit • Ardgowan Fisheries, Shielhill, by Greenock, Tel: 01475 522492, mobile: 07000 784775.(£15 per day (5 fish), £10 half day, any 4 hours (2 fish), £2 per session per angler for use of boat. £18 parent and child. Trout average 2lbs.)

AYR
Location • Ayr/Kilmarnock
Species • salmon, sea trout and brown trout
Permit • Linwood & Johnstone, Newsagents, The Cross, Mauchline, Ayrshire, Tel: 01290 550 219 (£6 – £20 per rod per day).
• J Gibson, General Store, Main Street, Auchinleck, Ayrshire, Tel: 01290 420 396 (Prices as above).
• Auchinleck Anglers' Association, G McClue, 61 Coal Road, Auchinleck, Ayrshire, Tel: 01290 423 491 (Prices as above).

BURNFOOT RESERVOIR
Location • Glasgow
Species • brown trout
Permit • P & R Torbet, 15 Strand Street, kilmarnock, Tel: 01563 541734 (Fishery managed by Kilmaurs AC, price on application)

CARMEL WATER
Location • Tributary of River Irvine
Species • salmon, sea trout and brown trout
Permit • T C McCabe, 8 East Park Crescent, Kilmaurs, Tel: 01563 538 652 (£8 – £20 per rod per day depending upon dates).
• P & R Torbet, 15 Strand Street, Kilmarnock, Tel: 01563 541 734 (Prices as above).
• J Steven, 25 New Road, Galston, Tel: 01563 822 096 (Prices as above).

CESSNOCK WATER
Location • Tributary of River Irvine
Species • salmon, sea trout and brown trout
Permit • T C McCabe, 8 East Park Crescent, Kilmaurs, Tel: 01563 538 652 (£8 – £20 per rod per day depending upon dates).
• P & R Torbet, 15 Strand Street, Kilmarnock, Tel: 01563 541 734 (Prices as above).
• J Steven, 25 New Road, Galston, Tel: 01563 822 096 (Prices as above).

CLYDE
Location • Glasgow
Species • brown trout, salmon and sea trout
Permit • The Anglers' Rendezvous, 18 Saltmarket, Glasgow, Tel: 0141 552 4662 (£5 per rod per day, concessions £3)
• Bruce MacMartin, Tackle & Guns, 920 Pollockshaws Road, Glasgow, Tel: 0141 632 2005(£5 per rod per day, concessions £3)
• William Robertson & Co. Ltd., 61 Miller Street, Glasgow, Tel: 0141 221 6687. (£5 per rod per day, concessions £3)
• Brian Peterson, The Fishing Shop, 24 Union Street, Greenock, Tel: 01475 888 085 (£5 per rod per day, concessions £3).
• Archie MacKinlay, Dunrod Angling Association, 2 Kincaid Street, Greenock, Tel: 01475 636 076 (£5 per rod per day, concessions £3)

COMMORE FISHERY
Species • rainbow trout
Permit • Commore Fishery tel.01505 850 572 (Prices on application)

GARNOCK
Location • Dalry/Kilwining
Species • salmon and sea trout
Permit • R Russel, R & T Cycles, Glengarnoch, by Kilbirnie, Tel: 01505 682 191 (£6 per rod per day, approx).
• McGuigan's Newsagents, 43 New Street, Dalry, Tel: 01294 832 360 (£15 per rod per day).
• The Craft Shop, Main Street, Kilwinning, Tel: 01475 674 237 (Prices as above) (Kilbirnie AC and Dalry Garnock AC. Principal tributaries Lugton Water and Rye Water. over/

Garnock, cont'd

Garnock salmon tickets £8 – £20 per rod per day depending on dates. Fishes best from July onwards after a spate).

GLEN WATER
Location • Tributary of River Irvine
Species • salmon, sea trout and brown trout
Permit • T C McCabe, 8 East Park Crescent, Kilmaurs, Tel: 01563 538 652 (£8 – £20 per rod per day depending upon dates).
• P & R Torbet, 15 Strand Street, Kilmarnock, Tel: 01563 541 734 (Prices as above).
• J Steven, 25 New Road, Galston, Tel: 01563 822 096 (Prices as above).

GRYFE
Location • Kilmacolm/Bridge of Weir
Species • salmon, sea trout and brown trout
Permit • Bruce MacMartin, Tackle & Guns, 920 Pollockshaws Road, Glasgow, Tel: 0141 632 2005 (Reserved for club members, guest tickets may be available).

GRYFE RESERVOIR
Location • Greenock/Largs
Species • brown trout
Permit • Archie MacKinlay, Dunrod AA, 2 Kincaid Street, Greenock, Tel: 01475 636076.

HARELAW DAM (RESERVOIR)
Location • Greenock/Kilmacolm
Species • brown trout
Permit • Brian Peterson, The Fishing Shop, 24 Union Street, Greenock PA16 8DD, Tel: 01475 888085. (£5 per rod per day, managed by Port Glasgow AC, stocked trout average half a pound).

HAYLIE FISHERY
Location • Largs/Kilbirnie
Species • brown trout, rainbow trout and American brook trout (fontinalis)
Permit • John Weir, Haylie Trout Fishery, Largs, tel. 01475 676 005

HOWWOOD FISHERY
Location • Johnstone/Dalry
Species • brown trout, rainbow trout and blue rainbow
Permit • John Cassells, Howwood Fishery, Bowfield Road, Howwood, Renfrewshire, Tel: 01505 702688 (£15 per rod per day (5 fish), £10 per 4 hour session (3 fish), £8 catch & release. 3 boats available, price on application)

IORSA
Location • Adrossan/Brodick
Species • salmon, sea trout and brown trout
Permit • Estate Office, Dougarie, Isle of Arran, Tel: 01770 840 259. Prices on application. Small spate stream in north of island flowing westward, fed by Loch Tanna. Small flies and trout rod tactics here).

IRVINE
Location • Kilmarnock
Species • salmon, sea trout & brown trout
Permit • T C McCabe, 8 East Park Crescent, Kilmaurs, Tel: 01563 538 652 (Important tributary of the River Irvine. The River Irvine Angling Improvement Association has done excellent work on this system, to enhance runs of salmon and sea trout. £8 – £20 per rod per day depending upon dates).
• P & R Torbet, 15 Strand Street, Kilmarnock, Tel: 01563 541 734 (Prices as above).
• J Steven, 25 New Road, Galston, Tel: 01563 822 096 (Prices as above).
• Alfi Coli, Game Sport of Ayr, 60 Sandgate, Ayr, Tel: 01292 263 822
• Linwood & Johnstone, Newsagents, The Cross, Mauchline, Ayrshire. Tel: 01290 550 219

KELVIN
Location • Glasgow
Species • brown trout
Permit • J & B Angling, 37 Eastside, Kirkintilloch, Tel: 0141 775 0083 (Season ticket £10).

KILBIRNIE LOCH
Location • Kilbirnie
Species • rainbow trout, ferox, roach and pike
Permit • Victor Donati, Hon. Secretary, 11 Briery Court, Kilbirnie, Tel: 01505 683923 (Excellent coarse fishery with specimen pike and good roach, as well as stocked rainbows. Day tickets £6.)

KILLEARN FISHERY
Location • Killearn House
Species • rainbow trout
Permit • David Young, Killearn Fishery, Killearn Home Farm, Killearn, Glasgow G63 9QH, Tel: 01360 550 994 (2.5 acre put and take fishery, with rainbows between 1.75 – 6 lbs. 4 hour session £15 (3 fish), £21 (5 fish limit) then catch and release, barbless flies only. Fishery is open from 9am – 6pm).

LAWFIELD DAM
Location • near Greenock
Species • rainbow trout and brown trout
Permit • Bill Mcfern, Lawfield Fishery, Kilmacolm, Renfrewshire, Tel: 01505 874182. (small stocked fishery with trout average 2 lbs. Bank fishing only. £15 for 8 hours (5 fish), £10 for 4 hours (3 fish). Catch and release after limit.)

LOCH ARKLET
Location • Stirling/Trossachs
Species • brown trout
Permit • W M Meikle, 41 Buchany, Doune, Perthsire, Tel: 01786 841692 (Boat £20 per day, electric motor hire £7 per day. See also Loch Katrine.)

LOCH BELSTON
Location • Sinclairston, B7046 Drongan/Skares road
Species • rainbow trout
Permit • Alfi Coli, Game Sports of Ayr, 60 Sandgate, Ayr KA7 1BX, Tel/Fax: 01292 263822.
• Linwood & Johnstone, Newsagents, The Cross, Mauchline, Ayrshire, Tel: 01290 550219. (Boat and bank fishing, rainbows average 1.5 lbs. 2002 prices on application).

LOCH BRADAN
Location • Dalmellington/Dailly
Species • brown trout
Permit • Caldons Campsite, Bregrennan, Newton Stewart, Wigtownshire, Tel: 01671 840218
• Forestry Commission, Creebridge, Newton Stewart, Wigtownshire, Tel: 01671 402420
• Kirrieoughtree Visitor Centre, Tel: 01671 402165.
• Forestry Commission, 21 King Street, Castle Douglas, Tel: 01556 502626. (£6.50 per rod per day, under 16 £3 per day).

LOCH BRECKBOWIE
Location • Dalmellington/Dailly
Species • brown trout
Permit • Caldons Campsite, Bregrennan, Newton Stewart, Wigtownshire, Tel: 01671 840218
• Forestry Commission, Creebridge, Newton Stewart, Wigtownshire, Tel: 01671 402420
• Kirrieoughtree Visitor Centre, Tel: 01671 402165.
• Forestry Commission, 21 King Street, Castle Douglas, Tel: 01556 502626. (£6.50 per rod per day, under 16 £3 per day).

LOCH KATRINE
Location • Stronachlachar
Species • brown trout
Permit • W M Meikle, 41 Buchany, Doune, Perthsire, Tel: 01786 841692 (Boat £20 per day, electric motor hire £7 per day. Concessions for OAPs and unemployed).

MACHRIE
Location • Brodick, Isle of Arran (west)
Species • salmon, sea trout and brown trout
Permit • Arran AA. Check with tourist Office, Brodick Pier, Tel: 01770 840 259 (spate river which fishes best in late summer, on a dropping river, Trout fly rod and small doubles, tubes produce best results).

NEWMILL DEER FARM FISHERY
Location • Lanark/Forth
Species • rainbow trout, stocked salmon
Permit • Dave Buchanan, Newhouse Trout & Deer Farm, Cleghorn by Lanark, Tel: 01555 870730. (£16 per rod per day (6 fish limit) £11.50 for 4 hours (3 fish limit) Big rainbows to double figures. Bait pool as well as fly fishing).

PORT-NA-LOCHAN
Location • Kilpatrick
Species • rainbow trout
Permit • Kinloch Hotel, Blackwaterfoot, Isle of Arran, Tel: 01770 860 444 (£10.50 per session, 4 hourrs (2 fish). Fishing tackle hire).
• Mr & Mrs C Bannatyne, Fairhaven, Catacol Isle of Arran, Tel: 01770 830 237 (Prices as above).

RAITH & PRESTWICK RESERVOIR
Location • Raith/Monkton
Species • rainbow trout
Permit • W & A Newall, Newsagents, 29 Main Street, Monkton, Ayrshire, Tel: 01292 479 175 (Prestwick reservoir is a 12 acre fishery and Raith is a smaller stocked fishery, with rainbows averaging over the pound, up to 4lbs. Further information from John Murphy, the Secretary, Prestwick Reservoir AC, 5 Raith terrace, Prestwick, SAE please).

SLIDDERY WATER
Location • Sliddery, Glen Scorrodale, Isle of Arran
Species • salmon, sea trout & brown trout
Permit • Arran AA. Check with Tourist Office, Brodick Pier, Tel: 01770 302140. (Arran AA manage the fishings on Sliddery and a number of other smaller streams on the island. Day tickets and week tickets available. Price on application. Small flies and trout rod adequate for this stream, which fishes best on a clearing spate in late summer.)

SPRINGWATER FISHERY
Location • Coylton Dalrymple
Species • rainbow trout
Permit • Daniel Wilson, Springwater Fishery, Drumgabs Farm, by Dalrymple, Ayrshire, Tel: 01292 560343. (3 separate pools restocked daily. Bank fishing only. Club house serves snacks.)

STINCHAR
Location • Girvan
Species • salmon and sea trout
Permit • Knockdolian water, The Factor, Knockdolian Estate, Alderside, Colmonell, Ayrshire, Tel: 01465 881 237(£15 – £90 depending upon dates, book well in advance. This is an excellent salmon and sea trout water with some beautiful and scenic fly water. Fishes best from mid-summer and into autumn, particularly following a dropping river).

• Bardrochat Water, Robert Anderson, Bardrochat Estate, Oaknowe, Colmonell, Ayrshire, Tel: 01465 881 202 (£15 – £90 depending upon dates, book well in advance).
• Dalreoch Water, Douglas Overend, Dalreoch Lodge, Colmonell, Ayrshire, Tel: 01465 881 214 (£15 – £90 depending upon dates, book well in advance).
• Hallow Chapel, Donald Trelford, Colmonell Ayrshire, Tel: 01465 881 249(£15 – £90 depending upon dates, book well in advance).
• Almont Beat, Donald Love, Almont, Pinwherry, Ayrshire, Tel: 01465 841 637 (Prices as above).
• Kirkhill Water, Mrs Shankland, Colmonell, Ayrshire, Tel: 01465 881 220 (Prices as above).
• Alasdair Ash, The Boar's Head Hotel, Colmonell, Ayrshire, Tel: 01465 881 371 (Call for advice re vacancies).

STRATHCLYDE COUNTRY PARK LOCH
Location • Motherwell
Species • brown trout
Permit • Strathclyde Country Park, 366 Hamilton Road, Motherwell, Tel: 01698 266 155 (£1.80 per rod per day).

ARDBRECKNISH HOUSE LOCH AWE
South Lochaweside, By Dalmally, Argyll PA33 1BH. Tel:
(01866) 833223, ardbreck01@aol.com
Loch Awe Boats: (01866) 833256

West Highland country house dating from 17th century
overlooking **Loch Awe**. Self catering apartments and
detached cottages. Rates from £135 per week and £800
for angling parties/ groups of 12. Unrivalled wild brown
trout fishing on Loch Awe, including the new British record,
a magnificent ferox of 30 lbs 8 oz, taken in 2000. Rainbow
trout, pike, char and occasional salmon, mainly late season.

BALLOCH HOTEL
Balloch, Loch Lomond. Tel: (01389) 752579

Good base for the 'Big Loch' offering excellent boat fishing
for salmon and sea trout, as well as coarse fishing for
specimen perch, roach and double figure pike. The **River
Leven** drains from the loch, and offers good budget
fishing for salmon and sea trout. Boating stations include
Macfarlane & Sons at Balmaha (01360) 870273, ideal for
the Endrick bank and good salmon drifts. Boats with
outboards £35 per day.

BOAR'S HEAD HOTEL
Colmonell. Tel: (01465) 881371

Good base for **River Stinchar**, one of Ayrshire's best
salmon rivers, offering particularly good fly fishing and
autumn sport. Contact Alasdair Ash at the hotel for
assistance in bookings and fishing lets, by arrangement with
various estates. Expect to pay from £15 in early season,
increasing through summer months to £90 or more in the
autumn per day per rod.

CLACHAN INN
10 Main Street, St John's Town of Dalry. Tel: (01644)
430241

Trout fishing available on **Carsfad Reservoir**,
Earlstoun Loch and **Stroan Loch**. Stocked rainbow
and brown trout. Boat and bank fishing from £5 per rod
per day plus boat charges. Carsfad Reservoir forms part of
the River Ken system and also produces large pike as well
as rainbows. Charges £10 per day and juniors £5.

COYLET INN
Loch Eck, Dunoon. Tel: (01369) 840322

Georgian coaching inn set on the banks of **Loch Eck**.
Fishing available on Loch Eck, fly fishing for salmon, sea
trout and brown trout. Trolling for migratory fish allowed.
Boat hire available and best for sport, although day tickets
also available for bank fishing. Day tickets also available for
Rivers Massan and **Cur** from Dunoon and District AC.
Both rivers fish best following spate conditions and can
produce both salmon and large sea trout. Charges £25 for
boats on Loch Eck, bank fishing £5 per day. Rivers Cur and
Massan £7 per day.

FORD HOTEL
Ford, By Taynuilt, Argyll. Tel: (01546) 810273 Fax: 01546)
810230

Comfortable, well-managed fishing hotel. **Loch Awe**
offers excellent sport with brown trout, escapee rainbows,
specimen pike and huge ferox. the new British Record trout
of 34lbs 8 oz came from Loch Awe in 2000. The previous
record stood at 25lbs 6oz taken in 1996. Some huge
rainbows have been taken in the past, up to 30lbs. The
hotel also has fishing on Cam Loch, a 12 acre fishery lying
between Loch Awe and Loch Avich and a series of other
lochans.
   Charges from £3 per day. Boats around £30 per day
including outboards and fuel.

GLENDARUEL HOTEL
Clachan of Glendaruel, Argyll PA22 3AA. Tel: (01369)
820274

Fishing for salmon and sea trout on the **River Ruel**,
affected nowadays by afforestation and prone to sudden
spates and quick acidic run-off. Also plagued in the past
with escapee rainbow trout from saltwater cages, which
are a menace with salmon and sea trout fry. Migratory fish
appear from late May early June, with the sea trout arriving
first.
   Fishing is leased by the Dunoon & District AC: charges
£12 per day. Charges for hotel fishings £15 per day
per rod.

KAMES HOTEL
Kames, Tighnabruaich, Argyll. Tel: (01700) 811489

Fishing on **Loch Asgog**, **Dam Lochs** and **Powder
Dam**. These fisheries are stocked and managed by Kyles of
Bute Angling Club, producing rainbow and brown trout,
averaging 10oz-12oz. Bank fishing fly only except for
Power Dam, where bait fishing is also allowed. Charges £5
per rod per day.

KILFINAN HOTEL
Kilfinan, By Tighnabruaich, Argyll. Tel: (01700) 821201

Comfortable hotel set in fine Highland scenery and sea
lochs. Good loch fishing for brown trout and the **Kilfinan
Burn** offers budget salmon and sea trout fishing from late
May through to autumn. This is a spate river which fishes
best late in the season, and produces around 20-30 fish in
a season. Charges £15 per day per rod.

KINLOCH HOTEL
Blackwaterfoot, Isle of Arran.
Tel: (01770) 860444

Arran has been called 'Scotland in miniature' and offers
good sea angling, excellent golf and a number of streams,
where in the right conditions and with rain, you can catch
salmon and occasional sea trout. This is light tackle country
with the best chance immediately after a spate; early late

are also favoured taking times. Kinloch Hotel has access to Port Na Lochan, a small put and take fishery stocked with rainbow trout averaging 1.5lbs offering bank fishing with fly and bait. £10.50 per 4 hour session and 2 fish. The hotel has fishing tackle for hire. Machrie Water fishes best after a spate and produces around 60 salmon and 40 sea trout each season. Small flies and single handed rod is all you require. And of course water! Permits available from the Machrie Water Bailiff (01770) 840241. Salmon and sea trout rod charges from £110-£200 per rod week.

KIRKTON INN
Dalrymple, Ayrshire. Tel: (01292) 560241,
www.kirktoninn.co.uk

Comfotable hotel with cosy restaurant and bar. Freezer facilities and drying rooms. Good base to fish the **River Doon** and other Ayrshire rivers and lochs, including **Loch Doon**. Reasonably priced salmon fishing: season runs from February to October, peaking in late summer and autumn. Few salmon are taken on the Doon before June and sea trout fishing has declined in recent years. Tuition is available.

KYLE OF BUTE HOTEL
Tighnabruaich, Argyll. Tel: (01700) 811674

Fishing on scenic 40 acres fishery **Loch Asgog**, **Dam Lochs** and **Powder Dam**. Stocked and managed by Kyles of Bute Angling Club, the lochs produce rainbow and brown trout, averaging 10oz-12oz. Bank fishing fly only except for Power Dam, where bait fishing is also allowed. Charges £5 per rod per day.

MILTON PARK HOTEL
St. John's Town of Dalry . Tel: (01644) 430286

The hotel has its own exclusive loch. Scenic **Barscobie Loch** covers around 13 acres and offers boat fishing for excellent brown trout, stocked rainbows and brook trout. Charges are £15 per day for two rods. Fly fishing by arrangement on lochs Brack, Moss Roddock and Earlstoun Loch on the River Dee system. Charges from £15-£17 per rod per day.

MORAR HOTEL
Morar, By Mallaig. Tel: (01687) 462346

Wonderful scenery and good fishing. Salmon and sea trout have declined in recent years due to intensive fish farming activity, but still some excellent wild brown trout in hill lochs. Magnificent **Loch Morar**, reputedly the deepest freshwater lake in Europe is 12 miles long and up to 1.5 miles in width. While both salmon and sea trout are in decline, the loch still produces in the order of 20-30 salmon each season and good brown trout. Fishing charges, please apply to the hotel.

PORTSONACHAN HOTEL
by Dalmally, Argyll. Tel: (01866) 833224

First class hotel on the lochside, with excellent restaurant and good cellar. An excellent bases from which to fish **Loch Awe**, whether for trolling for the giant ferox or the equally huge pike. Very good traditional loch-style fishing for brown trout as well as the ubiquitous rainbow trout escapees which while fewer in number can grow to double figures.

SHOREHOUSE INN
Lochgoilhead. Tel: (01301) 703340

Fishing available on River Goil which enters the saltwater at **Lochgoilhead**. Good spate stream for salmon and occasional sea trout. Some 30 fish taken each season. Fly fishing and bait allowed in high water conditions. Favourite pools include the Twin Tree Pool and Minister's Pool. Charges £15 per day and £50 per week.

THE ISLE OF COLL HOTEL
Arinigour. Argyll. Tel: (01879) 230334

Free fishing to residents of this traditional hotel on Loch Anlaimh and other lochs and lochans on the island. Brown trout in Anlaimh average around half a pound with occasional larger trout. Traditional flies work best. Bank fishing only, but most lochs are easily covered and wading is safe and easy. Trout fishing charges from £5 per day.

WHISTLEFIELD INN
Loch Eck, Dunoon

The 'old fisherman' at the oars of the boat in the field below this cosy hostelry has long-gone, but the renovated Inn serves excellent pub grub and also has an excellent dining room overlooking Loch Eck. Boats can be hired for salmon, sea trout and brown trout on Loch Eck. Loch Eck: Bank £5 per day, boats from £25 per day. River Cur and Massan £7 per day.

BALVAG

Location • Balquhidder
Species • salmon, sea trout and brown trout
Permit • Kings House Hotel, Balquhidder, Perthshire
FK19 8NY. Tel: 01877 384 646
(Charges under review. Boat available).
• Munro Hotel, Strathyre, by Callander,
Perthshire, Tel: 01877 384 263
(Charges under review).

BLACKWATER

Location • Bleaton Hallet
• Cray
• Finegand
• Glenkilrie
Species • salmon and brown trout
Permit • Bleaton Hallet: Pam Cameron,
Tel: 01250 882 269 (£20 per rod per day.
Max 4 rods. Fly fishing preferred).
• Cray: Pam Cameron, Tel: 01250 882 269
(£20 per rod per day. Over a mile of double
bank fishing for one rod (two rods by
arrangement). Maximum of two salmon per
day may be retained).
• Finegand: Brian Haddow, Tel: 01250 885 234
also e-mail: finegand@tesco.net
www.finegandestate.com
(Three separate beats. £40 per day per beat
for 2 rods until 31 July. £60 per day from 1
August to 15 October. Maximum of one fish
kept per rod per day. No worm fishing after
15 September. Cottages available to rent
at approx. £200 per week).
• Glenkilrie: Dave and Morag Houston,
Glenkilrie, Bridge of Cally,
Tel: 01250 882 241
(£10 per rod per day, maximum of three rods
allowed. Approximately one mile of single
bank fishing. Accomodation available).

BRAAN

Location • Dunkeld
• Amulree
Species • salmon and brown trout
Permit • Dunkeld: 'Kettles', Atholl Street, Dunkeld,
Tel: 01350 727 556 (£5 per day, £12 per
week. Juniors and OAPs half price. Fly fishing
only. 10 rod limit).

• Amulree: Amulree Post Office (Mon and Fri
only) Tel: 01350 725 200 (From £5 per day,
£12 per week. Juniors and OAPs half price.
Fly fishing only. 10 rod limit).
• Amulree Hotel, Amulree, Tel: 01350 725 218
£4 per day, £12 per week. Juniors and OAPs
half price. Fly fishing only. 10 rod limit.

BRAINCROFT LOCH

Location • by Crieff
Species • brown trout
Permit • Braincroft Farm, by Crieff,
Tel: 01764 670 140 (From £25. Maximum 3
rods, all fish under 12 inches to be returned).

BUTTERSTONE LOCH

Location • Dunkeld and Birnam
Species • brown trout
Permit • R Knight, Lochend Cottage, Butterstone Loch,
Tel: 01350 724 238 (Sessions are 9am – 5pm
and 5.30pm – dusk. Charges under review.
Fly fishing only. Fishing hut and toilets).
• Killearn Home Farm, Killearn, Glasgow
G63 9QH, Tel/Fax: 01360 550 994
Contact David Young.

CARLOGIE DAM

Location • Carnoustie, Angus
Species • brown trout
Permit • Carlogie Dam Fishings, Carlogie Farm,
Carnoustie, Angus, DD7 6LD,
Tel: 01241 853 128/Fax: 01241 857 308
email allansturrock@hotmail.com (4 hours,
2 fish £12 and 3 fish £16. 8 hours £21 for 5
fish, thereafter Catch and Release. Separate
C&R rate £5 for 4 hours, £10 for 8 hours.
Concessions available. Average weight 2lbs.
Hybrids include blue trout, steelhead trout,
gold trout and tiger trout. Fly only. B&B
accomodation available.

CASTLEHILL RESERVOIR

Location • Gleneagles, Auchterarder
Species • brown trout and rainbow trout, pike and perch
Permit • East of Scotland Water, Fife Division,
Craig Mitchell House, Flemington Road,
Glenrothes. Tel: 01592 614000

- East of Scotland Water, Fairmilehead, Edinburgh (Mon – Fri, 8am – 4pm). Tel: 0131 445 6462/01259 781 453 Boat £13 – £27 per day or evening. Bank – £4 to £10 per rod. Fly fishing only. Boat days Mon to Friday).

COWDEN LOCH
Location • Comrie
Species • brown trout
Permit • Lochview Farm, Mill of Fortune, Comrie, Tel: 01764 670 677 (Price on application. Caravan and fishing lodge available).

CROMBIE RESERVOIR
Location • Crombie Country Park, Monikie
Species • brook trout, brook trout and rainbows
Permit • Contact Monikie Angling Club Duty Bailiff, 10 – 10.30am, 1 – 1.30pm and 5.30 – 6.30pm, Tel: 01382 370 300 (Visitor prices £26 per boat (two rods, twelve fish limit). £15 for one visitor (six fish limit). Reduced prices for club members. Fly fishing only. Average weight 1lb).

DEAN
Location • Meigle
• Blairgowrie
Species • brown trout, rainbow trout and pike
Permit • Meigle: Kinloch Arms, Meigle, Tel: 01828 640 251 (£2 per day, £8.50 per season. Juniors and OAPs half price. Strathmore Angling Improvement Association. Certain stretches are fly only. Detailed map is available for 25p).
• Blairgowrie: Kate Fleming, Shooting and Fishing, 26 Allan Street, Blairgowrie, PH10 6AD, Tel: 01250 873 990 (£2 per day, £8.50 per season. Juniors and OAPs half price. Strathmore Angling Improvement Association. Certain stretches are fly only).
• James Crockart, 28 Allan Street, Blairgowrie, Tel: 01250 872 056 (Prices as above).

Location • Alyth
• Dundee
• Forfar
Species • brown trout and grayling
Permit • Alyth: Alyth Hotel, Alyth, Tel: 01828 640 251 (Prices as above).
• Dundee: Anglers Choice, 183 High Street, Lochee, Dundee, Tel: 01382 400 555 (Prices as above).

- Anglers Creel, 33 Exchange Street, Dundee, Tel: 01382 205 075 (Prices as above).
- Broughty Tackle Shop, 67 King Street, Broughty Ferry, Dundee, Tel: 01382 480 113 (Prices as above).
- Gows, 12 Union Street, Dundee, Tel: 01382 225 427 (Prices as above).
- Forfar: W R Hardy, Gunsmith 153/155 East High Street, Forfar, Tel: 01307 466 635 (£2 per day. Permit allows access to Strathmore Angling Association water on the river. Fly only. Size limit 10 inches).
- Canmore Angling Club secretary Alastair McIntosh, Tel: 01307 465 474 (Prices as above).

DOCHART
Location • Killin
Species • salmon, brown trout and grayling
Permit • News First, Main Street, Killin, FK21 8UJ, Tel: 01567 820 362 (£5 per day, £25 per week, juniors and OAP's half price. Rods and ghillies for hire. Minimum keepable size 10 inches).
• Captain Dowling, Kinnel House, Killin, Perthshire, Tel: 01567 820 590 (Prices on application).
• George Coyne, Head Keeper, Auchlyne Estate, Killin, Perthshire, Tel: 01567 820 284 (Prices on application).
• Mr T Taylor, Portenellan Lodge, Crianlarich, Perthshire, Tel: 01838 300 284 (Prices on application).

DRUMMOND LOCH
Location • Crieff/Muthill
Species • brown trout
Permit • Strathearn Tyres, School Wynd, Crieff, Tel: 01764 654 697 (£25 per boat, maximum 2 rods per boat. Fly only, no bank fishing, use of electric outboards and drogues only permitted).

DRUMMOND TROUT FARM AND FISHERY
Location • Comrie/St Fillans
Species • rainbow trout
Permit • Drummond Fish Farm, Comrie, Perthshire PA6 2LD, Tel: 01764 670 500 (2 hour ticket £3.50, concessions £3; 4 hour ticket £4, concessions £3.50; 8 hour ticket £7. Fish at £1.60 per lb. Rod hire £3. Six lochan inc. two beginners ponds and a 2 acre fly pond. Free tuition, snack bar, gutting and freezing service. Disabled access).

DUNALASTAIR WATER

Location • Tummel Bridge/Kinloch Rannoch
Species • brown trout and pike
Permit • David Kerr, Loch Garry Cottage, Dunalastair Estate, Kinloch Rannoch, Tel: 01882 632 354 (£17 per boat per day with 2 rods fishing).

EARN

Location • Lower Aberuthven
• Mill of Gask
• Braid Haugh
• Lawers
• Lochlane and Laggan
Species • brown trout, grayling, salmon and sea trout.
Permit • Lower Aberuthven: Jamie Haggart, Haugh of Aberuthven, Tel: 01738 730 206 (Salmon on application. Sea trout £8, trout and grayling £4, per day. Booking advised. Tuition available. Sunday fishing for trout and grayling).
• Mill of Gask: Jamie Roberts, Strathallan Castle, Tel: 01764 683 237 (Feb – April £8; May – July £5; Aug – Oct £12. No Sunday fishing).
• Braid Haugh: Braid Haugh Caravan Park, Crieff, Tel: 01764 652 951 (Salmon and sea trout, Feb – May, £10; Jun – Jul, £15; Aug – Oct, £20 per day. Brown trout, fly only, £5. Concessions £2.50. One salmon (or grilse) may be kept per day. No diving minnow. No Saturday tickets in October. No day permits after 15th October.
• Lawers: Lawers Estate, Lawers House, Comrie, Tel: 01764 670 050 (Cost on application. 2 rods per day, fly preferred, spinning allowed).
• Lochlane and Laggan: Tourist Information Centre, Crieff, Tel: 01764 652 578 (£5 – £45 per day according to season. No diving minnow. Three well equipped fishing huts. Fly only for trout. Tuition available).
• Contact John Young, Tel: 01764 670 361/ mobile: 07970 274 236 (Prices as above).

Location • Ruchill
Species • salmon and brown trout,
Permit • Watt-McKelvie Newsagents, Drummond Street, Comrie, Tel: 01764 670 294 (Adult day ticket £10, junior £5. Trout only £4).

Location • Kinkell Bridge
• Upper Strowan and Drummond
Species • salmon, sea trout and brown trout

Permit • Kinkell Bridge: Sandy Mackintosh, Tel: 01333 300 047 (£5 per day for brown trout, £10 for salmon and sea trout).
• Upper Strowan and Drummond: Tourist Information Centre, Crieff, Tel: 01764 652 578 (Salmon and sea trout, Feb – May, £10; Jun – Jul, £15; Aug – Oct, £20 per day. Brown trout, fly only, £5. Concessions £2.50. No salmon permits in October).
• A. Boyd, Newsagents, King Street, Crieff, Tel: 01764 653 871 (prices as above)

ERICHT

Location • Aberbothrie (Sunday fishing. Includes a stetch of the River Isla immediately upstream of the confluence with the Ericht)
• Blairgowrie
Species • salmon, sea trout and brown trout
Permit • Aberbothrie: Kate Flemings, Shooting and Fishing, 26 Allan Street, Blairgowrie PH10 6AD, Tel: 01250 873 990 (Salmon £15 per day, £60 per week. Trout £2 per day, £5 per week. Blairgowrie Angling Club water).
• Blairgowrie: James Crockart, 28 Allan Street, Blairgowrie, Tel: 01250 872 056 (Prices as above).
• TIC, 26 Wellmeadow, Blairgowrie, Tel: 01250 872 960 (Prices as above).

Location • Glenericht
• Lower Craig Hall
• Upper Craig Hall
Species • salmon and brown trout
• Glenericht: Roger McCosh, Glenericht Estate, Bridge of Cally, Perthshire, Tel: 01250 875 518 (Salmon, 15 May – 15 October, £40 per day. Fly fishing only. Check for other dates).
• Lower Craig Hall: Roger McCosh (see above)
• Upper Craig Hall: Latchie Rattery, Craighall, Tel: 01250 874 749 (£25 per rod per day. Maximum three rods. Lets available April – June and early September only. Approximately one mile of double bank fishing. Access from one bank only, not recommended for physically disabled. Fly fishing or spinning. Fishes best in medium to high water.

ERROCHTY DAM
Location • Kinloch/Calvine
Species • brown trout, pike and perch
Permit • David Kerr, Loch Garry Cottage, Dunalistair Estate, Kinloch Rannoch, Tel: 01882 632 354 (£17 per boat per day with 2 rods fishing).

GLENOGIL RESERVOIR
Location • Forfar
Species • brown trout
Permit • W R Hardy, Gunsmith 153/155 East High Street, Forfar, Tel: 01307 466 635 (Visitors £8 per rod per day (bank fishing). Boat hire £3 extra per day. Recommended 2 anglers per boat, maximum 3. 10am till half an hour after sunset. Fly fishing only. Electric outboards allowed. Size limit 10 inches. 4 fish per angler).
• Canmore Angling Club secretary Alastair McIntosh, Tel: 01307 465 474 (prices as above).

GLENSHERRUP RESERVOIR
Location • Glen Devon
Species • brown trout and rainbow trout
Permit • Glensherrup Trout Fishery, Glen Devon, Tel: 01259 781 631 (4 hours (2 fish and C&R) £12, 6 hours (3 fish and C&R) £14, 8 hours (4 fish and C&R) £16, 8 hours (5 fish and C&R) £18. Single, two man and three man boats, £18 – £38. Children under 12 with adult, free. Fly fishing only. Lodge, toilets, snacks and parking).

HEATHERYFORD FISHERY
Location • Kinross
Species • brown trout and rainbow trout
Permit • Heatheryford Trout Fishery, Dave Futong, Tel: 01577 864 212 (£18, 8 hrs, 4 trout; £15, 6 hrs, 3 trout; £12, 4 hrs, 2 trout. Fly only. Fishing instruction available on request).

ISLA
Location • Keithick
Species • salmon, sea trout and brown trout
Permit • Keithick: Kate Fleming, Shooting and Fishing, 26 Allan Street, Blairgowrie, PH10 6AD, Tel: 01250 873 990 (Salmon £15 per rod per day. Trout £2 per rod per day, £5 per week).

Location • Meigle
• Blairgowrie
Species • brown trout
Permit • Meigle: Kinloch Arms, Meigle, Tel: 01828 640 251 (£2 per day, £8.50 per

season. Juniors and OAPs half price. Strathmore Angling Improvement Association. Certain stretches fly only. Detailed map available for 25p).
• Blairgowrie: James Crockart, 28 Allan Street, Blairgowrie, Tel: 01250 872 056 (Prices as above).

Location • Alyth
Species • salmon, sea trout, brown trout and grayling
Permit • Alyth Hotel, Alyth, Tel: 01828 640 251 (Prices as above).

Location • Dundee
• Glenisla
Species • brown trout
• Dundee: Anglers Choice, 183 High Street, Lochee, Dundee, Tel: 01382 400 555 (Prices as above).
• Anglers Creel, 33 Exchange Street, Dundee, Tel: 01382 205 075 (Prices as above).
• Broughty Tackle Shop, 67 King Street, Broughty Ferry, Dundee, Tel: 01382 480 113 (Prices as above).
• Gows, 12 Union Street, Dundee, Tel: 01382 225 427 (Prices as above).
• Glenisla: Kirkside House Hotel, Glenisla, Tel: 01575 582 278 (Free).
• Various beats: W R Hardy, Gunsmith 153/155 East High Street, Forfar, Tel: 01307 466 635.

KERBET WATER
Location • Forfar
Species • brown trout
Permit • W R Hardy, Gunsmith 153/155 East High Street, Forfar, Tel: 01307 466 635 (£2 per day. Fly only. Small stream fishing. Size limit 10 inches).
• Canmore Angling Club secretary Alastair McIntosh, Tel: 01307 465 474 (Prices as above).

KINALDIE FISHERY
Location • Arbroath
Species • rainbow trout
Permit • G and J Hendry, Kinaldie Farm by Arbroath, Tel: 01241 830 241 (£10 for 2 fish per day. Juniors £5, OAPs £7.50. (special rates limited to 4 lbs of fish) 4 hours C&R £5. Two pools. One pool is fly only. £20 prize for the heaviest fish of the month. Fish up to 7lbs).

KINGENNIE FISHINGS

Location • Dundee
Species • brown trout and rainbow trout
Permit • Kingennie Fishings, Broughty Ferry, Dundee DD5 3RD, Tel: 01382 350 777/ Fax: 01382 350 400, Email kingennie@easynet.co.uk www.kingennie-fishings.com (Three pools. Cost from £10 – £25 according to pool, limits and hours. Speciman and Bankside pools are fly only. Any legal method for Woodside pool. Full facilities and STB 4 star lodges).

LAWERS DAM

Location • Killin
Species • brown trout
Permit • News First, Main Street, Killin, FK21 8UJ, Tel: 01567 820 362 (£5 per day, £25 per week, juniors and OAP's half price. Rods for hire. Minimum keepable size 10 inches).

LEDCRIEFF FISHERY

Location • near Dundee
Species • rainbow trout and brown trout
Permit • email piper.dam@virginnet.co.uk / Tel: 01382 581 374 (Boat 2 or 3 rods, 18 fish imit, £32 Mon – Fri, and £36 Sat – Sun. Boat 1 rod, 6 fish limit, £16 Mon – Fri, and £18 Sat – Sun. Sessions are 9.30am – 4.30pm, and 5pm – dusk. Bank fishing, 8 hours, 6 fish £16, and 4 hours, 4 fish £12).

LINTRATHERN RESERVOIR

Location • Alyth/Dykends
Species • brown trout, rainbow trout and hybrids
Permit • Lintrathen Angling Club, Tel: 01575 560 327 £32 per boat with 3 rods fishing.

LOCH AN DAIMH, GLEN LYON

Location • Glen Lyon
Species • brown trout
Permit • Mr W Mason, Croc-na-Keys, Glen Lyon, Tel: 01887 866 224 (£3 per rod per day. Fly fishing only, bank fishing from dam to island).

LOCHAN NA-LARAIG

Location • Killin
Species • brown trout
Permit • News First, Main Street, Killin, FK21 8UJ, Tel: 01567 820 362

LOCH BAINNIE

Location • Glenshee
Species • brown trout
Permit • Kevin Peters, Wester Binzean, Glenshee PH10 7QD, Tel: 01250 885 206

(£7 per rod per day, £30 per rod per season. Fly fishing only. Boat available. Access via Inverdrey Farm, SE Spittal of Glenshee).

LOCH BRANDY

Location • Angus
Species • brown trout
Permit • Clova Hotel, Glen Clova, Angus, Tel/Fax: 01575 550 350 Email: hotel@clova.com, www.clova.com (Free).

LOCH EARN

Location • Lochearnhead
Species • brown trout and pike
Permit • Loch Earn Fishings, Tel: 01764 681 257, Fax: 01764 681 550 (£6 per day, £15 per week, under 16s £2 per day, £5 per week. Season tickets available).
• Drummond Estates Boat Hire, Ardveich Bay, Lochearnhead, Tel: 01567 830 400 £6 per day, juniors £2 per day. Boat hire (max 3 rods) £15 – £29. Boats available 9am – 6pm).

LOCH EIGHEACH

Location • Kinloch Rannoch
Species • brown trout
Permit • Moor of Rannoch Hotel, Rannoch Station, Tel: 01882 633 238 (£3 per rod per day).

LOCH FASKALLY

Location • Pitlochry
Species • salmon, brown trout, ferox and charr
Permit • Dougal MacLaren, The Boat House, Loch Faskally, Pitlochry, Tel: 01796 472 919 (Bank fishing £3.75 per day, £14 per week. Boat with outboard, 2 rods, £35).

LOCH FREUCHIE

Location • Dunkeld and Birnam
Species • brown trout, rainbow trout and charr
Permit • Amulree Post Office (Mon and Fri only), Tel: 01350 725 200 (£3 per day. Juniors and OAPs £2. Under 15s free. Fly fishing only. Maximum 20 rods).
• Amulree Hotel, Amulree, Tel: 01350 725 218 (Prices as above).

LOCH GARRY (PERTHSHIRE)

Location • Perth/Inverness
Species • brown trout, ferox
Permit • Highland Guns and Tackle, Blair Cottages, Blair Atholl, Perthshire, Tel: 01796 481 303 (£5 per rod per day).

LOCH HEATH
Location • Angus
Species • brown trout
Permit • Clova Hotel, Glen Clova, Angus,
Tel/Fax: 01575 550 350
Email: hotel@clova.com, www.clova.com
(Cost on application. Situated in Glen Clova.
Vehicular access. Disabled access. New fishery
opened in 2001).

LOCH KINARDOCHY
Location • Tummel Bridge
Species • brown trout
Permit • Mitchell's of Pitlochry, 23 Atholl Road,
Pitlochry, Tel: 01796 472 613
(Boat £10 per day with 2 rods fishing. Tube
anglers [limited] £5 per day. Stocked by
Pitlochry AC).

LOCH LEE
Location • Glenesk, Brechin
Species • brown trout and char
Permit • Head Keeper, Invermark, Glenesk, by Brechin,
Tel: 01356 670 208 (£10 per boat per day
(up   to three anglers). No Sunday fishing. No bank
fishing. Fly fishing boat only).

LOCH LEVEN
Location • Kinross
Species • brown trout and rainbow trout
Permit • The Fishery Manager, Loch Leven Fisheries,
The Pier, Kinross, Perthshire,
Tel: 01577 863 407 (Boats £45 – £51
depending upon dates. Reduced prices some
afternoon/evening boats. Fly only 3 anglers
per boat).

LOCH MEALBRODDEN
Location • Crieff
Species • brown trout and rainbow trout
Permit • Abercairny Estates Ltd, Farm Office, Crieff,
Tel: 01764 652 706 (£20 per day including
boat for two rods. Fly only, boat hire from
dawn till dusk. No bag limit).

LOCH NAN EAN
Location • Glenshee
Species • brown trout
Permit • Kevin Peters. Wester Binzean, Glenshee
PH10 7QD, Tel: 01250 885 206
(£7 per rod per day, £30 per season. Fly
fishing only. 6 mile walk up Glen Thaitenich

LOCH RANNOCH
Location • Kinloch Rannoch
Species • brown trout, ferox and char
Permit • Loch Rannoch Hotel, Kinloch Rannoch,
Perthshire, Tel: 01882 632 201
• Dunalastair Hotel, Tel: 01882 632323
(boat & engine hire)
• Mr Legate, Glenrannoch House,
Tel: 01882 632307
• Mr J Brown, The Square, Kinloch Rannoch,
Tel: 01882 632268 (£4 per day, £14 per
week, season ticket £25. Under 12s and
OAPs free. Fly fishing and spinning only, no
bait allowed.)

LOCH SAUGH
Location • Drumtochty Glen
Species • brown trout and rainbow trout
Permit • Edzell Post Office, tell: 01356 642 200
(Stocked bt Brechin AA. £13 per rod per day,
bank fishing only. 4 trout limit. Average size
up to 2lb. Minimum size limit 10 inches.
• W Robertsons, Newsagent, 25 St Davids
Street, Brechin, Tel: 01356 622 685.
• Drumtochty Arms Hotel, The Square,
Auchenblae,Laurencekirk, Kincardineshire
AB30 1WS, Iel: 01561 320210

LOCH SHANDRA
Location • Glen Isla
Species • wild and stocked brown trout
Permit • Rob Pate, East Mill Farm, Glen Isla,
Tel: 01575 582 242 (Bank £10 per day, boat
£12 per day, 9am – 9pm. Limit of two stock
fish per rod. No limit on wild brown trout).

LOCH TAY
A major salmon and wild brown trout fishery,
14.5 miles long and averaging three quarters
of a mile wide, from the important spawning
tributary rivers Lochy and Dochart in the
west to Kenmore and the start of the River
Tay at the east end. The loch offers accessible
and reasonably priced salmon and trout fishing.
Location • Central
Species • salmon and brown trout
Permit • Central: Ardeonaig Hotel and Resturant,
Tel: 01567 820 400 (Cost on application.
3 boats with outboard motors).
• Loch Tay Highland Lodges, Milton of
Morenish, Killin FK2 8TY, Tel: 01567 820 323
(Salmon £40 per day (including boat and
permit, £45 on Saturdays. Trout £30 per day
and permit. Boat also available for half day,
£30, or full day, £45).

Location • East
Species • wild brown trout and brown trout
Permit • J. Duncan Miller, Loch Tay Lodges, Acharn, Tel: 01887 830 209 (Salmon £35 per day. (Trout £25 per day. Both include boat and outboard. Boat also available for hire for part day or weekly).
• Kenmore Post Office, The Square, Kenmore PH15 2HH, Tel: 01887 830 200 (£5 per day, Juniors and OAPs £2.50).

Location • West
• Killin
Species • salmon and brown trout
• West: News First, Main Street, Killin, FK21 8UJ, Tel: 01567 820 362 (£5 per day, £25 per week, juniors and OAP's half price. Tackle hire and boats/ghillies for hire. Minimum keepable size for brown trout 10 inches).
• Killin: Clova JR News Fishing Tackle Shop, Killin. Tel: 01567 820 362 (£5 per day, £20 per week. Boat hire £36 per day including fuel and permits).

LOCH TUMMEL
Location • Killikrankie/Tummel
Species • wild brown trout and ferox
Permit • Tourist Information Centre, 22 Atholl Road, Pitlochry, Tel: 01796 472 215 / Fax: 474 046 (£3 per day, £10 per week, £25 per season.
• Mitchell's of Pitlochry, 23 Atholl Road, Pitlochry, Tel: 01796 472 613 (Prices as above).
• Queen's View Visitor Centre, Forest Lodge, Strathtummel, by Pitlochry, Tel: 01350 727 284 (Prices as above).
• Tummel Valley Holiday Park, Strathtummel, by Pitlochry, Tel: 01882 634 221 (Prices as above).
• Loch Rannoch Hotel, Kinloch Rannoch, Perthshire, Tel: 01882 632 201
• Tummel Valley Park, Country Store, Kinloch Rannoch, Perthshire, Tel: 01882 632 306 (Prices as above).

LOCH TURRET
Location • Crieff
Species • brown trout
Permit • A Boyd, Newsagents, King Street, Crieff, Tel: 01764 653 871 (Check new season prices, bank fishing only).

LOCHAN A'MHUILLIN
Location • Perth
Species • brown trout
Permit • CKD Finlayson Hughes, Lyndoch House, 29 Barossa Place, Perth, Tel: 01738 451 600 Also Fax: 01738 451 900, email sporting@perth.ckdfh.co.uk (£28 per boat 2 rods. Fly fishing only).

LOCHAY
Location • Killin
Species • brown trout
Permit • News First, Main Street, Killin, FK21 8UJ, Tel: 01567 820 362 (£5 per day, £25 per week, juniors and OAP's half price. Rods and ghillies for hire. Minimum keepable size 10 inches).

LOWER FRANDY RESERVOIR
Location • Auchterarder
Species • brown trout and rainbow trout
Permit • Richard Philip, Kaimknowe Farm, Glendevon, Tel: 01259 781 352 (Contact Richard Philip, mobile Tel: 0780 154 7869, Fax: 01259 781 306, email: helen@glensherrup.fsbusiness.co.uk

LOWER FRANDY TROUT FISHERY
Location • Auchterarder
Species • brown trout and rainbow trout
Permit • Lower Frandy Trout Fishery. Tel: 01259 781 352 (Day boat (10am – 5pm) from £16. Evening boat (5.30pm – dusk) from £14. Bank 4 hour ticket £12 (2 fish and C&R), 8 hour ticket £16 (4 fish and C&R), 8 hour ticket £18 (5 fish and C&R). All day sporting ticket, catch and release £10. Children under 12 with adult, free. Fly fishing only. Lodge snacks, toilets and parking.

LUNAN
Location • Lunan Bay
Species • occasional salmon, sea trout and brown trout
Permit • T Clark and Son, 274 High Street, Arbroath, Tel: 01241 873 467 (£10 per rod per day – above and below the bridge).

LYON

Location •
- Cashlie
- Duneaves
- Innerwick, Glen Lyon
- Meggernie, Glen Lyon
- Slatich
- Timie

Species • brown trout

Permit •
- Cashlie: Mr Sinclair, Keeper's Cottage, Cashlie, Glen Lyon, Tel: 01887 866 237 (from £3 – £5, fly fishing only except in spate.)
- Duneaves: Richard Struthers, Duneaves Farm, tel: 01887 830 337 (Cost on application. Right bank only – Comrie Castle march to Glen Lyon Estate).
- Innerwick, Glen Lyon: W Drysdale, Innerwick, Keepers Cottage, Glen Lyon. Tel: 01887 866 218 (Salmon £12.50 until September. Trout £2.50. Fly fishing only).
- Meggernie: Glen Lyon Post Office, Bridge of Balgie, Glen Lyon, Tel: 01887 866 221 (£5 per rod, max 4 rods, fly only).
- Slatich: Mr A Walker, Slatich Farmhouse, tel: 01887 877 221 (Cost on application. Left bank only – Camusvrachan burn to Ruskich march dyke).
- Tirnie: David Campbell, Newsagent, Aberfeldy, Tel: 01887 829 545 (£5 per day. Left bank only – Keltneyburn to River Tay).

Location • Fortingall

Species • salmon and brown trout

Permit • Fortingall Hotel, Fortingall, Glen Lyon, Tel: 01887 830 367 (Salmon £25 per rod per day, trout £5 per rod per day, North bank only. Reduced rates for hotel guests).

MILL OF CRIGGIE TROUT FISHERY

Location • Montrose

Species • rainbow trout and brown trout

Permit • Mill of Criggie Trout Fishery, St Cyrus, Montrose, DD10 0DR, Tel: 01674 850 868 email Criggietrout@redhotant.co.uk (4 hour, 3 fish £12, 4 fish £15.50/8 hour, 6 fish £20 /4 hour C&R £7, 8 hour C&R £10. Concessions for OAPs and under 16s, Mon – Fri, 9am – 5pm only, 4 hour, 3 fish £10 / 8 hour, 6 fish £17. 4.5 acre fly-only fishery, stocked daily with brown and rainbow trout from 1.5lbs upwards. Open 9am – dusk. Snacks, tackle hire and tuition available. Parties and corporate groups welcome, prices on application).

MONIKIE COUNTRY PARK

Location •
- Island Pond
- North Pond

Species • brown trout and rainbow trout

Permit •
- Island Pond: Duty Bailiff, Monikie Angling Club, 10 – 10.30am, 1 – 1.30pm and 5.30 – 6.30pm, tel: 01382 370 300 (£26 per boat for two rods, 12 trout limit). £15 single rod, 6 trout limit. Reduced prices for club members. Fly fishing only. Average weight 1.75 lb.).
- North Pond: Duty Bailiff, Monikie Angling Club, 10 – 10.30am, 1 – 1.30pm and 5.30 – 6.30pm, tel: 01382 370 300 (£26 per boat for two rods, 12 trout limit). £15 single rod, 6 trout limit. Reduced prices for club members. Fly fishing only. Average weight 1.8 lb.).

NORTH ESK

Location •
- Burn House Beat
- Edzell

Species • salmon, sea trout and brown trout

Permit •
- Burn House Beat: The Burser, The Burn House, Glenesk, Brechin DD9 7YP, Tel: 01356 648 281 (£32 plus VAT (17.5%) per rod per day. Weekly lets for up to three rods between April and October. Fly and spinning allowed, worm fishing only in spate conditions).
- Edzell: Dalhousie Estates Office, Brechin, Tel: 01356 624 566 email dalhousieestates@btinternet.com (Weekly cost varies from £110 – £240, day tickets varies from £30 – £50, depending on dates. 50% deposit on booking. Maximum 3 rods. Single bank fishing (right bank). Beat is split into Upper and Lower halves with rotation at 13.00 hours. Fly only except during spate conditions).

Location • Kinnaber

Species • salmon and sea trout
- Martin Stansfield, Fortesk Castle, Aberlemno, Angus, Fax: 01307 850 449 (Prices per rod per day. 16 Feb – 31 March £100 (4 rods), April £100 (3 rods). No fishing May – August. September £100 (3 rods), Oct £120 (4 rods). Fly fishing preferred).

ORCHILL LOCH TROUT FISHERY

Location • Auchterarder

Species • rainbow trout

Permit • Orchill Loch Trout Fishery, South Lodge, Orchill, Braco, by Dunblane FK15 9LF,

Tel/Fax: 01764 682 287 (4 hours, 3 fish £12, 5 fish £20, evening 3 fish £12. Open every day 9am – dusk. Fly only. Regular stocking. Open all year).

PIPER DAM
Location • near Dundee, off A923 Dundee – Couper Angus road
Species • brown trout and rainbow trout
Permit • email: piper.dam@virginnet.co.uk / Tel: 01382 581 374 (Boat 2 or 3 rods, 18 fish limit, £32 Mon – Fri, and £36 Sat – Sun. Boat 1 rod, 6 fish limit, £16 Mon – Fri, and £18 Sat – Sun. Day sessions are 9.30am – 4.30pm, and 5pm – dusk. Bank fishing, 8 hours, 6 fish £16, and 4 hours, 4 fish £12. Electric motor hire £10 per session. Open all year round, weather permitting).

RESCOBIE LOCH
Location • Forfar/Burnside
Species • brown trout and rainbow trout
Permit • Booking at Rescobie boathouse from 8am – 10am. Otherwise, honesty system allows anglers to obtain a permit.
Tel: 01307 830 367 (Price varies from £5 – £30 per rod depending on dates, concessions etc. Electric outboards allowed. Fly only. Size limit 12 inches.

SANDYKNOWES FISHERY
Location • Rhynd Road, Bridge of Earn
Species • rainbow trout and brown trout
Permit • Fishery Manager, Sandyknowes Fishery, Collage Mill Trout Farm, Bridge of Earn, Tel: 01738 813 033 (£10 per 4 hour session, bag limit 4 fish. OAPs £8 for 3 fish limit).

SOUTH ESK
Location • Brechin
• House of Dun
• Kincraig
• Kinnaird Lower Beat
• Kinnaird Upper Beat
• Fortesk
• Inshewan
• Kirriemuir
Species • salmon, sea trout and brown trout
Permit • Brechin: Brechin Leisure Centre, Inch Park, River Street, Brechin, Tel: 01356 623 088 (£1 for adults, 50p for children under 14. Maximum of 6 rods per day, bookable 24 hours in advance. Fly only. From the weir below Brechin Castle to Brechin Bridge).
• House of Dun: National Trust for Scotland,

House of Dun, Montrose, Angus, Tel: 01674 810 238 (Weekly rates per rod inc VAT; 16 Feb – 19 Mar, £78; 26 Mar – 16 Apr, £90; 23 Apr – 14 May, £120; 21 – 28 May, £178; 4 – 18 Jun, £215; 18 Jun – 2 Jul, £280; 9 – 16 Jul, £320; 23 Jul – 13 Aug, £390; 20 – 27 Aug, £450; 3 – 17 Sep, £500; 24 Sep – 31 Oct, £530. 33% deposit required. Fly and spinning only. 3/4 mile double bank, five named pools. Various accomodation available from the National Trust, Tel: 01674 810 264).
• Kincraig: Graham Carroll, Fishing Tackle, 15 Church Street, Brechin, Tel: 01356 625 700 (£10 – £15 per rod per day. Beat extends for 1/2 mile and has been in private hands for a number of years. Historically good sea trout and late salmon fishing).
• Kinnaird Lower Beat: Southesk Estates Office, Haughs of Kinnaird, Brechin, DD9 6UA, Tel: 01674 810 240/ Southesk@aol.com (Cost on application, from around £350 per week for four rods. Sea trout from June. Salmon and grilse from July onwards).
• Fortesk: Martin Stansfield, Fortesk Castle, Aberlemno, Angus, Fax: 01307 850 449 (Call fishing manager Harry Millar Tel: 01307 818 581, Fax: 01307 850 449. Day or weekly lets available during September (3 rods) £40 per rod per day. October (4 rods) £45 – £50 per rod per day. 12 double bank pools and 4 single bank pools. Fly fishing preferred. Syndicate rods occasionally available for sea trout).
• Inshewan: CKD Finlayson Hughes, Lyndoch House, 29 Barossa Place, Perth, Tel: 01738 451 600 email sporting@perth.ckdfh.co.uk (From £55 per rod per day. Let on a daily or weekly basis for up to 4 rods. Split into 2 rod beats. Fishing huts and full time ghillie. Vehicular access. 20 pools. Excellent sea trout fishing).
• Kirriemuir: Mr W Dick, Secretary Kirriemuir Angling Club, Tel: 01575 573 277 (Visitors £15 per day, £75 per week for 2 miles of the South Esk, 5 miles of River Prosen and over 1 mile of the River Isla. No Saturday permits except for members. No worm fishing. Spinning in high water only. Excellent fishing).

Location • Kinnaird Middle Beat
• Kinnaird Upper Beat
• Kinnaird Powmouth Beat
• Clova Beat
• Finavon Castle

South Esk cont'd

Species • salmon and sea trout

Permit • Kinnaird Middle Beat: Southesk Estates Office, Haughs of Kinnaird, Brechin, DD9 6UA, Tel: 01674 810 240/ email Southesk@aol.com (Cost on application, from around £600 per week for four rods. Good autumn salmon beat).

• Kinnaird Powmouth Beat: Southesk Estates Office, Haughs of Kinnaird, Brechin, DD9 6UA, Tel: 01674 810 240/ email Southesk@aol.com (Let by the day from April onwards. April – August £18 per rod per day, September – October £25 per rod per day. Two rod beat. Short beat that occasionally provides good salmon and sea trout fishing).

• Kinnaird Upper Beat: Southesk Estates Office, Haughs of Kinnaird, Brechin, DD9 6UA, Tel: 01674 810 240/email Southesk@aol.com (Cost on application, from around £1200 per week for four rods. Good spring salmon fishing).

• Clova beat: Clova Hotel, Glen Clova, Angus, Tel/Fax: 01575 550 350, email hotel@clova.com, www.clova.com (£22 per day. Max 8 rods).

• Finavon Castle: CKD Finlayson Hughes, Lyndoch House, 29 Barossa Place, Perth, Tel: 01738 451 600 email sporting@perth.ckdfh.co.uk (From £320 – £890 per week for 2 rods. (Third rod is reserved by the estate). Approximately one mile of double bank fishing. Good sea trout fishing from June – August).

• Permits for various beats on several Tayside rivers including South Esk available from Ally Gowans APGAI, fishing trips, instruction and guiding arranged. Tel: 01796 473 718, Fax: 01796 473 718 and email ally@letsflyfish.com. Professional guiding and fly fishing instruction service for individuals, groups or corporate. Use of tackle included. Spey casting tuition).

RIVER TAY

Location • Aberfeldy Angling Club waters
• Borlick Farm
• Edradynate and Grantully
• Findynate
• Kenmore
• Murthly

Species • salmon, sea trout, brown trout and grayling.

Permit • Aberfeldy Angling Club Waters: Wade Newsagents, 31 Bank Street, Aberfeldy PH15 2BB, Tel: 01887 820 397

(Permit 1 – Bolfracks south bank only. Permit 2 – Aberfeldy town (fly preferred but other methods allowed). Permit 3 – Both banks of Derculich, Findynate, Cloichfoldich, Lower Grantully, Pitcastle and Pitnacree beats. South bank only on Ballintaggart and Sketewan. Specified waters £5 per day, £15 per week. Season associate membership also available, concessions for OAPs and juniors).

• Borlick Farm: R Kennedy, Borlick Farm, Aberfeldy, Tel: 01887 820 463 (£4 per rod per day. Any legal lure. Salmon £23 – £28 per day. Trout £5 per day. Weekly permits also available, and rod hire).

• Edradynate and Grantully: Robert Cairns, Tel: 01887 829 319 (Cost on application. Ghillie and boat available, fly casting tuition).

• Findynate: David Stirling, Findynate Lodge, Strathtay, Pitlochry PH9 0LP. (From £15 per rod per day, max 3 rods. Two half mile double bank beats, six pools, lovely fly water).

• Kenmore: The Post Office, 1 The Square, Kenmore, PH15 2HH. Open 7 days/week, Tel: 01887 830 765 (Visitor day permits £5 adults, £2 juniors and OAPs. Weekly permits £25. Annual permits £60 adults, £10 juniors and OAPs. Strictly fly only, 2 trout limit. Excellent fly water. Kenmore AC water).

• Kenmore Hotel, The Square, Kenmore, PH15 2NU, Tel: 01887 830 205 Fax: 01887 830 262 and email reception@kenmorehotel.co.uk, www.kenmorehotel.com. Cost varies from £15 – £50 per day depending on season. Reduced prices for hotel guests. Allocation of pools is on a daily basis and hotel guests have preference).

• Murthly: Murthly Post Office, Station Road, Murthly, Tel: 01738 710 383 (£4 per day, concession rate £2. Fly or bait fished on rod, reel and line. No Sunday fishing. Dawn to dusk).

• Estate Office, Douglasfield, Murthly, Tel: 01738 710 303, Fax: 01738 710 579 (Brown trout £4 per day, £16 per rod per day. Boat and boatman available).

• Spittlefield Post Office, Tel: 01738 710 229 (Prices as above).

• Estate Office, Douglasfield, Murthly, Tel: 01738 710 303 / Fax: 01738 710 579 (Price varies from £25 – £150 according to season. Two 5 rod beats, one 3 rod beat. No natural baits. Boat and boatman available. Fishing availability limited due to syndication).

Location • Aberfeldy
        • Dunkeld House
        • Lower Kerock and Delvine
        • Upper Newtyle and Lower Newtyle
Species • salmon
        • Aberfeldy: D Campbell, The Square,
           Aberfeldy, Tel: 01887 829 545 (From £5 per
           day. To suit individual and fishing safaris.
           Also Loch Tay and various hill lochs).
        • Dunkeld House: Hilton Dunkeld House Hotel,
           Dunkeld, Tel: 01350 728 370/
           Fax: 01350 723 959 (Cost on application.
           Boat and bank fishing, 6 rods per mile,
           ghillies and equipment hire).
        • Lower Kerock and Delvine: CKD Finlayson
           Hughes, Lyndoch House, 29 Barossa Place,
           Perth, tell: 01738 451 600
           Also Fax: 01738 451 900 email
           sporting@perth.ckdfh.co.uk. (£20 – £80 per
           day. Boat and ghillie available).
        • Upper Newtyle and Lower Newtyle:
           Youngs Garage, Birnam, Tel: 01350 727 276
           (Cost varies throught the season. Boat and
           bank fishing. Boat and boatman available).

Location • Estuary
        • Dalguise
Species • salmon and brown trout
Permit • Dalguise: CKD Finlayson Hughes, Lyndoch House,
           29 Barossa Place, Perth, tell: 01738 451 600,
           Fax: 01738 451 900 email
           sporting@perth.ckdfh.co.uk . (£20 – £60 per
           rod per day including shared boat and ghillie.
           Middle river beat immediately below Lower
           Kinnaird. Comfortable fishing hut).
        • Estuary: Dundee City Council, Leisure and
           Parks Department, Floor 13, Tayside House,
           Dundee DD1 3RA, Tel: 01382 434 187
           (Free. Both sides of the river shore adjoining
           or opposite Dundee, excluding private
           property. Good sea trout fishing at times).

Location • Lower Kinnaird
Species • salmon and sea trout
Permit • Kinnaird Estate, By Dunkeld,
           Tel: 01796 482 440 (Cost from £30 – £128
           per rod per day. Maximum 6 rods).

Location • Kinnaird (North bank)
        • Kinnaird Upper (South bank)
        • Stenton
        • South Bank
        • Upper Newtyle and Lower Newtyle
        • Weem Water
Species • brown trout

Permit • Kinnaird (north bank): Ballinluig Inn,
           Ballinluig, Tel: 01796 484 242 (£3 per day,
           fly only).
        • Kinnaird Upper (south bank): Ballinluig Inn,
           Ballinluig, Tel: 01796 484 242 (£3 per day,
           fly only.
        • Stenton: CKD Finlayson Hughes, Lyndoch
           House, 29 Barossa Place, Perth,
           Tel: 01738 451 600 (From £240 per day,
           3 rods. Boat and ghillie available).
        • South Bank and Upper Newtyle:
           Kettles, Atholl Street, Dunkeld,
           Tel: 01350 727 556 (£4 per day, £12 per
           week. Juniors and OAPs half price. Fly
           fishing only).
        • Upper Newtyle and Lower Newtyle:
           Gordonian Fishings, Tel: 01821 642 312
           (Cost varies throught the season. Boat and
           bank fishing. Boat and boatman available).
        • Weem water: Mr T Sharp, Laigh of Clunie
           Steading, Edradynate, Aberfeldy,
           Tel: 01887 840 469 (North bank only).

WEST WATER
Location • Brechin
        • Edzell
Species • salmon
Permit • Brechin: Brechin Angling Club Secretary Bill
           Balfour, Tel: 01356 622 753 (£10 – £17 per
           rod per day, depending on dates. Maximum
           of 2 fish per day. Week permits allow four
           fish to be retained. Various beats extending
           over several miles of river. Access unsuitable
           for children or physically impaired persons).
        • W Robertsons, Newsagent, 25 St Davids
           Street, Brechin, Tel: 01356 622 685
           (£10 – £17 per rod per day, depending on
           dates. Maximum of 2 fish per day. Week
           permits allow four fish to be retained. Various
           beats extending over several miles of river.
           Access unsuitable for children or physically
           impaired persons).
        • Edzell: Edzell Post Office, Tel: 01356 642 200
           (£10 – £17 per rod per day, depending on
           dates. Maximum of 2 fish per day. Week
           permits allow four fish to be retained. Various
           beats extending over several miles of river.
           Access unsuitable for children or physically
           impaired persons).

AILEAN CHRAGGAN HOTEL
Weem, Aberfeldy, Perthshire PH15 2LD.
Tel: (01250) 873512
AltamountHouse@aol.com

Ideally located for the upper reaches of the **River Tay** and excellent centre for touring.

ALTAMOUNT HOUSE HOTEL
Blairgowrie.
Tel: (01250) 873512, AltamountHouse@aol.com

A magnificent Georgian Country House set in 6 acres, within walking distance of Blairgowrie. Enjoy fresh local produce prepared by their award winning chef. Good centre for trout lochs, stillwater fisheries and salmon and sea trout on **River Tay** and tributaries. Trout fishing from £5 and salmon fishing from around £25 per day.

AMULREE HOTEL
Amulree, By Dunkeld, Perthshire.
Tel: (01350) 725218

Proprietor Graham Stewart is a keen and experienced angler, happy to advise guests on the extensive fishings available form this comfortable hotel. The **River Braan** offers splendid fly fishing for wild brown trout in delightful surroundings. A number of hill lochs and lochans including **Loch Freuchie** offer variety for the trout angler. From below the Falls of Hermitage through Strathbaan and to its confluence with the River Tay at Dunkeld Bridge, the River Braan is a major spawning tributary receives good runs salmon and the fishing is preserved. Charges £5 per day which included fly fishing for brown trout on the Upper River Braan and Loch Freuchie.

ARDEONAIG HOTEL
Ardeonaig, South Loch Tayside by Killin, Perthshire.
Tel: (01567) 820400
Fax: (01867) 820282

Excellent base for **Loch Tay** offering good trout fishing and trolling for salmon, from early spring throughout the season to October 15. 16 miles long and up to a mile wide, the loch produces some exceptionally large fish and around 400 salmon each season. Brown trout average around 8oz but ferox to double figures are present in the loch and a previous British Record brown trout (16lbs) came from **Loch Faskally** at the head of the **River Tummel**.

Escapee rainbow trout are also present and drop down to over-winter in the **River Tay** at Kenmore, where they cause havoc, destroying large numbers of eggs during the salmon spawning. Boat charges including fishing £30-£50 per day for two rods. Ghillies/ boatman available. Bank fishing from around £5 per rod per day.

AUCHTERARDER HOUSE
Auchterarder, Perthshire, PH3 1DZ.
Tel: (01764) 663646
Fax: (01764) 662939
auchterarder@wrensgroup.com

Excellent base for touring Perthshire's rivers and lochs and with good visitor access to nearby golf courses. Auchterarder House has its own private trout fishery available to guests.

CLOVA HOTEL
Glen Clova, By Kirriemuir, Angus.
Tel: (01575) 550222

Excellent base for **River South Esk** with 3 miles of excellent sea trout fly fishing available to guests for £22.00 per day. The Kirriemuir AC has 7.5 miles of excellent fishing downstream in Glen Cova. Charges from £15.00 per day. (01575) 573277.

COSHIEVILLE HOTEL
Keltneyburn by Aberfeldy.
Tel: (01887) 830319

Pretty and hospitable old coaching inn close to **Loch Tay** and upper beats on the River Tay, River Tummel and Glen Lyon. Excellent hill loch fishing for brown trout and inexpensive salmon fishing on the main river beats and association water by arrangement. Trout fishing from £5 per day.

DUNALISTAIR HOTEL
by Kinloch Rannoch, Perthshire.
Tel: (01882) 632323

Excellent wild brown trout fishing, high average weight on **Dunalistair Loch** which extends to 1.5 miles and up to half a mile wide. trout are stocked annually and average around 2lbs with plenty of larger specimens. Also good fishing on **River Tummel** and **Loch Rannoch**. Early season can produce large ferox from the Tummel immediately below Loch Rannoch, which can run to double figures. Dunalistair Loch: Boats are £17 per day for two rods, available from Dunalistair Estate (01882) 632354. Brown trout fishing in river and hill lochs from £5 per day.

FARLEYER HOUSE HOTEL
Aberfeldy, Perthshire, PH15 2JE.
Tel: (01887) 820332
Fax: (01887) 829430
reservations@farleyer.com
www.farleyer.com

Access to some of the best private beats on River Tay for salmon. Special courses for beginners and fly fishing and casting instruction. Various tuition and angling packages, with special rates for non-fishing guests.

FORTINGALL HOTEL
Fortingall, By Aberfeldy, Perthshire.
Tel: (01887) 830367

Situated above **Loch Tay** on the **River Lyon** at the entrance to beautiful Glen Lyon. Much of the fishings has been retained by the estate, but the hotel still offers some good salmon fishing at a reasonable price on the picturesque River Lyon, including the productive Peter's Pool which can produce salmon from early February onwards. Other lets can sometimes be available. Well-situated for lochs and the **Rivers Tay** and **Tummel.** Trout fishing from £5 per day. Salmon rods from £25-£50 per rod per day.

FOUR SEASONS HOTEL
St Fillans, Perthshire.
Tel: (01764) 685333

Close to **Loch Earn**, a busy fishery which is covered by a Protection Order. Angling is controlled by Loch Earn Fishings who stock the loch each season with 7,500 brown trout, between 10oz and 2.5lbs. Fish grow on quickly and the loch can produce beautiful brown trout up to 7lbs and larger. All legal methods are allowed, although fly fishing using traditional loch-style techniques still produce some of the best baskets. The loch is heavily fished and also used for other watersports, so early and late are best times for success. Day tickets cost only £5.00 for adults and under 16s fish for £1. Boat charges range from £15 for short 4 hour hires, to £29 for a full day, inclusive of outboard motor and fuel.

HILTON DUNKELD HOUSE HOTEL
Perthshire.   **SEE AD ON PAGE 45**
Tel: (01350) 727771

Dunkeld House Hotel on the banks of the **River Tay**, has its own private beats with best results harling from the boat. A ghillie/boatman is included in the costs of the main lets, although bank rods are also available. Good fly fishing and spinning, with harling producing most of the early spring and autumn salmon. Some excellent wild brown trout and specimen grayling in the Tay here, which offer good summer sport with the dry fly and traditional wet fly from late spring through to September. Fishing charges on application to the hotel.

KENMORE HOTEL
Kenmore, Perthshire.
Tel: (01887 830205

Famous fishing hotel and centre for festivities at the start of the Tay season on January 15th. Fishing on the river and **Loch Tay** from January 15th through to 15th October, with a chance of fresh fish from opening day throughout the season. The hotel also offers Spey-casting courses and instruction. Boats may be hired from the hotel for Loch Tay from £30-£50 per day with outboard for two

rods. Ghillies/ boatmen can be arranged. River charges vary with beats and time of year. Salmon fishing £25-£50 per day in the spring, £30 per day for summer lets and twice or more in the autumn.

LOCH RANNOCH HOTEL
Kinloch Rannoch, Perthshire.
Tel: (01882) 632201

Good centre for wild brown trout fishing on **Loch Rannoch** and hill lochs. Some very large ferox trout are taken every season from Rannoch. The upper **River Tummel** can produce excellent sport with wild brown trout on dry fly and normal downstream wet fly tactics. Dunalistair Water, an excellent loch with large, beautifully marked trout. Can be dour but worth the effort, with trout averaging close to 2lbs and plenty of larger fish. Some big pike are also present in the loch. Bank fishing from £3-£5 per day. Dunalistair £17 per day for two rods, booked through the estate (01882) 632354. See also Dunalistair Hotel.

MEIKLOUR HOTELS AND FISHINGS
Perthshire.
Tel: (01250) 883206

Prime salmon fishing on some of the best beats on the **River Tay** including Meiklour, Lower Islamouth, Upper Islamouth. The Islamouth fishings were sold earlier this year and restrictions may apply. The River Tay is famed for its large salmon, particularly in the autumn, although large fish run also in July. Signs of substantially improved spring runs in 2001. Good fly and spinning water for bank anglers, but many of the fish are taken harling from boats. Kynoch, Rapala and similar plugs favoured: Blair spoons, Toby , devons and Waddingtons all take fish. Shrimp and prawn have been banned on Tay for some years and most anglers return their hen fish and coloured cock salmon in the autumn months. A voluntary scheme of returning spring fish or donating them live to the hatchery stripping programme is also showing positive signs for future stocks on this famous river. Charges and availability on request, but expect to pay upwards of £100 per rod per day and more for an autumn let.

MOOR OF RANNOCH HOTEL
Rannock Station, Perthshire.
Tel: (01882) 633238

Excellent wild brown trout on a number of lochs, including **Loch Rannoch**, which produces large ferox every season. **Loch Laidon** is a large loch on Rannoch Moor which offers good bank fishing. Trout are mainly small around 6oz, but the loch produces some very large fish every season in the 8-11 lbs range. Also **River Gaur** and **Garbh Ghaoir Burn**: best on a dropping spate with some good browns. Loch Eigheach, the source of the River Gaur also holds trout around half pound, but with some much larger fish. Wading not advised. Bank fishing from £3-£5 per day.

ROSEMOUNT GOLF HOTEL
Blairgowrie, Perthshire.
Tel: (01250) 872604/ (01250) 874496,
info@rosemountgolf.co.uk

A golfing hotel with every amenity for anglers as well as being situated close to the middle **River Tay** and tributaries. Good grayling fishing as well as wild river brown trout. Salmon fishing available by arrangement on rivers Tay, **Isla** and **Ericht** as well as loch fishing. DBB en-suite from £42.00. Fishing rates on application.

SPITTAL OF GLENSHEE HOTEL
Glenshee, Perthshire.
Tel: (01250) 885215

Winter and spring skiing country, but good centre too for river and loch fishing. The **Shee Water** forms part of the Tay system which produces upwards of 250 fish each season and offers good, well-priced salmon fishing. An important spawning stream, it joins the River Ardle to form the River Ericht and thence to the River Isla and eventually the mighty Tay. Good loch fishing too. Salmon fishing from £40 per two rod beat to £50 per rod per day in the autumn. Catch and release is encouraged and anglers are restricted to two salmon per day.

SUNBANK HOUSE HOTEL
50 Dundee Road, Perth, PH2 7BA.
Tel: (01738)624882
Fax: (01738) 442515
www.sunbankhouse.com

Delightfully located in own grounds overlooking the **River Tay**, this fine early Victorian mansion is a short walk from the centre of Perth, it provides an ideal base for exploring central Scotland and its delights. A cast of Miss Georgina Ballantine's record salmon of 64 lbs, taken from the Tay at Delvine in 1922 is displayed in Perth Museum. The Perth Town Water offers accessible sport for salmon and sea trout on a budget and fishing can also be arranged on private beats on request. Specimen roach and perch are also present around Perth harbour reaches. Charges for salmon and sea trout, restricted to 20 tickets per day cost £10 and £15 from mid-season until October 15 from the Department of Leisure and Recreation, 5 High Street Perth (01738) 475000. Private beats from £30-£50 per rod per day and considerably more in the autumn.

THE BRIDGE OF CALLY HOTEL
Bridge of Cally, Blairgowrie.
Tel: 01250 886 231

Comfortable fishing hotel offering special rates and private facilities for angling parties. Excellent fishing on the **River Ericht**, a tributary of the **Isla**, for salmon and occasional sea trout, peaking in autumn. Important spawning stream for the Tay system.Spinning allowed on Blairgowrie AA water but excellent fly water as well. The hotel has access to single and double bank fishing for 4 miles of the Ericht and by arrangement on the Craighall Beat and River Isla. Charges from £30-£60 per day depending on beats and season.

THE ROYAL DUNKELD HOTEL
Dunkeld, Tayside.
Tel: (01350) 727322
Fax: (01350) 728989

Former coaching inn in the picturesque town of Dunkeld on the north bank of the **River Tay**. Good fly fishing for trout and grayling on the river and salmon lets can be arranged. As well as the river Tay, there are some excellent hill lochs above Dunkeld, some stocked with rainbows as well as native brown trout. Traditional loch-style techniques, drifting main close to the shoreline or around islands. Bank fishing can also be productive. DBB 3 nights from £140.00. Trout fishing from £5-£20 per day, boat and bank fishing.

Western Isles

LOCH BAIL-FHIONNLAIDH
Location • Benbecula: Peinylodden/Market Stance
Species • brown trout
Permit • (Malcolm MacPhail, Head Keeper, Garynahine Estate, Isle of Lewis, Tel: 01851 621 383 Fishing let with Garynahine Lodge for parties of up to 12 anglers).
• Sportsworld, 1 Francis Street, Stornoway, Tel: 01851 705 464 (call for advice)
• South Uist Angling Association, 1 Ardmore, Eochdar, South Uist, Outer Hebrides, Tel: 01870 610 325 (£6 per rod per day approx).
• John Kennedy, Bornish Stores, Bornish, Isle of South Uist, Tel: 01878 710 366 (Prices as above).
• Colin Campbell Sports, Balivanich, Benbecula, Tel: 01870 602 236 (Prices as above).

LOCH EILEAN IAIN
Location • Benbecula: Peinylodden/Market Stance
Species • brown trout
Permit • Shell Bay Caravan Site, Liniclate, Benbecula, Tel: 01870 602 447 (£6 per rod per day approx).
• South Uist Angling Association, 1 Ardmore, Eochdar, South Uist, Outer Hebrides, Tel: 01870 610 325 (Prices as above).
• John Kennedy, Bornish Stores, Bornish, Isle of South Uist, Tel: 01878 710 366 (Prices as above).

GRIMERSTA
Location • Benbecula: Garynahine/Miavaig
Species • salmon, sea trout and brown trout
Permit • Colin Campbell Sports, Balivanich, Benbecula, Tel: 01870 602 236 (£6 per rod per day approx).
• Shell Bay Caravan Site, Liniclate, Benbecula, Tel: 01870 602 447 (Prices as above).

LAXADALE LOCHS
Location • Harris: Glen Laxadale
Species • salmon and sea trout
Permit • Lochboisdale Hotel, Lochboisdale, Isle of South Uist, Outer Hebrides, Tel: 01878 700 332 (£25 per boat per day for trout, £35 per boat per day for sea trout & salmon. Ghillies available. Book in advance).
• Harris Hotel, Tel: 01859 502 154 (Call for further information).

BEAG-NA-CRAOIBHE
Location • Lewis: Stornoway/Balallan
Species • brown trout
Permit • Sammy MacLeod, The Anchorage, Ardhasaig, Tel: 01859 502 009 (Call for further information).

RIVER BLACKWATER
Location • North Lewis
Species • salmon and sea trout
Permit • Mr M Morrison, Handa, 10 Keose Glebe, Lochs, Stornoway, Isle of Lewis, Tel: 01851 830 334 (Also accommodation).

LOCH BA UNA
Location • Benbecula: Market Stance
Species • brown trout and sea trout
Permit • Simon Scott, Estate Manager, Grimersta Estate Office, Isle of Lewis, Tel: 01851 621 358, Fax: 389 (Fly fishing only).
• Simon Scott, Estate Manager, Grimersta Estate Office, Isle of Lewis, Tel: 01851 621 358, Fax: 389 (Fly fishing only).
• Finlyson Hughes, 29 Barossa Place, Perth, Tel: 01738 451 111 (Fly fishing only).
• South Uist Angling Association, 1 Ardmore, Eochdar, South Uist, Outer Hebrides, Tel: 01870 610 325 (Call for further information).

LOCH BEE, EAST
Location • South Uist
Species • salmon, sea trout and brown trout
Permit • John Kennedy, Bornish Stores, Bornish, Isle of South Uist, Tel: 01878 710 366 (Call for further information).

LOCH COIRIGEROD
Location • Lewis
Species • trout
Permit • Colin Campbell Sports, Balivanich, Benbecula, Tel: 01870 602 236 (Call for further information).

LOCH GEIMISGARAVE
Location • Harris: Flodabay
Species • brown trout, sea trout and salmon
Permit • Shell Bay Caravan Site, Liniclate, Benbecula, Tel: 01870 602 447 (Call for further information).

LOCH KEOSE
Location • Stornoway/Balallan
Species • brown trout and sea trout
Permit • Simon Scott, Estate Manager, Grimersta Estate Office, Isle of Lewis, Tel: 01851 621 358/Fax: 389 (Call for further information).

LOCH LANGAVAT
Location • Lewis
Species • salmon, sea trout and brown trout
Permit • Robin Davidson, Morsgail Estate, Isle of Lewis.
• Head Keeper, Uig and Hamanavay Estate, Tel: 01851 672 421 for further information.
• John MacLeod, Valtos Cottage, Laxay, Lochs, Stornoway, Isle of Lewis, Tel: 01851 830 202 Call for advice (Head Keeper, Soval Estate).
• Robin Davidson, Morsgail Estate, Isle of Lewis.

LOCH MORSGAIL
Location • Garynahine/Miavaig
Species • salmon, sea trout and brown trout
Permit • Sportsworld, 1 Francis Street, Stornoway, Tel: 01851 705 464 (Call for details).

LOCH NA CRAOIBHE
Location • Lewis
Species • brown trout
Permit • Sportsworld, 1 Francis Street, Stornoway, Tel: 01851 705 464 (Call for details).

LOCH NAM FALCAG
Location • Lewis
Species • brown trout
Permit • Malcolm MacPhail, Head Keeper, Garynahine Estate, Isle of Lewis, Tel: 01851 621 383 (Call for details).

LOCH NAN CULAIDHEAN
Location • Stornoway/Garynahine
Species • salmon, sea trout and brown trout
Permit • South Uist Angling Association, 1 Ardmore, Eochdar, South Uist, Outer Hebrides, Tel: 01870 610 325 (£6 per rod per day, boats £5 approx).

LOCH OLAVAT
Location • Benbecula
Species • brown trout
Permit • John Kennedy, Bornish Stores, Bornish, Isle of South Uist, Tel: 01878 710 366 (£6 per rod per day, boats £5 approx).
• Colin Campbell Sports, Balivanich, Benbecula, Tel: 01870 602 236 (Prices as above).
• Shell Bay Caravan Site, Liniclate, Benbecula, Tel: 01870 602 447 (Prices as above).
• Mrs Mackinnon, Finsbay Loch, South Harris, Outer Hebrides, Tel: 01859 530 318 (£12 per day approx. Boat available for disabled anglers).

LOCH TARBERT
Location • Harris/Flodabay
Species • brown trout, sea trout and salmon
Permit • Mrs Mackinnon, Finsbay Loch, South Harris, Outer Hebrides, Tel: 01859 530 318 (£12 per day approx. Boat available for disabled anglers).

LOCH TUNGAVAT
Location • Garynahine/Timsgarry
Species • brown trout, sea trout and salmon
Permit • Scaliscro Lodge Hotel, Scaliscro, Uig, Isle of Lewis, Tel: 01851 672 325/Fax: 393 (Free to residents, otherwise £12 per day).

LOCHS SGIBACLEIT, SHROMOIS, AIRIGH, THORMAID
Location • Seaforth Head
Species • salmon, sea trout and brown trout
Permit • Scaliscro Lodge Hotel, Scaliscro, Uig, Isle of Lewis, Tel: 01851 672 325/Fax: 393 (£60 per rod per day, approx).

VATANDIP
Location • Stornoway/Garynahine
Species • brown trout and sea trout
Permit • Sportsworld, 1 Francis Street, Stornoway, Tel: 01851 705 464 (Call for details).

Brew up in the hills above Scaliscro Lodge, and a strap of heather-smoked brownies to go with freshly baked bread and perhaps a wee dram.

ANGLERS RETREAT
1 Ardmore, Lochdar, South Uist, Western Isles HS8 5QY
Tel: (01870) 610325, anglers.retreat@virgin.net

Share the secrets of this Hebridian anglers paradise: choose from numerous lochs, all with, hard-fighting wild brown trout. Traditional flies include Black Pennel, Soldier Palmer, Invicta, Grouse and Claret, Grouse and Mixed. Kingfisher or Silver Butcher also does well. Boat and bank fishing with rods from £5 per day.

ASSAPOL HOUSE HOTEL
Bunessan, Isle of Mull, Argyll
Tel: (01681) 700258 Fax: (01681) 700445

Comfortable fishing hotel and self-catering accommodation is also available through Scoor House (01681) 700297. **Loch Assapol** offers inexpensive fishing for salmon, sea trout and brown trout, although sea trout particularly fewer in numbers. Brown trout average 8oz but with a chance of much bigger fish. Bank fishing £5 per day and £8 for boats.

BROADFORD HOTEL
Broadford, Isle of Skye
Tel: (01471) 82220

Fishing available on a number of lochs and rivers in the area. The hotel has 1.5 miles of the small **River Broadford** which offers good light tackle fishing for salmon and sea trout. This is a spate stream which needs water to produce fish. Sea trout are present from late June onwards with salmon arriving about a month later. The river fishes best on a dropping spate through to October. Catch and release is encouraged and coloured fish should be carefully returned from late summer onwards.The hotel charges £8-£10 per day for the river and from £5 for loch trout fishing.

CASTLEBAY HOTEL
Castlebay, Isle of Barra, OS31 P267 SFF
Tel: (0871) 810223

Loch Tangusdale is the best of nine brown trout lochs on the island, with a high average weight of around 2lbs. Loch na Doirlinn produces specimen browns up to 5lbs but has a reputation of being dour. Sea trout are occasional taken in **Loch an Duin** and can also be taken fly fishing and spinning the shoreline, normally during the first two hours of the flood tide. Bank fishing only for trout costs £5 per rod per day and tickets are available from the hotel or the Tourist Information Office, Castlebay (0871) 810336.

COLINSAY HOTEL
The Isle of Colinsay
Tel: (01951) 200316, Fax: (01951) 200353,
Colinsay.hotel@pipemedia.co.uk

Special fishing breaks available for excellent trout fishing. Traditional casts include Black Pennel, Soldier Palmer, Invicta, Greenwell's Glory and silver butcher. Good sea angling: boat fishing for codling, pollack, coalfish and skate. Shoreline can produce flatfish, pollack (lythe), coalfish (saithe), wrasse and mackerel.

GIGHA HOTEL
Island of Gigha, Argyll
Tel: (01583) 505254, Fax: (01583) 50524

Comfortable fishing hotel in lovely countryside. **Mill Loch** was previously stocked with farm salmon and rainbows, but the current owner William Howden is encouraging the wild brown trout stocks to re-establish themselves. Trout average 8oz with some bigger fish, offering good fly fishing. Free fishing for hotel guests on Mill Loch and other adjacent lochans.

HARRIS HOTEL
By Tarbet, Isles of Lewis & Harris.
Tel: (01859) 502154

Good centre for brown trout fishing and improving salmon and sea trout on the **Laxadale Lochs**. The Laxadale system is currently under change of ownership and enquiries should be made to the hotel. The **River Laxdale**, **Fincastle Loch** and the tiny **Loch Laxdale** as their names imply also offer salmon and sea trout as well as good brown trout. Lets are sometimes available from around £15-£25 per day (01859) 550202/ 550317. Fishing on trout lochs costs around £5 per rod per day.

ISLE OF COLONSAY HOTEL
Colonsay, Argyll PA61 7YP
Tel: (01951) 200316 Fax: (01951) 200353

Beautiful Island in the Hebrides, accessible by regular ferry from Oban with stunning landscapes and wonderful beaches. Good sea angling. Loch Fada and a number of other trout lochs available, offering good fly fishing. Traditional loch style fishing, with best drifts producing free-rising wild brown trout, 12oz up to the pound mark. In a good wave, fish short and use something bushy like a Soldier Palmer on the top dropper. Charges bank fishing £8 per day. £12 for boat fishing.

ISLE OF RASSAY HOTEL
Isle of Rassay
Tel: (01478) 660222

A choice of good trout lochs including **Loch a'Mhullinn**, **Loch na Meilich** and **loch a'Chadha**. Trout average around half a pound but 1lb plus fish are regularly caught. Traditional flies work well. Charges a modest £7 for a week's excellent fly fishing.

KILLIECHRONAN HOUSE HOTEL
Aros, Isle of Mull PA72 6JU
Tel: (01680) 300403 Fax: (01680) 300463

The **River Ba** which runs from Loch Ba for little more than 2 miles to the head of the sea loch at Killiechronan, is an excellent spate river which produces around 80 salmon and twice that number of sea trout each season. Some very large sea trout are also taken on the loch, including a specimen of 19lbs. recent seasons has seen a dramatic decline in returning sea trout and small average fish, although large sea trout are still occasionally taken.

River charges from £20 per day and boats, including outboard and experienced ghillie cost £75 per day for two rods. Estate fishing is also let through Knock House (01680) 300356 with tenants of the estate lodge receiving priority.

LOCHBOISDSALE HOTEL
Isle of South Uist, Western Isles HS8 5TH.
Tel: (01878) 700332/700367
hotel@lochboisdale.com

One of Scotland's great fishing hotels, whether the fish are taking or not! Great hospitality and great facilities matched by the wonderful wild brown trout of the **Machair** lochs, and well-priced salmon and sea trout fishing throughout the summer and early autumn. John Kennedy is the man to speak to for your best choice of fly, including one or two designed by John himself. Special package rates from the hotel depending on lochs and season.

LOCHMADDY HOTEL
Isle of North Uist, HS6 5AA
Tel: (01876) 500331/2 Fax: (01876) 500210

Situated on the Isle of North Uist, you can enjoy Hebridean hospitality and home cooking after your day by river, loch and shoreline. A great fishing hotel offering excellent sport with wild brown trout, sea trout and salmon. Good runs of salmon from spring through to autumn, peaking with the grilse, summer salmon and sea trout in July. Brown tout fishing free to guests. £6 per day and £20 per week for non-residents. Loch Grogarry £33-£49 for boat and two rods per day. Special inclusive fishing packages on application to the hotel.

SCALISCRO LODGE
Uig, Isle of Lewis HS29EL
Tel: (01851) 672325 Fax (01851) 672393

Excellent sporting lodge offering excellent value-for-money fly fishing for salmon and numerous hill lochs with excellent wild brown trout fishing on limestone lochs. Special group package rates and fishing charges on application to the lodge.

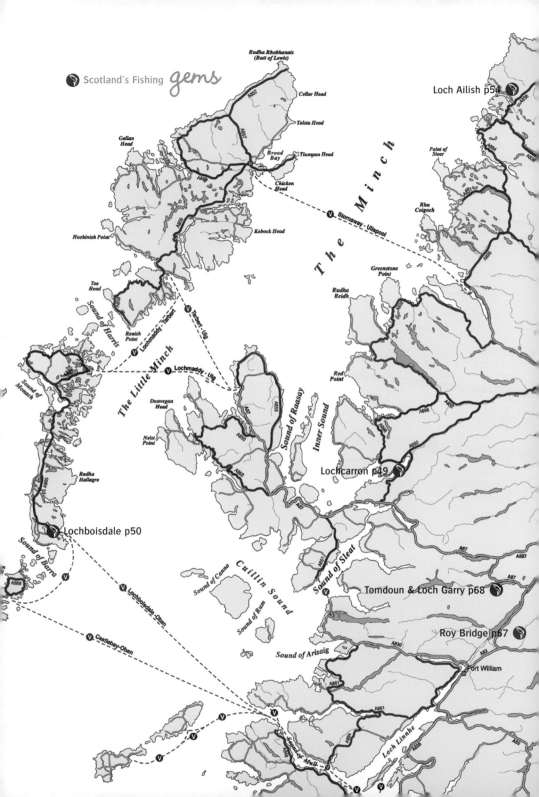

Scotland's Fishing *gems*

Loch Ailish p54

Loch Ailish p54

Rudha Rhobhanais
(Butt of Lewis)

Cellar Head

Tolsta Head

Galian
Head

Broad
Bay

Tiumpan Head

Point of
Stoer

Chicken
Head

T h e   M i n c h

Rhu
Coigach

V Stornaway - Ullapool

Hushinish Point

Kebock Head

Greenstone
Point

Toe
Head

S o u n d   o f   H a r r i s

Renish
Point

V Lochmaddy - Tarbert

V Tarbert - Uig

Rudha
Reidh

Red
Point

V Lochmaddy - Uig

T h e   L i t t l e   M i n c h

Dunvegan
Head

Neist
Point

S o u n d   o f   R a a s a y

I n n e r   S o u n d

Sound of
Monach

Rudha
Hallagro

Lochcarron p49

Lochboisdale p50

C u i l l i n   S o u n d

Sound of Canna

S o u n d   o f   S l e a t

Tomdoun & Loch Garry p68

S o u n d   o f   B a r r a

V

V Lochboisdale - Oban

Sound of Rum

Roy Bridge p67

V Castlebay - Oban

Sound of Arisaig

Fort William

V

V

V

S o u n d   o f   M u l l

V

L o c h   L i n n h e

Loch Awe p57

Loch Lomond p64

Firth of Lorne

Loch Linnhe

Sound of Mull

Sound of Jura

Sound of Bute

Kilbrannan Sound

Firth of Clyde

Coul Point

Rhinns Point

Laggan Bay

Helensburgh

Dunoon

Gourock

Greenock

Port Glasgow

Alexandria

Dumbarton

Johnstone

Paisley

Barrhead

Kilwinning

Ardrossan

Irvine

Kilmarnock

Troon

Prestwick

Ayr

Bennane Head

Larne - Cairnryan

Belfast - Stranraer

Stranraer

Loch Ryan

Luce Bay

Burrow Head

Scotland's Fishing gems

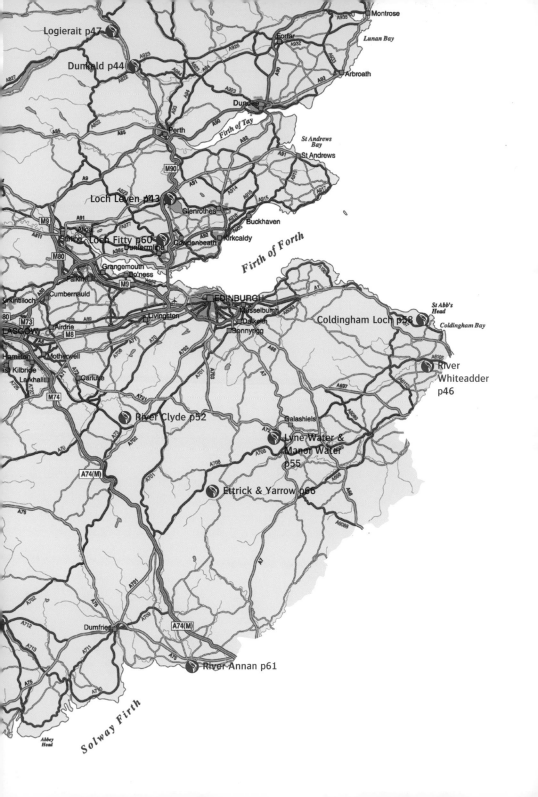

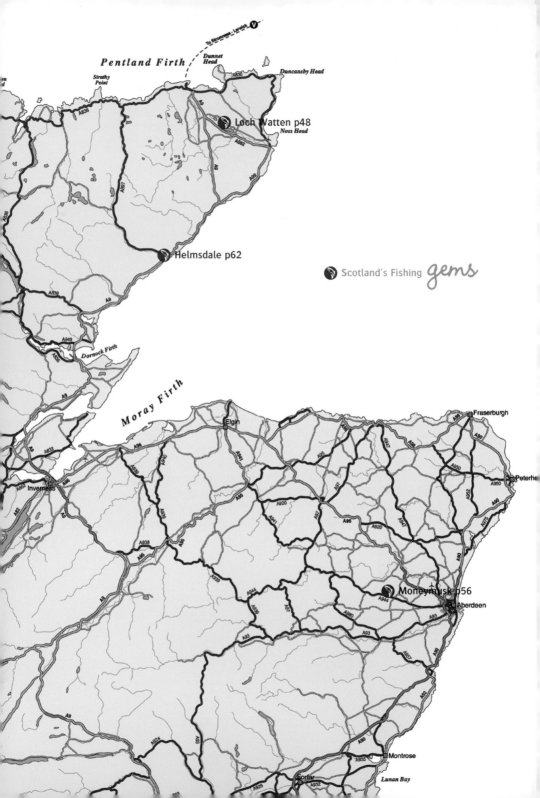

Pentland Firth

Dunnet Head

Duncansby Head

Strathy Point

Loch Watten p48

Noss Head

Helmsdale p62

Scotland's Fishing *gems*

Dornock Firth

Moray Firth

Elgin

Fraserburgh

Inverness

Peterhead

Moneymusk p56

Aberdeen

Montrose

Lunan Bay

Forfar